10.00

AF694325

The Killing of Olive Taylor

A Story of Judicial Misconduct and Other Felonious Acts

By

J. Edward Kloske

Point of View Publishing

This is a work of non-fiction

Copyright 2009 by J. Edward Kloske

All Rights Reserved – Portions of this book includes material that may be subject to other copyright provisions and if so are used here with permission, and portions of this book may include material in the public domain and not subject to copyright provisions. Portions of this book under copyright by the author may not be used for any purpose, including electronic conversion in any form, without the written permission of the author, except for brief excerpts used in published reviews.

Manufactured in the United States of America

Published by

Point of View Publishing

Direct all inquiries to the publisher at

Post Office Box 1324
White House, TN 37188-1324 USA

First Edition

Publisher's logo is a trademark of Point of View Publishing

Library of Congress Control Number: 2009942177

ISBN 978-0-578-04436-1

In memory of my uncle Ernest Charles Pugh
Master Sergeant
United States Marine Corps
Retired
1932 – 2007

He served his country with pride and honor

-

And for my grandfather Edward George Kloske
1888-1953

I wish I could have known him longer

ACKNOWLEDGMENTS

I would like to give thanks and praise to the staff of the following organizations for their help in locating the many records that make up the details of this incredible story:

The National Archives and Records Administration
Pacific Region – San Francisco
The California State Archives – Sacramento
State of Oregon – Multnomah County Circuit Court
San Joaquin County Superior Court
San Joaquin County Library
Stockton, California
United States Department of Homeland Security
U.S. Citizenship and Immigration Services
Lee's Summit, Missouri

To our family genealogists who helped tell the family side of this story while providing important details and historical perspective on the Taylor Family:

Debbie Stevens
Ernest Charles Pugh
Kathryn Oehlman Latham

With special thanks for the editing assistance to
Donna Angeron Browning

PREFACE

For some inexplicable reason I have yet to discover, an alarming number of public officials and employees believe that they can fail in their jobs and responsibilities without consequences. That would be regardless of the harm that they do to others simply because they were well intentioned at the time and acted or not without malice. Not unlike someone who pulls a man out of a wrecked vehicle and kills him in the process of saving him, even though there was no obvious imminent threat to the man at the time of the rescue. Those things generally happen because somebody who was not properly trained or experienced attempted something way beyond their knowledge, skill or ability.

I had been researching my family history for many years when I discovered a story of government incompetence so extraordinary it begged to be told. A man born in Greece came to the United States as an immigrant in 1907 and eventually managed to let his self-determined level of importance steer him towards snuffing out the life of my great-great grand aunt in a public school classroom in the San Joaquin Valley of California in 1932. She was teaching class at the time of her death and was killed in front of a number of her students.

This book is about how all of that happened, and more. It is most certainly about people who worked for government at various levels, people who were paid to represent our ancestors' interests, enforce their laws, uphold the publics trust, and who failed miserably in that particular time of need. It's about lawyers of marginal ability, enforcers of the law who appeared clueless as to its provisions, investigators who just couldn't seem to investigate, and judges who just flat had no business being judges. It's about detectives, some considered exemplary in their field, who couldn't detect all that much, international flight to avoid prosecution, state and federal bureaucrats and diplomats, all hot on the trail of a man who out thought them at every turn while trying miserably to bring him to justice.

This book is strewn with tales of missed opportunities, comedies of errors, downright insufficiency, and a justice system that failed the victim at practically every turn. My research discovered this story in the musty records of a host of government agencies and jurisdictions. What this book attempts to do is what the public record does not do: put the whole sequence of events in one place rather than in multiple places with no real connection from one place to another. Sure, some case law has been written about the legal aspects associated with specific involvement of the courts, but a lot of that did little to illuminate how the people associated with those events contributed in some fashion or other to the ultimate outcome of the story.

Everything that I will present for your consideration happened a very long time ago, but those events unfortunately mirror so much of what we still see and hear in our society today. I have no way of knowing what was in the minds of the many people who unknowingly contributed to this story, but I can certainly raise questions in light of the known evidence they left behind.

While reading through all of the research and reference materials I have uncovered, I have tried very hard to view it all from the perspective of somebody sitting on a jury and having this information presented to them much the same way one would expect in a trial or before a grand jury. I must confide that I am not a lawyer, nor have I ever formally attended law school in pursuit of a legal degree. Unless you are a lawyer yourself, that should increase your comfort level considerably. It is generally recognized that in order to practice law you actually have to be a lawyer. Most places still require most judges to also be a lawyer before they can actually serve as a judge. It is never necessary to be a lawyer to sit on a jury. It is also not necessary to be a lawyer to enforce the law or investigate the criminal conduct of others. When certain human events end up before a jury the need for a lot of lawyers rises considerably. The lawyers are all there to help explain various matters to you, including the judges, but you have to listen very carefully to what they say, and particularly to witnesses to critical events, or experts making certain technical or scientific declarations of fact.

I should also point out that my opinions, conclusions and observations presented here are not intended as legal advice, and should not be construed as such. What I am going to be doing here is giving you a different perspective. One that looks at events through the eyes of someone charged with the task of finding guilt or innocence, based on the evidence known to have existed, and the laws in effect during the period that this book will cover.

There will be times when you will probably ask yourself whose side am I on. Let me tell you up front, I am on the side of justice here, no matter who they are, or what they did or didn't do. The refreshing part of this book is that you will also meet a few highly competent lawyers, and judges who actually understood not only legal mandates, but the limitations that our laws impose as well.

The essential focus of this book is the law, and the people who enforce the law, break the law, and defend the accused. The only authority over anything in this story is the law. Without laws, and people who interpret and enforce them properly, there is no justice, only anarchy. A little common sense from a number of people you will meet in this book might have helped circumstances greatly. This started out as Olive Taylor's story, but grew into something way beyond her untimely and unfortunate death. This is actually a story of justice gone awry. It needed to be told. May Olive Taylor rest in peace.

Olive Luella Taylor
Circa 1910

Revenge is a kind of wild justice, which the more man's nature runs to, the more ought law to weed it out.

- Sir Francis Bacon
England 1561-1626
From an essay on Revenge

CHAPTER ONE
OLIVE LUELLA BAILEY

She was born in Humboldt County, California in the town of Powellville in 1882. She was the daughter of Charles Massie Bailey, a Virginian, who came to California along with everybody else with gold fever around 1850 at age 19. Charles eventually met and married Nancy Maria Hite of Indiana. They married in the Camp Grant community of Humboldt County in 1877. Together they would provide Olive with three brothers, two of them born in New Mexico between 1886 and 1890. The couple each had children from previous marriages, so it was quite a bunch under one roof. All together, Charles and Nancy raised the population by six sons and six daughters, a few in Humboldt County, and a few more in the Sonoma County town of Healdsburg. Olive's father was a farmer, a cattleman, a miner, a hunter, and a hotelkeeper. His first wife was a full-blooded American Indian, whom he met while prowling the Eel River in Northern California in 1860. Nancy was the homemaker and keeper of the household. Her parents were born in Michigan, and she made the trip from Indiana to California in a covered wagon. Charles, having left Virginia to do a little farming with his brother Hardin in Missouri, took the train.

Olive came to Healdsburg with the family when she was a young girl, where she spent most of her formative years, and graduated from high school there. She decided she wanted to be a teacher herself, and after graduation enrolled in the Fresno State Teachers College at Fresno,

California. By the time she completed her studies in Fresno, part of the family had relocated to Santa Rosa, California, and so did Olive. There she often taught as a substitute teacher and for a short while at Windsor Grammar School. While in Santa Rosa, Olive met the love of her life in the form of one Ethan Allen Taylor, no connection to the furniture company. Ethan was a mechanic, an engineer and a machinist. A daughter, Mildred was born in 1906. They moved to Arizona for a few years, where Ethan tried his hand at mining in 1910, and Olive taught children the wonders of learning. By 1920 the family was back in Santa Rosa, Ethan working on cars, Olive raising Mildred and teaching part time as she was needed to fill in for other teachers. By 1924, the family had moved to Stockton California and San Joaquin County. Olive was teaching elementary school for the Castle School District. Ethan owned a service station, the old fashioned kind where you filled up your gas tank and also got your windshield cleaned, plus your water and oil levels checked. You didn't have to drive to the edge of the property to top off the air in your tires, the air hose being located right next to the gas pumps. Ethan also did automotive repairs at the station. Mildred had followed in her mother's footsteps and became a teacher herself at the Stockton High School, and in later years would teach at Pleasanton, California. Olive's mother, Nancy, had moved from Santa Rosa to Stockton and was living with the Taylors there in 1932. The Taylors were part of a very large family, and visitations both in Stockton and in Santa Rosa were the norm, as various family members traveled back and forth between the two communities. Then there were the family reunions that were popular in that era. They drew quite a crowd when they had a family gathering, most often in Santa Rosa and on the Russian River in Northern California.

Family elders recall that Olive had a passion for teaching, and thought of her profession as more of a calling than just a job. As with most such things in life, the people who are best at what they do, do it with little fanfare or recognition. The only public testimonial I have been able to find came from Mrs. Mary B. Castle, Secretary of the Castle School Board of Trustees in San Joaquin County who said that Olive Taylor was highly regarded by the parents of the school district, which is no surprise. Olive made friends easily wherever she had lived, and was clearly a favorite among the many children she had taught over the years.

San Joaquin County was among the original California counties that saw their official beginning in the state in 1850. The early years saw the county as a gateway for mining, but that changed with the arrival of the railroad and a shift toward food production outside of its local market area. By the late 1800's, another shift saw an increase in smaller land holdings and greater diversification in crops. This shift greatly expanded the role of the county as a major supplier of produce and fruit. This era saw the development of over 4,500 farms representing in excess of 700,000 acres producing vegetables, fruits, and other important crops. The San Joaquin County valley region proved itself to be a natural for agriculture. The climate and soils of the valley were well suited to a wide variety of crops, among them several varieties of grapes to fuel the many wineries in the area. The whole county was (and still is) a patchwork of farms and fields and orchards. Better still, was the abundant supply of water from artesian wells that supplied most of the ranch and farm water in the area. A huge agricultural industry drives the need for a lot of labor, not only for harvest but also to package produce and pack trucks and train cars for shipment to multiple destinations across the country. Hard work and dedication to the industry can yield a decent living not only for the native born, but also for multitudes of people emigrating from foreign lands.

For Olive Taylor and her family, their world would be changed in 1930. She was teaching the elementary and middle grades at the Castle School near Manteca, California. A Greek had come to San Joaquin County with his new wife fifteen years earlier, and from that marriage would eventually come several children. Olive had an encounter with the man over those same children in 1930, but didn't give it much thought. The Greek moved his children to a different school. Problem solved in her view, nothing to be greatly concerned about. Teachers occasionally had disagreements with the parents of their students. Just as parents need to maintain order in their households, teachers need to maintain order in their classrooms, right? Olive didn't know it then, but the clock had begun counting down the last two years of her life.

CHAPTER TWO
TOM COUMAS

Spyridon Dem. Symroyannis was the name he started out with on October 29, 1889. Or perhaps it might have been Spyros Smyrnoyiannis. Two different judicial courts in Greece seem to think he was one or the other. In fairness to both of those courts, the original documents were in Greek and later translated into English. Perhaps his last name is correct, as his official birth record in Greece has identified his father as Demetrios Symroyannis. His mother was known as Thogshony Throvopoulu, Throvopoulu supposedly being her maiden name. Her son's place of birth was Roino, Mantineia, District of Arcadia Greece, and where he generally remained until he was 17 years of age. On December 20, 1906 he boarded a ship, named the S.S. Perugia (in Naples, Italy) under the name Spiros Smirsiany. I have no idea how he got from Greece to Italy, or why he changes names like some change their underwear, but the Perugia eventually bumped into the pier at New York City on January 4, 1907. Smirsiany identified himself to the ship's manifest as a laborer and was here to visit his cousin, Giorgio, the authorities later thought in Chicago, although the majority of his meanderings within the United States went mostly unnoticed.

People who are smart about discovering who goes where and when, next thought Smirsiany surfaced in Portland, Oregon in 1910 and filed an application to become naturalized as an American citizen on November 29, 1910 under the name Speros Smernogeon. The record gets a little fuzzy about what happened next, but on or about September 29, 1911, Smirsiany was single, living in Portland and working as a waiter at an establishment called the Commercial Club under the name Spiros Smirnagianis. Smirsiany, now Smirnagianis decided his name was much too complicated for living in the United States, so he hired a lawyer by the name of Milton Reed Klepper to help him get his name legally changed to Tom Coumas. The record is even fuzzier about how Smirsiany managed to get documents that identified him as Smirnagianis, although probably nobody cared, or asked, perhaps the least of which was attorney Klepper.

Klepper, who later in life would go on to become very prominent in Oregon political circles as a member of the Oregon State Assembly, filed a petition on Smirnagianis behalf before the Multnomah County Court, where a judge whose signature is practically illegible and therefore will remain anonymous, agreed with the Klepper/Smirnagianis declaration of difficulties and embarrassments in conducting business in America with difficult names, and probably also without attention to Smirnagianis identity or if at all or very little, decreed that Smirnagianis would be henceforth known to the world as Tom Coumas. The judge came to that conclusion on February 5, 1912 after due notice was published for the requisite period in *The Sunday Welcome* with nobody coming forward to raise a fuss in particular over the matter. Hard to say if anybody inquired into Smirnagianis' legal status in the United States, such as a visa or a passport or some sort of immigration document, or something that would cause somebody in authority such as an officer of the court or a judge that Smirnagianis was in the country legally and was who he claimed to be. Also never mind the fact that he lied about who he was and filed a petition with the court under a fictitious name which surely must have been a violation of something in Multonomah County at the time. Justice is blind because nobody is watching or paying any attention to what other people are doing. Unless you are the old guy down the street who peeks out of his blinds on a regular basis and can tell you almost everything going on down to the hour of the day, but nobody bothers to ask, but that is a different story from this one.

Armed with his brand new identity courtesy of Multonomah County, Coumas filed a new request to become a U.S. citizen, again at Portland, but this time with the Circuit Court, still single, with no children, and at the age of 24 years on November 13, 1913. Then on February 25, 1914, Tom Coumas along with all else so inclined in court that day, stood upright and raised his right hand and swore the oath of allegiance to the United States of America. This allegiance swearing business is something that the United States government takes very seriously, particularly on the part of folks from foreign lands who really want to become one of us and make our home their home. The Circuit Court having considered all of the therefore's and what-have-you's, and having satisfied itself that requirements and conditions were met, approved the application and Tom Coumas became a citizen of the United States on April 2, 1914. I have to wonder if his immigration documentation that he used to enter the country in 1907 had been changed from Spiros Smirsiany to Tom Coumas, or he showed the Circuit Court his decree changing his name from Spiros Smirnagianis to Tom Coumas, which probably did not match his immigration documents. I mean the official court order regarding this clearly identifies him as being a "subject of Greece", would not somebody connected with the Court have reviewed his papers to verify that he was who he claimed to be?

On January 1, 1915 Coumas married Margaret Mary Debauw in Vancouver, Washington just north of Portland and the Columbia River. Coumas declared on that occasion that the name of his father was Demetrius Smyrnogeas. I recognize that some of these names have somewhat complicated spellings but how hard can it be to remember the name of your own father?

Margaret was the daughter of Cornelius Debauw and Felicita Caroline Seghers, a musician and music teacher from Baasrode, Belgium. Margaret was born in Oswego, Oregon in 1893. Cornelius was a trombone player in the Oswego Band, and died in a drowning accident in Oregon when Margaret was four years old. Following their marriage in Vancouver, Tom and Margaret relocated to Manteca, California that same year. There, Tom would pursue life as a laborer of one sort or another, and he and Margaret would start a family.

It wasn't a good start for either of them. Their first two of six died prematurely. Of the four surviving Coumas children, there were three sons and a daughter. Their eldest, a son was confined to a reform school at age 13. Another son died at age 16. In 1928 Margaret was admitted to the state mental hospital at Stockton, California. Margaret's sister, Henrietta, was previously thought to have been admitted to a state mental hospital in Oregon, according to a Debauw family member.

By 1932, Coumas had acquired a housekeeper by the name of Clara Hickman who was living with Coumas' two sons and daughter in Manteca. The daughter was 9, and the two boys were ages 8 and 3 years. The girl and the older boy were students in Olive Taylor's class at the Castle School near Manteca, having enrolled there on April 7th. For a year prior to that date, these two were attending the Lincoln school in the same general area of San Joaquin

County. Teachers at the Lincoln school referred to the Coumas children as "incorrigible". Mrs. Hickman had been with the Coumas family since December of 1931. Margaret was still in the mental hospital at Stockton. Tom Coumas held a variety of jobs usually involving produce, farming and the grocery trades. One source indicates that Coumas once worked for the Economy Fruit Market. Later, that same source claimed that the correct reference to Coumas' employment was at the Public Market. One of the more interesting aspects of researching a story like this it that the information sort of comes in spits and spurts from a wide variety of sources. Often, you have to snip and glue several pieces together to come up with the history of it all and a timeline for it. Equally important is to recognize that the validity of most information is subject to the accuracy and perception of the person reporting or recounting their recollection of it. One thing is historical fact; the Coumas children were about to trigger an event in Olive Taylor's classroom that would change the lives of several families forever.

CHAPTER THREE
DARK DAY IN APRIL

April 20, 1932 – It may have been a day that started out like any other in San Joaquin County. Ethan Taylor would have been at his service station. Olive would have headed out to the Castle School as she had since 1924. The Coumas children also went to the Castle School that morning, including four other students in Mrs. Taylor's class - Frances Fisher, Athena Bouzeneris, Frances Aguilar and Mary Kondratenko. All four lived in Manteca in 1932. Athena was 16 years of age, and Frances Fisher was 17, both born in California. I do not know the age of Frances Aguilar or where she was born. She may have been about 15 years old, but I can't say with certitude that she was. Athena's parents were born in Greece. Mary Kondratenko was probably 14 years of age, and she came to the United States in 1923 with her family from Russia by way of Canada. Perhaps a great part of the frustration that I have with this story is the lack of information about the principal people that are associated with it. Nothing in any official record I have reviewed tells me how many children were in Mrs. Taylor's class on April 20th, their grade level, or the ages of all of the children present. However, these four girls would eventually bear witness to a terrible event and are therefore an important part of the story.

I would have also liked to have found a list somewhere, perhaps generated by someone in authority, of the adults on the premises of the Castle School on this day. Two others were accounted for, a man by the name of William J. Duval, the 74-year-old janitor at the school, and his wife Rosiann. There is no mention in the numerous newspaper accounts that would follow the events of this day of any principal, teacher (other than Mrs. Taylor), or other school official or employee on the school grounds with the exception of the Duval's. One newspaper account mentions that the county superintendent of schools, John R. Williams, was at the school later in the day, but his name does not appear in any official record I have reviewed.

At around noon that day, the Coumas boy threw his lunch on the classroom floor. The boy screamed and swore at Mrs. Taylor when she told the boy to pick up his lunch from the floor. Mrs. Taylor used her ruler to deliver several slaps to the boy's hand. Later that day, Mrs. Clara Hickman, the Coumas housekeeper called at the school and began arguing with Mrs. Taylor and creating a disturbance in her classroom. The time of day of this occurrence is not fixed, but came from early newspaper accounts quoting informed sources. Mrs. Hickman was alleged to have called Mrs. Taylor names, and demanded that the Coumas children be given a transfer to another school. Bear in mind that the Coumas children had only been attending this school for 6-7 days prior to this incident, and that Olive Taylor had issues with these same children two years previous. In any event, Mrs. Taylor granted the transfer request, providing Mrs. Hickman with the requisite transfer slip. It was not reported where the Coumas children were at the time of this exchange between Mrs. Taylor and Mrs. Hickman. It is highly probable that the Coumas children had been excused, the regular class session having ended for the day, and had returned to their home, complaining to Mrs. Hickman about Mrs. Taylor and being disciplined by her. It was not reported if the Coumas daughter played any role in the incident while in the classroom, she being the eldest of the two Coumas children. Mrs. Hickman, for reasons unknown, then went to the school to confront Mrs. Taylor.

A little after 4:00 p.m. that day, Tom Coumas went to the school and confronted Mrs. Taylor, demanding to be told why she had disciplined his son. An argument ensued, words were exchanged, and Coumas pulled out a .32 caliber pistol and shot Mrs. Taylor twice, one round penetrating her side just under her arm, and the other penetrating her leg. The janitor, Duval having followed Coumas into the classroom tried to grab Coumas' arm and Coumas shot him twice, striking the janitor in the face and hand. Mrs. Duval, who was in the classroom at the time Coumas confronted Mrs. Taylor, tried to go to her husband's aid and Coumas fired a shot at her. Mrs. Duval, not hit by Coumas' bullet, ducked behind a desk and then Coumas fled the building. All of this came from newspaper accounts quoting official sources but not naming those sources.

Olive Taylor was prone face down on the classroom floor. It is not known who, if anyone went to her aid. Six students witnessed the attack and fled the classroom in several directions from the school. Some of the students went to the nearby home of rancher Arlo Gustafson and explained to him what had happened at the school. Mr. Gustafson then called the San Joaquin County sheriff's office to report the incident.

First arriving at the school were Crawford Hitchcock, Chief of the Manteca Police Department and San Joaquin County Sheriff's Deputy Jack Cassidy. The sum total of time these officers of the law spent on the premises was two minutes. I have not found any official document that details who had control of the crime scene following the departure from the premises of Hitchcock and Cassidy. I have not uncovered any official document that details any investigation of the crime scene that would include the collection of evidence of any kind from the scene other than Mrs. Taylor's personal property. I have yet to find any official document that consists of the interview of any witnesses to the crimes committed, a list of people on the premises at the time of the crimes being committed - nothing that indicates when or if the coroner arrived and took possession of Mrs. Taylor's remains or who determined she died at the scene, nothing that indicates who arranged for medical treatment of Mr. Duval or how and by whom was he transported to the San Joaquin General Hospital, or a report on the nature of his injuries from any medical practitioner. There is no report in the official record of any law enforcement representative having taken a statement from Mr. Duval regarding his injuries. There does not seem to exist any report that details the recovery of any shell casings, or bullets from the classroom or the victims of the shootings. There was a newspaper account that reported that school district superintendent John R. Williams was among the "first" to arrive at the scene, but I have found no report of any interview having been conducted or statement taken from Mr. Williams. The reporter also noted that the Coumas children were considered unruly by Mrs. Taylor and that she had often complained about their behavior in her classroom, and that these same children had a tendency to cause trouble. The reporter does not say to whom Mrs. Taylor complained, what sort of trouble they caused, or who was the source of that information.

Sometime after 5:00 p.m. on April 20th San Joaquin County Sheriff's Deputy Ivan E. Hitt arrived at the Castle School to take photographs of the crime scene. Deputy Hitt worked in the sheriff's office identification bureau performing criminal photographic and investigation work of some thirteen years standing. Deputy Hitt took several photographs of Mrs. Taylor on the floor of her classroom.

There are no photographs in the official records of any bullet holes in the structure of the classroom where the shots were fired, no photographs in the official records of any shell casings discovered in the classroom, and the room in which the shootings took place was not photographed on all four sides, only the front of the room where Mrs. Taylor fell to the floor. Official records do not include any photographs of Mr. Duval with regard to the physical injuries he received at the hand of Tom Coumas.

A hand drawn diagram of the classroom appeared in a newspaper story (*The Stockton-Record*) on April 21, 1932 indicating the position of Mrs. Taylor where she had fallen in that room, but the source of the drawing is not named by the newspaper, and no diagram of any kind showing the position of the persons in that classroom at the time of the shooting was included in the official record of the incident.

Security of the crime scene is fundamental criminology and vital to any case the state might bring to preserve the integrity of any evidence that might have been collected at the scene and to prevent potential contamination by all manner of persons who might otherwise have access to the scene. I was unsuccessful in recovering any investigatory or evidentiary records from the Manteca Police Department regarding this incident. I should point out however, that it would appear that the Castle School property was outside the Manteca city boundary, and therefore may not have been within their lawful jurisdiction. Still, one would have thought that Chief Hitchcock would have filed a report of some sort. Surely the Chief talked to somebody at the school to determine what had happened and who was responsible, but if such a conversation or inquiry took place, I haven't been able to find a record of it. Unfortunately the San Joaquin County Sheriff had no investigatory records of the shooting either, and as you will soon learn, had practically the entire force out looking for Tom Coumas, including Chief Hitchcock and Deputy Cassidy. Coumas was on the run, and all manner of law enforcement officers were on the hunt to find him.

CHAPTER FOUR
COUMAS RUNS

A man by the name of Harvey M. O'Dell was the sheriff of San Joaquin County in 1932. He was elected to office the previous year, and served in that capacity until 1939. I'm not sure what role sheriff O'Dell played in the attempted apprehension of Tom Coumas. Reports I have reviewed do not mention the county sheriff regarding the shooting at Castle School. He was mentioned in several newspaper stories as being the man directing the search for Coumas, but he did not appear to be one of the law enforcement officials actually out looking for Coumas.

One newspaper reported that the "entire" sheriff's office, armed with shotguns, teargas and side arms searched the Manteca area on the evening of 20th of April without success. Somebody was feeding a lot of information to the area newspapers about the shooting because multiple newspapers were carrying a lot of details about local efforts to find Coumas. In addition to Chief Crawford, and Deputy Cassidy, Sheriff's Deputies Ernest G. Hill, Louis Totman, Martin Ansbro, and Amos Ford were searching for Coumas. San Joaquin County Assistant District Attorney Harry C. Stanley and shorthand reporter Edwin S. Parker were also assisting in the search but to what extent was not mentioned by the reporter. Perhaps Mr. Stanley was interviewing witnesses and Mr. Parker was keeping notes, but I have yet to see any such documents on the public record.

Hitchcock and Cassidy went to the Coumas home, but did not find him there. Deputy Hill later found part of Coumas' family at the nearby home of Peter Kaloutsis, a local farmer and reported friend of the Coumas family. Coumas' green Essex sedan was found abandoned at the Kaloutsis residence, but not Coumas. One newspaper reported that Coumas had been cornered at the residence of a friend in Manteca on the evening of April 20th and that a shotgun squad had been dispatched to the scene. Nothing in any official report confirmed that part of the news story. The same story claims that the authorities had no idea how many people comprised the Coumas family or the whereabouts of the family during the hunt for Coumas.

I don't know who notified Mrs. Taylor's family of her death. I do know that Mrs. Taylor's brother Floyd P. Bailey was notified late in the day on April 20th. Floyd, himself an educator and president of Santa Rosa Community College in Santa Rosa, California traveled to the Taylor home that same evening. Other relatives were living at the time in the San Francisco Bay Area, and were aware of the incident. Mrs. Taylor's daughter, Mildred, was working at her school in Pleasanton, California also near the Bay Area. It would certainly appear that a lot of false information and rumors were circulating in the aftermath of the shooting. Many of the accounts given in several newspaper publications differed wildly from official records. Duval was recovering from his wounds the following day at the Stockton General Hospital and was expected to survive, one news source noted. Yet, Duval himself would later testify that he found shell casings on the floor when he returned to the classroom at Castle School. Exactly when he returned has never been documented in any official record.

Somebody in authority was giving very specific details of the circumstances regarding Coumas' flight, but most of these have not been corroborated in any official public document. Here are the "facts" that the media were reporting on the subject: Coumas left the school and drove to his home in Manteca; he gathered up his three children and Mrs. Hickman and drove the family to the home of a man by the name of Peter Pappas, where Coumas left Mrs. Hickman and Coumas' daughter; Coumas then drove to the home of an unidentified acquaintance where Coumas burned his sweater, then forced the friend to drive him and his two sons to the Kaloutsis residence. There Coumas left the boys, abandoned his vehicle and apparently fled on foot. The unidentified acquaintance called the police after Coumas had left the Kaloutsis property.

I find the account of what was reported to have occurred with regard to the unidentified acquaintance somewhat troubling. Nothing on the official record makes any mention of Coumas having burned his sweater or any witness having been interviewed who made any statement in that regard. I found no mention of any law enforcement account where this same person was "forced" to drive Coumas and his sons to the Kaloutsis residence. Nor have I seen any law enforcement account that this mystery person called any law enforcement agency with that information. The reason I find it troubling is that if this account is true, then Coumas committed the crime of kidnapping in forcing that person to drive him anywhere. Another news story reported that Coumas threatened to kill his daughter when he returned to his home from the school after the shooting, and that she tried to take the gun away from her father who was apparently threatening her with it. That "fact" has never been confirmed in any official public document.

Actually Coumas was all over Manteca on the night of April 20th, visiting with all manner of persons with whom Coumas was acquainted, but the "entire" sheriff's office and the Manteca Police Department could not find him.

Coumas, having lived in the area for 17 years was certainly no stranger, and Chief Hitchcock knew Coumas. On April 21st a local newspaper published an article on the shooting that was accompanied by a photograph of Coumas that Hitchcock had retrieved from the Coumas residence the previous day, so clearly the authorities had circulated information about Coumas and that he was a wanted man.

Here is what the official record says about the whereabouts of Coumas following the shooting. A man by the name of William Pappas claimed that Mrs. Hickman asked that he come to the Coumas home. Mr. Pappas arrived at the Coumas home at about 4:30 p.m. on April 20th. Mr. Pappas observed Coumas leaving his residence with his two sons in his green sedan, but that the daughter and Mrs. Hickman had been left behind. Mr. Pappas then took Mrs. Hickman and the daughter to his home. If newspaper accounts are to be believed, Coumas then went to the Kaloutsis residence in Manteca. The official record confirms this, but the time of day is not given. At about 6:00 p.m. Coumas showed up at the home of Christ Morogiannis in Manteca. They had discussions about the events at the Castle School and Coumas left. At about 9:00 p.m. Coumas returned and had further discussions with Morogiannis, then left again. At about 10:00 p.m. Coumas showed up at the Pappas home. It is not clear when he left the Pappas residence, or where Coumas spent the night.

The following morning, April 21st Coumas showed up at the ranch of Joe Coniglio in Manteca, at around 8:00 a.m. and demanded that Coniglio drive Coumas to Modesto, California about 15 miles south of Manteca. Another man happened by at that point, a friend of Coniglio's who had his car with him. Coniglio convinced the man to drive Coumas and himself to Modesto. Once there, Coumas threatened Coniglio's family if Coniglio told the authorities where they had taken Coumas in Modesto. What is most interesting about this encounter is that Coumas was armed and exhibited the weapon in a threatening manner, keeping the gun exposed throughout the trip to Modesto.

On the evening of the 21st of April a man approached the night policeman at the jail in the town of Mill Valley, California and asked to be lodged for the night. Mill Valley is located in Marin County just north of San Francisco. The policeman, Andy Bickerton, accommodated the man and locked him up in a cell. Bickerton then left a note at the adjacent fire hall to release the man from his cell the following morning. Apparently the jail was unattended at night. At just after sunrise on the morning of April 22nd, a fireman by the name of Alexander Silveria released the man who thanked Silveria and walked away. The man who had been locked up overnight in the Mill Valley jail was believed to have been Tom Coumas. A description had been issued by the authorities and published in many area newspapers. Coumas was said to have been five feet seven inches tall and weighing 167 pounds. He had brown hair, brown eyes and was dark skinned.

Coumas had a cousin living in nearby San Mateo, California by the name of John Smyrnos. San Mateo is a community south of San Francisco where Smyrnos operated a candy store. As the story goes, Smyrnos had managed to annoy Coumas over the settling of an estate involving another family member and that Coumas had threatened Smyrnos. Apparently Smyrnos feared for his life, and when news of the shooting in Manteca was reported in the local papers, the San Mateo police thought it necessary to assign a guard at the Smyrnos home.

On May 8, 1932 the Honorable James Rolph, Jr. Governor of the State of California offered a $500 reward for information leading to the arrest and conviction of Tom Coumas. The reward was both the idea and granted at the request of Sheriff O'Dell. All of which really didn't matter. Coumas had vanished and nobody could find him.

CHAPTER FIVE
THE CORONER

The coroner of San Joaquin County was a man by the name of Charles C. DeYoung. I'm really not sure what qualified the man for the job. He was a partner in a funeral home business in Stockton, California in 1920 and in 1930. It was not uncommon for funeral home operators to serve as county coroners in that state and were generally elected public officials. I don't know his background in law nor if he even had one. I also have no idea how long he had been coroner in 1932 or the extent of his experience as a coroner, in pathology or in criminal forensics.

Section 1510 of the California Penal Code reads in part, "When a coroner is informed that a person has been killed, or has committed suicide, or has died under such circumstances as to afford a reasonable ground to suspect that his death has been occasioned by the act of another by criminal means, he must go to the place where the body is, cause it to be exhumed if it has been interred, and summon not less than nine nor more than fifteen persons, qualified by law to serve as jurors, to appear before him forthwith, at the place where the body of the deceased is, to inquire into the cause of death." For the record, that quote is from a 1928 copy of the Penal Code, but there is no reason to believe this section of the law had changed by April 1932.

Section 1514 of the same code requires, "After inspecting the body and hearing the testimony, the jury must render their verdict and certify the same by an inquisition in writing, signed by them, and setting forth who the person killed is, and when, where, and by what means he came to his death; and if he was killed, or his death occasioned by the act of another, by criminal means, who is guilty thereof."

What I was able to find, by way of a finding of a coroner's jury, in compliance with the sections quoted, was a one-page form headed by the title "Coroner's Record". The form indicates that Olive Luella Taylor was in "residence" at the place of her death for "many years" and had been in California for "life". I'll leave it up to you to find something odd in that information in the record. The date of the "investigation" was April 20, 1932. The "informant" is given as "Ethan A. Taylor" and he is listed as the only relative. Mrs. Taylor's remains were released to "B.C. Wallace, Park View Cemetery, 4/22/32."

Under "Description of Accident (and) description of remains" was entered, "Deceased was shot and instantly killed by a revolver at the hands of Tom R. Coumas, Manteca, who was enraged because Mrs. Taylor had chastised Coumas' Children at school. Coumas came into the room of the Castle School where deceased was teaching, and shot Mrs. Taylor. The Janitor, W. J. Duval, tried to protect Mrs. Taylor, but Coumas shot at him and Duval fell down wounded. Coumas fired three shots at Mrs. Taylor. The shooting occurred at 4:00 PM just as Mrs. Taylor was about to leave for home, with some children." Under "Witness to accident" is listed "Mrs. and Mrs. W.J. Duval, Manteca, Calif."

This is the sum total of the statement of the coroner regarding this "accident". There is no record of a coroner's jury ever having been convened as required under state law. There appears no reference to any additional pages, photographs or exhibits. I do know that Sheriff's Deputy Ivan Hitt did take photographs of Mrs. Taylor's remains at the county morgue after she had been moved there. When all of that happened is not noted in DeYoung's record.

Under the section of that record titled "Property on body" is indicated "none". However under the section just below it titled "Disposition of property" is a notation "as below".

What is "below" is a listing in the form of a receipt for a number of what appears to be personal affects, which may have represented the contents of Mrs. Taylor's purse, and some jewelry in the form of a ring and a broach. No mention of a purse. This section of the record indicates that Ethan Taylor received this property from Charles DeYoung on April 21st, 1932. The record does not note who collected these materials, or where, or when, or under what circumstances. There is no description of the scene where she was felled, the condition of her body when examined at the scene, or any other relevant information. Relevant information might have included an analysis of the direction of the bullets trajectory in relation to the victim, for example.

Of interest to me is that Coumas' name as expressed here is Tom "R." Coumas. I have no idea where the "R." came from. He certainly did not have an "R." in his name when he had it changed in Oregon in 1912. Another interesting "detail" is the mention of the gun used in the shooting as a "revolver". It is interesting because nothing about the gun or its ammunition is noted in this record. Nothing is mentioned here about the retrieval from Mrs. Taylor of any bullets, or the caliber. Witnesses in the classroom that afternoon would later testify to a number of shots possible for a revolver to contain, but Duval would later testify that he (Duval) found shell casings on the floor of the classroom. Anybody out there know of any revolver that ejects shell casings as the gun fires? Generally when you take statements from witnesses you take them separately so you can attribute the content of such statements to the person who actually made them. This is critically important to the investigation and in making determinations about the possible violations of various laws from whatever conduct or circumstances that is being investigated. Also, it is very helpful to note any questions asked of witnesses by the person investigating something and the responses of such witnesses to such questions. It is also an effective tool for the accuracy of the official record to have a witness write out a statement, have the statement typewritten, the witness review the statement for accuracy and then have the witness sign and date the statement. Even more disturbing - there is no record that I have found that indicates that Mr. DeYoung testified as to his "investigatory" findings in any proceeding regarding this "investigation".

Section 1512 of the Penal Code allows a physician or surgeon to be summoned by the jury to inspect the body or hold a post-mortem examination for the purpose of providing a professional opinion as to the cause of the death.

There was a physician called to examine Mrs. Taylor by the name of Dr. William P.J. Lynch. Dr. Lynch was in private practice in Stockton, in 1930. The coroner's record indicates that the cause of death established by Dr. Lynch was "Exsanguination due to bleeding from ascending aorta as result of gunshot wound." Unfortunately that is the sum total of Dr. Lynch's observations in this record. Nothing about the "three shots" fired at Mrs. Taylor, nothing about any other wounds to her body. And there were other wounds. Dr. Lynch did not apparently think it necessary to note where the bullets entered her body and the path that they took through it. For the benefit of those not familiar with the term, exsanquination is the process by which one loses blood from a body part. Put another way, the bullet ripped a hole in her aorta, the main artery in the human body and she bled to death. There is greater detail over the contents of her purse here than the details of her injuries. Her death certificate holds more information than the coroner's record. At least on that document Dr. Lynch declares her death a 'homicide", from "bullet wounds" and was "shot through Aorta". The coroner, Mr. DeYoung, certifies on the death certificate that both an "investigation" and an "autopsy" were conducted. Would you categorize this effort on the part of Mr. DeYoung as an "investigation"? There may have existed at the time a legitimate reason why the state law was ignored in this particular instance, although I'm at a loss to conceive what that reason might have been. Public agencies tend to ignore the law when it suits their purposes to do so, and enforce it when it suits their purposes to do so. I always thought taking an oath of office to uphold the law meant all of the law, all the time, but we just know that is seldom the case and a huge part of the problems we have always had with our system of justice. It is possible that the "extended" report issued by DeYoung and Dr. Lynch just became separated from the original record form, or was simply misplaced or just plain lost over the years. It's possible. Given the amount of records I have been able to uncover in this shooting, I would lean toward "this is all there is". Particularly since the record makes no reference to any "attachments". Not very impressive considering these findings, such as they were, would serve as part of the evidence for what would eventually become a charge of murder of Olive Taylor and attempted murder of Mr. Duval.

CHAPTER SIX
GUARD DARRAH

Guard Clement Darrah, born in California in 1895 was the district attorney of San Joaquin County in 1932. He was admitted to the California bar in 1922, and elected district attorney in 1927. This was not a man with vast experience in the somewhat complicated field of lawyering, as it were. Someone once said that the strength of your case is often determined by the skill of your lawyer. This is particularly important when an outrageous criminal event, such as Coumas caused, begs judicial resolution. Mr. Darrah was the People's lawyer as district attorney. By his own statement on the public record, Mr. Darrah believed that his duty and responsibilities were to "investigate and institute criminal proceedings in [San Joaquin] county; to present evidence to the Grand Jury and present and prepare indictments for the Grand Jury to return after evidence had been adduced [presented] warranting such action on the part of such Grand Jury; to draw up and return informations [accusations] into court, and generally to act as the legal advisor for, institute proceedings for, prosecute and defend civil actions for the County of San Joaquin and its officers."

He was also in the grape business in San Joaquin County. Specifically the city of Lodi, under the Elephant brand. He was the packer and shipper of flame Tokay grapes during the 1920's. I share that with you for the sole purpose of illustrating that by association, Mr. Darrah would have had some experience with the agricultural labor market in San Joaquin County, and the cultural habits of immigrants who worked in the county. How is that important you ask? Well, the local authorities were looking for a man whose trade involved the peddling of fruit and vegetables among other pursuits, and who lived in a community of farmers and ranchers, many of whom were immigrants from Greece. The question that is most assuredly begged is, if he is not here, where then could he be? Surely the "investigation" into Coumas' background would indicate that he was a man of Greek origin. While I think it would have been patently unfair to hold Mr. Darrah accountable for the apprehension of Coumas, I would think it reasonable that he was the recipient of whatever information regarding Coumas was "adduced" to him by the local law enforcement agencies involved in the matter. The Castle School would seem to be an excellent potential repository of information about the parents of the children in their charge and that Coumas' country of origin might have been noted. One would think that somebody in law enforcement searched Coumas' personal affects in his residence, and one would think that discovery of letters, papers or documents indicating a connection to Greece would have been highly probable. Failing that, any number of investigators working on the case could have just asked somebody in the community. For example, Deputy Sheriff Hill might have raised the subject with the Kaloutsis family when he found the Coumas children there on April 20th.

Newspaper accounts published shortly after the shooting made note of Assistant District Attorney Harry C. Stanley assisting in the search for Coumas. No report of his notes, findings or reports appears on the public record in the matter of his involvement in the case.

CHAPTER SEVEN
SAN JOAQUIN COUNTY GRAND JURY

DA Guard Darrah did indeed convene a Grand Jury into the matter of the shootings at the Castle School. The foreman was F.A. Dougherty, Jr. Nothing much can be told about what took place before this jury, when they met, who they heard, what was presented, who was present, or where they met, only that it occurred prior to or on May 12, 1932. There is nowhere to be found the nature of any evidence presented against Tom Coumas before this jury. The person responsible for recording any sessions held by this Grand Jury regarding Coumas has not been identified in any document on the public record and the transcript could not be produced by San Joaquin County as far back as 1934, two years after the shooting. Now please recall that the Governor of California had issued a reward for Coumas, something that rarely occurs in real life; a schoolteacher was shot and killed in her classroom in front of several students, something one could surely label an equally rare if not sensational event; the teacher was a prominent and well known member of the local community; the school janitor was wounded in the same altercation; the janitors wife was also threatened, and the district attorney of the county of record loses the Grand Jury transcript?

All that being said, this Grand Jury returned an indictment against Coumas in 1932 charging him with two felonies of one count each; murder and assault with a deadly weapon with intent to commit murder. For those who may wish a clarification, a Grand Jury indictment is defined in section 917 of the California Penal Code as "an accusation in writing presented by the Grand Jury to a competent court charging the person with a public offense." As for the date of that "accusation", well I think it was May 12th. The original date written is May 4th, but that is crossed out, and the 12th written in its place. No, the change is not initialed. I have no idea if this is a true copy of the original filed with the "competent court", or some persons working copy with inked in corrections. It was provided to me by the San Joaquin County Superior Court, so the document must be on the public record. The jury found that Coumas did on April 20, 1932 willfully, unlawfully and feloniously, and with malice aforethought kill and murder one Olive Taylor, a human being and that Coumas did, at the same place, with the same weapon, on April 20, 1932 willfully, unlawfully and feloniously commit an assault upon the person of William Duval with a deadly weapon, with intent on the part of him, the said Tom Coumas, to commit murder contrary to the form, force and effect of the Statute in such cases made and provided, and against the peace and dignity of the People of the State of California. The indictment is signed by Guard C. Darrah, as District Attorney for San Joaquin County.

Now there is an interesting anomaly with regard to the body of this indictment. The witnesses that were "examined" before this particular Grand Jury are listed as being William Duval and Martin Ansoro. I'm certainly not sure, but the only person in this case that bears any resemblance to the name Martin Ansoro is San Joaquin County Deputy Sheriff Martin Ansbro, unless of course the newspaper reporting the name of Ansbro got it wrong. I will go with Ansbro, because it can be verified that Ansbro is the correct spelling of his name. But even more curious than that is the copy of this indictment on the official record has the designation "Mrs." written in ink before the typed name of William Duval. Does this mean that Mrs. Duval is the one who testified before this Grand Jury, not her husband William Duval? Even more curious is that the name of Martin Ansbro (Ansoro) is crossed out in ink and the name of Crawford Hitchcock is written in ink. Does this mean that it was actually Crawford Hitchcock that testified before the Grand Jury? Even more curious than that - are these all the witnesses in this thing? What about the other law enforcement personnel involved in the "investigation"? What about the coroner, the medical examiner, the kids in the classroom, the people with whom Coumas had contact before and after the shooting? What about the housekeeper, Mrs. Hickman? Who testified as to Duval's injuries? What of the other people Coumas threatened with his pistol? I count at least two kidnappings in this deal, and a whole slew of people assaulted with a deadly weapon, not the least of which would seem to be Mrs. Duval. There seemed to be a number of witnesses to all of that, if you can believe the news accounts of the day. Interestingly enough the California Penal Code sections that the Grand Jury concluded Coumas violated are not referenced in the indictment. Since Grand Jury indictments are generally filed with the Court, one would think it would be helpful to the Court to cite the statutes involved. This Grand Jury did not, but for your benefit I will. The crime of murder in California in 1932 was found in Section 187 of the Penal Code. It reads, "Murder Defined. Murder is the unlawful killing of a human being with malice aforethought." This is a tricky thing to charge somebody with, particularly due to the penalties that are associated with it including execution. So, one must look to the evidence in the case to support the definition of the conduct, and malice before the actual deed is the most difficult part to prove. The accused must demonstrate by conduct or other evidence that intent to kill with malice was evident in the execution of the act. Malice is express in the law when there is manifested a deliberate intention to unlawfully take the life of a fellow human being. Malice is implied when no considerable provocation appears, or when the circumstances attending the killing show an abandoned and malignant heart. Under Section 188 of the same code, malice can be either express or implied. It's up to a trial jury to decide the merits of the circumstances of the act, and whether the act meets the criteria under the law to reach a finding of murder. District attorneys are responsible for presenting evidence that will support the charge of murder when such charges are brought against an accused. It serves no useful purpose to have an accused found not guilty of a murder charge because the evidence does not support the charge. The accused cannot be made to stand trial again once tried on a charge in the original indictment, and found not guilty by a jury.

Assault with a deadly weapon was a little fuzzy in the California Penal Code of that era, and several sections of the code are involved depending on how the assault is perpetrated and the result of the assault. Essentially the Penal Code section in play is 217, and the key to conviction here is the intent of the person charged with the attempt. The evidence presented must support a conclusion that the accused intended to cause the death of another person. And all of which must be proven beyond a reasonable doubt, and the verdict of guilty must be unanimous at trial. Interestingly, Section 921 of the same code requires that a Grand Jury "ought to find an indictment when all of the evidence before them, taken together, if unexplained or uncontradicted, would, in their judgment, warrant a conviction by a trial jury." On the other hand, Section 920 offers that a Grand Jury if by examination of the evidence submitted could cause them to believe that other evidence might explain away the charges against the accused, they should order that such evidence be produced and that the district attorney be directed to subpoena the requisite witnesses to appear before them.

Of course the reality of the Grand Jury process is that the jury pretty much does whatever the district attorney recommends. I have always found this an incredibly unfair aspect of our criminal justice system due to the irreparable harm often caused someone unfairly accused of criminal conduct, more often than not on equally incredibly thin and vaguely circumstantial evidence. I say unfair because law enforcement types often shoot their mouths off in public about a particular case (or quietly whispering "facts" to the media as anonymous informed sources) rather than confine their accusations to a court of law, where such matters are required by law to be adjudicated. Contributing to this is that the Grand Jury process is largely in favor of the prosecution and the defendant or accused is not heard by the jury. However, that does not mean that the jury has no obligation to question the nature of evidence submitted, and in particular any aspect of that evidence that may not support the charges levied or the test of law in bringing those charges before the jury for the purpose of returning an indictment against the accused, in this case, Tom Coumas.

Unfortunately we can't review that here because the transcript is missing, so we just don't know what evidence this particular Grand Jury considered in reaching its conclusions regarding Coumas.

I have not been able to find in the public record a copy of a warrant for the arrest of Tom Coumas on any charge. The crimes were committed on April 20th, and the Grand Jury did not return an indictment until either the 4th or the 12th of May. I have no way of knowing which indictment date is the valid date. The indictment can serve as a warrant when filed with the court of jurisdiction, but why did this process take two weeks at the minimum (May 4th) or three weeks if you accept the May 12th date? Did anybody seek a search warrant for the Coumas residence? I have not found a copy of one, if it ever existed.

News of any efforts to apprehend Coumas pretty much dried up by the end of May 1932. Coumas was nowhere to be found, and nobody seemed to have a clue as to where he might be. But clues are clues and there was one man in America who was famous for giving clarity to the smallest of clues. Guard Darrah had a card up his sleeve and was about to put it in play.

CHAPTER EIGHT
ELLIS PARKER

He was Chief of Detectives for the Burlington County, New Jersey police headquartered in Mt. Holly, New Jersey. Chief Parker was internationally known for the brilliance of his detective work, and gained considerable fame, if not some controversy, for his work on the Charles Lindbergh baby kidnapping. He was born in New Jersey about 1872, and although I do not know when he entered police work, by 1932 he had accumulated at least 32 years experience in the crime solving business. He also knew Guard Darrah, and Darrah new Parker. Sometime around October of 1932, when the trail of Tom Coumas was growing colder by the hour, and no amount of searching produced the slightest results, Darrah asked Parker to look into the matter.

There are certain premises in police work that are assumed to be givens. One such premise is that criminals on the run often make contact with family members and seek refuge in the homes of parents and other family members.

Darrah had given consideration that Coumas might have returned to Greece, but he was being sought as Tom Coumas. Of course that offered up a dead end. Parker started by writing to all state vital records offices in the U.S. trying to find any record of Coumas' marriage to wife, Margaret. Washington responded with a record that indicated Coumas said he was a cook at the time of the marriage and was a naturalized citizen of the U.S. Parker then wrote to immigration officials in Washington, D.C. and was able to uncover Coumas' immigration records. Parker suggested to Darrah that he have restaurants checked to determine if Coumas had found employment in California as a cook. A check on a restaurant in Merced, California uncovered a man who said he had hired Coumas, but that Coumas had since disappeared. The geographic location of Merced caused Parker to conclude that Coumas was heading for Mexico and possibly from Mexico to Greece. Parker wrote to authorities in Mexico in search of Coumas, but nobody had seen the man there.

Parker knew a professor of the Greek at Princeton University by the name of Edward Capps, who had spent time in Greece and was well acquainted with the country. Parker had learned that Coumas was born in Roino, Greece from the Washington marriage documents, and asked Professor Capps if he could find out anything on Coumas in Roino. Capps also knew several U.S. officials at the embassy in Athens, and other Greek officials from time spent in Greece as an American Red Cross Commissioner and the United States Minister to Greece under appointment of President Woodrow Wilson. Professor Capps' credentials with regard to both his knowledge and presence in Greece were impressive, but he could not find Tom Coumas. Capps contacted an old friend at the embassy in Athens, Lincoln MacVeigh, who during his diplomatic career served as both Minister to Greece and Ambassador to Greece. Still there was no sign of Coumas in Greece, which Ellis Parker found astonishing.

Meanwhile, the Portland, Oregon police, aware that Coumas was wanted for murder in California, uncovered Coumas' name change documents from 1912 and immediately notified Parker that the man he was looking for was Smyrno Smyrnogranis. Parker again contacted the

Mexican authorities who armed with the new name for Coumas turned up a cook by the name of Smyrno Smyrnogranis who had boarded a steamer at Tampico bound for Brazil. Parker tracked the steamer through several ports of call, and then sent another letter to Greece but this time asking for a search for Tom Coumas as Smyrno Smyrnogranis. By the time that letter arrived in Greece, authorities there had already arrested Coumas. Be that as it may, and even granting certain latitudes for missing timelines and a detailed record of who did what and when, Chief Parker may not have exactly uncovered the route Coumas took to Greece, but may have played a large role in solving the mystery of Coumas' whereabouts. Clearly the San Joaquin County officials were in contact with the authorities in Greece, as well as our embassy there. It was Darrah who notified Parker by telegram of Coumas' arrest in Greece. What is somewhat troubling about all of this is that Coumas was not arrested in Greece until June of 1934. Darrah brought Parker into the case in October 1932. So the whole process of running Coumas down in Greece took 21 months?

And interestingly enough, you may recall that the name Coumas used in his name change petition in 1912 was Spiros Smirnagianis, not Smyrnos Smyrnogranis. Research into a story like this causes one to uncover and consider a wide variety of sources, and record keeping is not always precise and often gets muddied through translation and transcription. But, facts are facts and when they are part of an official record, hard to ignore or simply excuse.

What bothers me is when did the San Joaquin County detectives conclude that Coumas was from Greece and might have family there and somebody maybe ought to check Greece to see if maybe he had gone there. Margaret Coumas was in the mental hospital in Stockton, and surely the hospital administration had a record of her family and other information about her, possibly including her husband. Did anybody follow that thread? Did the San Joaquin County investigators speak with the authorities in San Mateo who were guarding Coumas' cousin, himself a Greek immigrant, regarding where Coumas might have fled? Then there were the local residents in Manteca who were both friends and acquaintances of Coumas and with whom he had left his children. Which begs another question; where were the Coumas children, and did anyone consider the California law, which makes it illegal to abandon ones children in that state?

Mexico found evidence of a trail of Smyrnos Smyrnogranis, a name supplied by Chief Parker, given to him by the police in Oregon, who obviously had the wrong name. So was the guy who boarded the steamer in Tampico the wrong guy?

Tom Coumas, on the other hand had an entirely different recollection of this journey from Manteca to Greece.

Meanwhile, Guard Darrah still had a problem. Coumas had been found, but Greece had him in custody and Darrah wanted him back in the United States for trial in San Joaquin County.

CHAPTER NINE
EXTRADITION

Coumas was arrested by the Greek police at his grocery store in Roino. He had been a very busy man since arriving back in Greece during the summer of 1932. At first he had been living at his parents' farm, doing chores for his father. The first time the police visited Coumas was not to arrest him but to deliver a summons and tell him he was required to serve a four-month term in the Greek army. As Coumas tells the story, he tried to explain to the police that he was an American citizen, but the authorities were not convinced. In fact the police told Coumas, we hear that all the time when we tell Greeks they have to serve their required time in the military. There existed a provision in Greek law that said persons of a particular age could avoid the military obligation by paying a specified sum of money to the government. Coumas did not have the requisite amount, and thus in November 1932 entered the Greek army where he served as a medical aide and remained for a period of four months.

When he was discharged from the army the following February, he had little funds and no job. So he got married. As he would later explain the situation, a letter had come from Manteca to his parents in Roino bearing the news that Coumas' wife, Margaret, had died in Stockton, California. Coumas' uncle in Greece knew a Greek family who had a daughter and through the girl's father introductions were made. The girl had some money of her own and after they were married, Coumas used those funds to buy a grocery store in Roino. Coumas was tending his store in June of 1934 when the police came calling, this time to arrest him for the crime of murder, and other crimes for which he was wanted in the United States.

A short newspaper story appeared on July 15, 1934 that reported that acting California Governor Frank. F. Merriam had signed extradition papers asking for the return of Coumas from Greece to the United States.

Unknown to Coumas at the time, and apparently preceding the arrest of Coumas in Greece, the U.S. State Department under Cordell Hull had become involved in the hunt for Coumas, including the White House and then President of the United States, Franklin D. Roosevelt. Various dispatches were flying back and forth between Washington and the American embassy in Athens. Included in those dispatches was a Presidential Warrant for the arrest of Coumas along with an official request that Coumas be extradited to the United States to stand trial on the charges in San Joaquin County. I would assume that Governor Merriam's request eventually found its way to Greece through U.S. State Department channels, but by that time Coumas had already been arrested in Greece.

Earlier in 1934, Guard Darrah convened another Grand Jury after the Greek Government made a demand for the evidence supporting the original California indictment in 1932. That evidence could not be provided due to the court reporter problem, and the missing Grand Jury transcript. The only thing Darrah could do was to call another Grand Jury into session and amend the original indictment and produce a refreshed version of the original indictment.

Coumas sat in the Tripolis jail for three months while the U.S. and Greek governments went back and forth over claims on him were argued. Ultimately the Greek government agreed to hold an extradition hearing on Coumas, and San Joaquin County was given the opportunity to present their evidence in substantiation of the charges against him.

That hearing was convened by the Council of the Court of Appeals at Nauplia on August 28, 1934. The court had for its consideration numerous documents provided to it by various representatives of the U.S. Government, and San Joaquin County. Among these were the amended indictment with the statements of several witnesses, a statement from District Attorney Darrah, and Coumas' immigration records. The Court of Appeals at Nauplia consists of a number of justices of which three participated in this hearing, two attorneys representing the government of Greece and two attorneys representing Coumas.
The hearing took but a day, and concerned itself with the various points and authorities of law. It was not a hearing about the rights of Tom Coumas. This was strictly a jurisdictional hearing to decide who in fact had legal jurisdiction over Coumas, and whether or not the evidence supported the crimes with which he was charged by San Joaquin County. No U.S. representative is named in the record on this hearing as having appeared personally and was heard by this court during this hearing. Coumas did not testify, leaving his legal interests to the lawyers representing him.

In order to appreciate the challenges this court faced in reaching its ultimate conclusions, we need to go back to San Joaquin County and take a look inside the March 14, 1934 Grand Jury.

CHAPTER TEN
SAN JOAQUIN COUNTY GRAND JURY II

Spryos Smyrnogranis, Spira Smyrnogianas, Spiros Smyrnogiania, Spiros Smyrnogiani, sometimes written as Spiros Smirsiany, Speros Smernogeon, Spero Smernogeon, Spiros Smirnagianis, Spiros Smernagian, Speros Smirnogianis, Spiro Smirnagianis, Spiros Syminogean, Spiros Smyrnogeau and sometimes written as Thomas Coumas – all known aliases used by Tom Coumas according to the amended indictment of this Grand Jury on March 14, 1934. Why this man felt that he needed to use all of these various different names in his various endeavors remains known only to him, since I have not seen any document that attempts to explain it, or even ask him about it.

Be that as it may, this amended indictment is issued in all of those names. Guard Darrah is taking no chances with identity issues on this round.

The indictment names as witnesses the following: 1) William Duval, 2) Frances Fisher, 3) Mary Kondratenko, 4) W.S. Worcester, and 5) Rudy Weber. The charges levied are essentially the same, murder of Olive Taylor and attempted murder of Duval.

To refresh your memory William Duval was the school janitor, Frances and Mary were students in class on April 20th, and Rudy Weber (who hasn't been mentioned previously) was an investigator in the San Joaquin County

Sheriff's office. I can't tell you anything about W. S. Worcester since I have no statement he might have given before this Grand Jury, or what he might have testified about. I can tell you his first name was Wilbur. As a general rule, only evidence sufficient to prove the commission of the crimes charged against the accused are presented before a grand jury and generally do not represent the sum total of evidence that might be presented at trial. The district attorney is only trying to get an indictment here, not a conviction. Henry F. Ellis, age 70 was the foreman of this Grand Jury, and the indictment is signed by both Guard Darrah and Assistant District Attorney Harry C. Stanley. The Clerk of the Superior Court was Eugene D. Graham for both the 1932 and 1934 indictments. Hugo P. Braasch was the Deputy Clerk in 1932, and in 1934 it was Guard Darrah's father-in-law, Thomas U. Stroup. Yes, Darrah was married to Stroup's daughter, and yes, her father worked in the San Joaquin County Superior Court as a Deputy Clerk, the same court where Darrah did his deeds as County District Attorney. I don't know that this particular information is particularly helpful, but I'll let you make up your own mind about that.

Clearly, once somebody in San Joaquin County concluded that there existed a possibility that Coumas had fled to Greece, there were communications going back and forth between San Joaquin County and various people attempting to locate Coumas, not the least of which Ellis Parker, Edward Capps, and officials of the U.S. State Department. Since Coumas had not been arrested in Greece at the time this Grand Jury was convened, it was probably only convened to deal with the loss of the transcript in support of the May 12, 1932 indictment. It is also possible that this amendment may have only served as justification for the Presidential Warrant, and the official request of the Greek government to locate and arrest Coumas should he be found in Greece. Indictments are often sealed, and these must be no exception because none of the witness statements are on the public record in San Joaquin County. But one thing is certain - the authorities in Greece knew that Mrs. William Duval was Rosiann Duval, and that Worcestor's first name was Wilbur. This suggests to me that Mrs. Duval was the witness named in the witness list for the 1932 original indictment, rather than Mr. Duval. Interesting that Darrah would choose her rather than the man who was shot and wounded by Coumas. Not that she would not have constituted an important witness. There were only two witnesses named in the 1932 indictment, and as such I would have thought Mr. Duval would have been the stronger witness then. It couldn't be that he was excluded because one of the crimes charged was committed against him. After all, he is named as a witness in the 1934 amended version, but not Mrs. Duval. However you slice it, we will never know what these six witnesses testified to in either Grand Jury proceeding since the records of their testimony do not appear to exist.

Back in Greece, it is now August 1934 and the Court of Appeals is considering all of this at Coumas' extradition hearing at Nauplia.

CHAPTER ELEVEN
NAUPLIA

When I indicated that the testimonies of the witnesses in the Grand Jury indictments of Coumas were not on the public record, I was referring to the Coumas case file in the custody of the San Joaquin County Superior Court. They were however alive and well in the hands of the Court of Appeals in Nauplia, along with numerous other documents supplied to the Greek court by not only San Joaquin County, but the U.S. Government essentially through the American embassy in Athens.

The essential issue before the Greek court was an official request dated August 1, 1934 that Coumas be extradited to the United States to stand trial for his crimes committed in San Joaquin County. The U.S. authorities claimed Coumas was an American citizen, subject to U.S. laws and was hiding in Greece simply to avoid prosecution in the U.S. for his crimes. That was the basis for Coumas arrest in Greece in June of 1934. What seems to be indicated here by the various dates involved is that certainty on the part of the various authorities that Coumas was in fact in Greece did not begin to materialize until around April/May/June 1934, fully two years after the shooting took place in California. The Greek arrest warrant for Coumas was issued on June 23, 1934.

Part and parcel to all of this was the necessity for Coumas to be identified as the person that the Americans were seeking. For this purpose, photographs that were liberated from the Coumas home in Manteca by Crawford Hitchcock had been supplied to the court in Greece, along with information that he had been naturalized in Oregon in 1914, and that his name had been changed to Tom Coumas from Spiros Smirnagianis. The Greek government having thoroughly investigated the identify issue, and later by Coumas' eventual admission, that he was actually one Spyros Smyrnoyiannis born in Roino, Greece in 1889. Having confirmed all of that, also confirmed that by virtue of birth, Coumas was a citizen of Greece.

The American government took the position that when Coumas stood upright on February 25, 1914 in Portland, Oregon and spoke the oath of allegiance to the United States he essentially divested himself of citizenship in any other country on earth, and perhaps the United Federation of Planets. This is a major sticking point in the craw of the old federal Immigration and Naturalization Service (INS) and has been cited by the federal government many times in future legal events involving Coumas.

This is what Tom Coumas supposedly said out loud in Portland that day,

> "*I hereby declare on oath that I absolutely and entirely renounce and abjure all allegiance and fidelity to a foreign prince, potentate, state or sovereignty of whom or which I have heretofore been a subject or citizen; that I will support and defend the Constitution and the Laws of the United States of America against all enemies, foreign and domestic; that I will bear true faith and allegiance to the same; that I will bear arms on behalf of the United States when required by law; or that I will perform non-combatant service in the Armed Forces of the United States when required by law; or that I*

> *will perform work of National importance under civilian direction when required by law; and that I take this obligation freely without any mental reservation or purpose of evasion, so help me God."*

The general premise held by the United States from that day forward is that Coumas, by taking that oath was no longer a citizen of any country except the Unites State of America.

What constantly amazes me in our country is how many people there are that are charged with enforcement of our laws who do not understand the laws they are required by law to enforce or just do not know that the laws they are required by law to enforce even exist. Let me explain. Coumas did not have the legal power or authority to make that oath in Oregon, therefore the United States had no legal power or authority to make him a U.S. citizen. The Court of Appeals at Nauplia cleared all of that up. It seems that under Greek law, specifically Act No. 120 of January 2, 1914 (an Act of which Coumas was probably unaware since he had been living in the United States since 1907) that being naturalized in a foreign country is not sufficient to cause one the loss of Greek citizenship. Further, a Greek citizen may not divest oneself of Greek citizenship without the permission of the Minister of Foreign Affairs (of the Greek government), by presidential decree.

You would certainly think that the very people who were in the immigration business in the United States would have known that people immigrating from Greece after January 2, 1914 and who sought naturalization in the United States would have to show proof that the Greek government had given their permission to divest themselves of their Greek citizenship, because as a Greek citizen they were subject to Greek law no matter where on earth they might be, and therefore could not simply sweep it away by taking an oath to the contrary in the United States. That would certainly seem to be the case, unless of course the United States recognized and accepted dual citizenship in 1914, which it would appear that they did not or one would think that the oath would not have had that renouncing and abjuring stuff in it.

The Court of Appeals at Nauplia also observed that a treaty was signed between the Greek and American governments on May 6, 1931 that essentially says that neither country can be compelled to give up one of its own citizen criminals to and on the demand of the other. Treaties carry a very high level of precedence over other more junior laws, and rank above federal law in the United States. That is why the United States Congress cannot pass a law that compels somebody to do or not do something that would violate the provisions of a treaty, and the President of the United States cannot order anybody to do something or not do something that would violate a treaty. Unless of course it might involve people who lived here before the establishment of the United States on the continent commonly referred to as North America, but that is another whole different book.

So, under Article 8, of the Treaty of Extradition between Greece and America, the extradition of their own citizens is strictly forbidden. Coumas was not going to be delivered to the American government by the Greek Government, and so the extradition request was denied.

There did remain the not so small matter that as a Greek citizen he was liable for his conduct while in the United States but under Greek law. The examination of that conduct would await another day and another court. This court was only concerned with the matter of the extradition request, which for the reasons previously stated here were denied. It was not the purpose of this court or this hearing to decide merit or validity of the charges conveyed in the San Joaquin County March 14, 1934 Indictment. Coumas was ordered released from his detention by the court on August 28, 1934.

CHAPTER TWELVE
DEPOSITIONS

The Greek government was not yet done with Tom Coumas. Just because extradition was denied, it did not mean that Greece did not take the charges against Coumas in the United States very seriously. Following the decision of the Court of Appeals at Nauplia, the Greek government undertook an investigation of their own into Coumas' conduct in the United States in 1932. Remember that citizens of Greece are accountable to Greek law; no matter where they might be, or in what country any offenses might have been alleged.

On October 16, 1934 the Minister of Foreign Affairs, through the district attorney of the Superior Court of Tripolis, Greece sent a dispatch to the Consulate General of Greece in San Francisco. In that dispatch, the Minister gave notice that an investigation was underway into the San Joaquin County allegations and requested that new depositions be taken from witnesses William Duval, Rosiann Duval, Frances Fisher, Mary Kondratenko, Rudy Weber, Wilbur Worcester and any other witnesses that should be considered as necessary and material to the acts for which Coumas was accused. The dispatch included four photographs of Coumas taken in Greece and required that each witness be shown those photographs and the following specific questions asked; 1) Is the person in the photographs the person who committed the crimes for which he is accused? 2) Does the witness have absolute confidence in the identity of the person who committed the crimes as being the person who appears in the photographs shown? 3) Did the witness know the accused prior to the commission of the crimes? 4) Did the witness know the country of Coumas' birth, and under what circumstances, or if only just an acquaintance, if the witness had any special connection with Coumas or a business relationship, or only knew him by sight? 5) Did the witness know how long Coumas had lived in San Joaquin County, in what city, and his address? The dispatch encouraged speed in handling the request for these depositions, citing limitations under Greek law in which a person can be held without proceeding to trial. And the best news of all, Coumas had been arrested again in Greece on September 13, 1934 on a new warrant. The Consul General of Greece added a caveat to the dispatch that the depositions must all be taken on the same day under Greek law and depositions taken on any other day would be excluded from consideration in the investigation. By letter, the Consulate conveyed all of these criteria to District Attorney Guard Darrah on December 13, 1934. Guard Darrah was going to get another shot at Coumas, and he was going to take it.

On December 19, 1934 the San Joaquin County Grand Jury was yet once again called into session with Foreman Ellis presiding, and Mr. Darrah representing the People. Nobody was in attendance to represent Tom Coumas. Darrah assembled fifteen witnesses for this session with Herman G. Spalinger recording testimony. I do not know for certain the exact order of their appearance before the Grand Jury, but it appears this was the order of appearance from the transcript, and this is the same witness list later certified by the San Joaquin County Superior Court: 1) William J. Duval, 2) Dr. William P.J. Lynch, 3) Rosiann Duval, 4) Ivan E. Hitt, 5) Mary Kondratenko, 6) Frances Fisher, 7) Frances Aguilar, 8) Athena Bouzeneris, 9) William Pappas, 10) Aristea

Kaloutsis, 11) Christ Morogiannis, 12) John Soukos, 13) Joe Coniglio, 14) Crawford Hitchcock, and 15) Rudolph Weber.

Since I don't know conclusively the order of their appearance on this occasion, I'm going to have them appear here under these general groupings; student witnesses who were in the classroom at the time of the shooting; Mr. and Mrs. Duval in that order; law enforcement personnel; friends/associates of Coumas; and the medical examiner. In the interest of time and space I'm going to paraphrase their testimony, but I will share actual testimony when I think it will illustrate a point or has some significant bearing on the charges against Coumas. I should also point out, in order to save some additional time and space that each witness was asked during their depositions to identify Coumas from a number of different photographs, some that were in Coumas possession in Manteca, and those submitted by the Greek authorities in October 1934. Also you should keep in mind that this Grand Jury is meeting to take depositions from witnesses on the charges levied in the March 14, 1934 indictment, roughly 30 months after the shooting at Castle School in Manteca. I also don't know if all of these witnesses were in the room when others gave testimony. Reading the law on the matter, one could conclude that only the person giving testimony may appear as testimony is given and that only the witnesses giving testimony may appear. It would seem to me that in the interest of avoiding prejudicing the witnesses you would have them testify without the other witnesses in the room. Of course these witnesses have had ample opportunity to discuss the case amongst themselves, particularly since they are all from the same small community and given the passage of time since the shooting. This session did not result in any changes to the March 14th indictment and no additional charges were added as a result of the testimony of these witnesses.

Mary Kondratenko

Mary states that she was in the classroom at the Castle School at about 4:00 p.m. on April 20, 1932 and that the regular session of school had closed for the day. She indicates that others in the classroom at that time were Mrs. Duval, Olive Taylor, and five other girls (students). She says that she heard shots, saw Tom Coumas in the classroom, saw the gun in his hand, and saw him fire those shots. She tells Darrah that she knew Coumas from when he used to peddle vegetables. Darrah then asks her:

> "Q. You just tell us, then, what you saw and heard after this man, Tom Coumas, came into the school-house. A. He went in and comes up to the teacher; he says, 'You are a public teacher, you can't treat my children like this, 'he said. She took a step back, [s]he says, 'Listen here' – and he told her to shut up and he swore; then he pulls out this here gun and shoots at her. She just twisted and fell; we started to run. That's all I saw. Q. How many shots did you hear fired? A. I heard two shots that I can remember. Then we ran through the door; I didn't hear anything else. Q. What did Mrs. Taylor do immediately after the shot was fired? A. She just twisted to the side and fell to her face. Q. Right there on the floor? A. Right there."

In the original transcript of Mary's deposition, when Mary quoted Coumas as saying "he says", I added the [s] because I think Mary meant to say "she", as in Mrs. Taylor said, "Listen here – ". This would be consistent with other testimony taken for the purpose of these depositions. Perhaps the court reporter heard her wrong or the deposition was transcribed incorrectly.

Darrah then takes Mary through a series of photographs asking her to identify Coumas as the man who shot Olive Taylor, and Mary confirms positively that the man in the photographs is Coumas and is the man she saw shoot her. Then Darrah resumes his questioning of Mary:

> "Q. Did you see Mrs. Duval in the school room that day? A. Yes. Q. This was when, do you recall the time? A. April 20th. Q. Of what year? A. 1932. Q. Did you see what Mr. Duval was doing? A. He just walked in the class room and he was in back of – he was in the class room, he was in back of Mr. Coumas, and I had my side to him; I did not see Mr. Duval do anything; I just saw Mrs. Taylor fall, and I turned around and started Running. Q. And to what place did you run? A. Ran to the stage in the back; he was toward the front. Q. There were some other girls, you say, with you? A. Yes. Q. Who else was with you? A. Two other girls with me, and then three other girls with me then; the other girls were on the other side of the room. Q. Then did you remain at the school building there until the officers came? A. No, we waited, watched Mr. Coumas drive away, and I went down to Mrs. Gustafson's place and telephoned. Q. How did Mr. Coumas leave? A. In his car. Q. Did anybody go with him? A. No. Q. Do you know Mr. Coumas' children? A. Well I know one of the girls, and a boy. Q. Did you see them there this day Mrs. Taylor was shot? A. They were there that day. Q. What became of the children after the shooting, do you know? A. I don't know."

Darrah, then referring to a photograph that shows Olive Taylor lying on the classroom floor, asks Mary:

> "Q.....do you recognize anything on that photograph? A. Yes, that is Mrs. Taylor. Q. That is

where she was laying when you were running out of the room? A. Yes. Q. Did you notice the seats, those were the seats in the class room? A. Yes."

What we have here is a witness to what the Grand Jury has concluded was a murder. What we do not seem to have is a district attorney with any sort of planned approach to questioning the witness. Keeping in mind that Darrah is under no obligation to divulge all the facts in this case; just the one's he believes are important. That being said, when I read this statement it occurred to me that Darrah might have asked: 1) the names of the other girls, 2) where were they in the classroom when Coumas walked in, 3) what did Mrs. Taylor say to Coumas, 4) did Mrs. Duval say anything to Coumas, 5) did Mr. Duval say anything to Coumas, 6) was Mr. Duval already in the classroom when Coumas walked in, and what was Mr. Duval doing when he was in the classroom, 7) where was Mrs. Taylor in the classroom when she was shot, 8) where in the classroom did Mrs. Taylor fall, 9) what were the names of the Coumas children in the classroom that day, 10) were the Coumas children in the classroom at the time of the shooting, 11) did you see Mrs. Clara Hickman come to the classroom that day, 12) did you see what happened when Mrs. Hickman came to the classroom that day, 13) did you hear or see what Mrs. Taylor did or said when Mrs. Hickman came to the classroom that day, 14) was it just you or did other girls go with you to Mrs. Gustafson's, 15) who were the other girls that went with you, 16) when you ran to the stage who was in the front, 17) at Mrs. Gustafson's who telephoned, and who was telephoned. And possibly another point was when Darrah asks Mary about the time and she gives the date. Did he mean the time of day, or was he asking her for the date of the shooting? And maybe, just maybe I would be curious enough to ask what Mrs. Duval was doing, and where in the classroom was Mrs. Duval when Coumas came into the room. And yes, maybe one more question for this witness; Mary testified that she was in the building until Coumas drove away from the school. At least she said she watched Coumas drive away from the school. Is it possible that she could see the classroom from the stage where she said she ran, and if so, why didn't Darrah ask her if she saw Mr. Duval shot by Coumas? Or for that matter why didn't Darrah ask her if she saw Coumas point the gun at Mrs. Duval? Perhaps Darrah knew the answers to those questions and therefore did not ask them. I can't overemphasize enough that if these questions are obvious to me, surely they would arise in Greece where these depositions are destined. What I am looking for is a witness supporting the charge of attempted murder of Mr. Duval.

Athena Bouzeneris

Athena confirms that she was in the classroom on April 20th and that the regular session had concluded, with some students remaining in the classroom. She indicates that Mr. and Mrs. Duval were not in the classroom at the close of school – Darrah does not ask her the time of day for any of this – but came in later. Athena also confirms that Tom Coumas came into the classroom that day, but again, Darrah does not ask her the time of day that he entered. I don't know about 1932, but most classrooms have clocks that everybody can see, but maybe this information is not relevant to Mr. Darrah's purposes here. Darrah then asks Athena to identify Coumas from the various photographic exhibits, which she does, tentatively, but then at the urging of Darrah, positively. Mr. Darrah:

> "Q. When he [Coumas] came into the school room, where were you at that particular time? A. I think I was standing close to the window by the table. Q. Did you notice him as he came through the door? A.

Yes. Q. Did he say anything? A. Well, he was talking, but I forgot what he said. Q. Was there anybody else talking? A. I don't remember. Q. Now, to the best of your recollection, you just state all that you heard and saw from the time that Mr. Coumas came in through the door? A. Well, he was hollering outside; he was talking to somebody, then he came through the door, he was mad, and we were just listening to him, and I don't know, he just took out the gun and shot her. Q. Did you see the gun? A. Yes. Q. What was it, a pistol? A. Yes. Q. It wasn't a gun you shoot with two hands? A. No. Q. Just a one-handed gun, a pistol, was that it? A. Yes. Q. All right, how many shots did you hear fired? A. I don't remember. Q. Did you hear more than one? A. I don't remember if I did or not. Q. What happened to you after the shots were fired? A. I ran up to the stage. Q. You ran, did you? A. Yes. Q. What happened to Mrs. Taylor, did you notice? A. No. Q. Well, when you ran, did you run out of the room? A. I run up to the stage. Q. Then where did you go? A. I went with the other girls and telephoned at Mrs. Gustafson's. Q. After you telephoned, what did you do? Did you go back to the school or some other place? A. I forget whether I went back or not. Q. Do you remember my questioning you that afternoon? A. I remember somebody questioning me. Q. You were back at the school house there, were you? A. Oh, yes. Q. So you must have come back? A. Yes. Q. When you came back where was Mrs. Taylor? A. She was on the floor. Q. She was on the floor – now [Darrah takes up a photograph of Olive Taylor lying on the classroom floor and shows it to the witness], do you recognize that person as Olive Taylor? A. Yes. Q. And was the position she occupied then? A. Yes."

The witness was then dismissed. If a witness says they do not recall something and the lawyer asking the questions plows ahead leading the witness into a different response, isn't that called leading the witness? If Darrah interviewed this girl at the school on April 20th, did he not ask her to give a statement, and if so, why didn't he use her statement from that date to refresh her memory? Again I have a problem with the lack of time establishment, particularly as it relates to her return to the classroom. This witness was also not asked if she saw Duval shot, and did not establish who was "telephoned". And as with the previous witness, Darrah did not establish who Gustafson was and where that person was in relation to the school. Also keep in mind these statements are being taken for the benefit of authorities in another country halfway around the planet who probably had not ever been in San Joaquin County save Coumas. Some additional questions that could have been asked might have been, "When you saw Mr. Coumas with the gun, where was he pointing it?" And perhaps, "When you returned to the classroom, who else was in the room at that time, other than Mrs. Taylor?" What troubles me here is that I find it somewhat logical to conclude that some minutes had passed since this witness went to the Gustafson ranch to report the shooting, and the time it would have taken to explain that to whomever at the ranch, and then return to the school. Why then, was this girl allowed back into the room, which by then surely must have been a crime scene? I also think it would have been helpful for Mr. Darrah to ask the witness to clarify what she meant by saying Coumas was mad. "Mad in what way, or what made you think he was mad?"

Frances Aguilar

Again Darrah takes the witness through the fundamentals of establishing her residency, that she was at the school on April 20th, and that the witness had known Olive Taylor. Darrah starts by asking Frances what, if anything, she saw at the school on April 20th:

> "A. You mean at the time of the happening? Q. Yes. A. Well, I was sitting about the third seat or second or third row from the left and I saw this man coming in, and he started telling her about what she had done, and he told her that she was a public teacher and she shouldn't have done that. Q. Shouldn't have done what? A. Whipped his child; I think she had whipped his child. She says, "Well, listen here" – she started in explaining and he told her to shut up and swore at her; I did not see the pistol, I ran out. Q. Did you see her falling to the floor? A. No. Q. Did you hear her? A. No, I didn't hear her, because I covered my ears; I ran out and covered my ears. Q. And do you know who the man was? A. Yes, Tom Coumas."

Darrah then takes the witness though the photos for identification purposes and Frances confirms Coumas identity. Darrah then shows Frances a photograph of Olive Taylor on the classroom floor and asks:

> ".....do you know who that is? A. Yes, Mrs. Olive B. Taylor. Q. Was she your school-teacher at the time? A. Yes, sir. Mr. Darrah: That is all."

Ok, has anybody yet actually seen this shooting, of anybody, in this classroom? Curious that Darrah doesn't ask Frances if she saw Mrs. Taylor "whip" Coumas child.

Frances Fisher

Darrah takes the witness through her residency, whether she knew Olive Taylor, and if she was at the school on April 20th. He does not ask if she was in the classroom on that day, just "at the Castle School". Mr. Darrah then asks Frances,

> "Q. What, if anything, did you see there at that time? A. Why I was there when Tom Coumas killed the teacher. Did you want me to tell what happened? Q. Yes. A. Well, I was in there sitting in one of the seats in the school, and he came in the door; he stood there just a little ways from the door, he started hollering right away, shouting at her, calling her names; he asked her why she whipped his little boy, and she just said, "Well, listen here" – that's all she said. Q. She said what? A. "Well, listen here" – that's all she said. Well, Mr. Duval was outside, he was – I don't know, he was getting some coal for the fire; he came in and they were all there, he got between Mrs. Taylor and Tom Coumas, and the man started shooting and I saw the teacher fall, then I began to run; I run out the door, and I went down the road to Mrs. Castle's. Q. Did you see who shot her? A. Tom Coumas. Q. Did he have a pistol in his hand? A. Yes. Q. Did you see him shoot it? A. Yes. Q. And how many times did he shoot it, do you know? A. No, I don't. Q. Was the teacher making any attack upon him at the time he shot her? A. No; he just shot her. Q. What was she doing? A. She just stood there looking at him; she did not say hardly anything. Q. And was she attempting to strike him in any way? A. No. Q. Was anybody attempting to strike him? A. No. Q. Did you see when he shot Mr. Duval? A. No, I didn't see him when he shot Mr. Duval."

Darrah then takes the witness through the photo identification routine, which Frances says she is positive the pictures are of Tom Coumas, and that the photo of Mrs. Taylor on the classroom floor is representative of the position on the floor the witness saw Mrs. Taylor lying. And Darrah excuses the witness.

Some of the photos show Coumas with a mustache, and some do not. Some of the witnesses in their identification of Coumas comment at the time of the shooting he was not wearing a mustache.

We have now heard from every student who was in that classroom on April 20th and from whom Darrah took testimony. We know from this testimony that there were six female students in the classroom on that day and four were deposed. We know the four witnesses did not identify by name the other girls who were in the classroom that day. We have nobody yet who saw Mrs. Duval threatened, or Mr. Duval shot. We have no idea who Mrs. Gustafson or Mrs. Castle was, or where they were in relation to the school building. We do not who was called. We have one of the witnesses who saw Coumas leave, but she was not asked for a description of the vehicle. We have two witnesses who make reference to the Coumas child being whipped, but it has not been established if any of these witnesses actually saw the child being whipped by Olive Taylor. Mr. Darrah also did not ask any of these witnesses if Mrs. Clara Hickman, the Coumas housekeeper, came to the classroom that day and if they saw any exchange between Hickman and Taylor. Darrah did not ask any of these witnesses if the Coumas children were in the classroom at the time of the shooting. Perhaps I am being too picky here, but these seem like fundamental matters of evidence to me, particularly when you are trying to illuminate the circumstances for the benefit of the Greek government's investigation into the charges brought forward by this Grand Jury.

CHAPTER THIRTEEN
THE DUVALS

I am separating out the Duval's from the other witnesses giving new or original depositions on December 19, 1934 because in addition to Olive Taylor, Mr. Duval has been previously identified as a shooting victim, and that Mrs. Duval was also threatened by Tom Coumas in that same classroom on April 20th. Plus the students who gave depositions didn't have all that much to impart regarding the roles played by the Duval's that day.

William J. Duval

Mr. Duval was sworn and asked by Darrah to confirm his name and if he was at the Castle School on April 20th and Duval did and said he was. Darrah did not ask Duval about his residency or if he knew Olive Taylor, nor did Darrah ask Mr. Duval why he was at the school that day or establish him as an employee of the school or in what capacity. Darrah asks Duval:

> "Q. And what did you see happen there, at that time [April 20th], if anything? A. Well, I drove into the school yard at ten minutes after four o'clock – I looked at my watch just as I drove in. I stepped up on the sidewalk, or on the back porch, and a man came up behind me and tapped me on the shoulder, and asked me where the school-ma'am was. I told him that she was in the school room I thought,

because I could hear someone in there – her car was standing there right beside mine. He never said anything; he turned and walked in the school-room and he walked right up to her. She was in the back aisle of the school-room, which was right back to the door that he entered. She seemed to be instructing a little girl there. He walked right up to her and when he went in the door, the door stayed open – it did not close. I did not know him; had never seen the man before, and he commenced to talk to her in a loud voice – in a very rough way – and I turned and looked to see what it was, what was going on. When he was talking so loud and so rough I stepped inside; and when I stepped inside I heard him call her a hard name. Q. What name? A. Well, he called her a damn bitch, that is all I heard that he said that I understood. I understood that plainly – and he was shaking his fist in her face. I walked in there and there was rows of seats coming down to this aisle, and I had to step over to one side; there was still a seat here, I stepped over, and he thought I stepped in between him and her. When he was talking and acting the way in which he was, it come to my mind who he was, because she had told me once the man who lived up the road had two children there and she had to correct them; he told her if she ever put her hands on him again he would beat her to death, that is all I know about her then. Well, I stepped in between him and her and he turned around – turned half way around – and looked at me. He had on a short coat, or kind of a jacket. He did not say nothing. She seemed to have stepped back and he run his hand in this pocket and pulled a gun. When he pulled the gun I made a grab for the gun – this all happened in about ten seconds, not more than twelve at the outside – I got hold of something, anyway, I did not get hold of the gun, I know that; I think I got his wrist that held the gun. There were two shots there like that, I did not know where they went of course; then, I heard a third shot. Q. Is that all you heard? A. The next shot was the fourth shot that got me; I went down. After I came back from the hospital, I went to the school-house; I wanted to see if I could see anything about where those bullets went. There was one bullet in – went right straight up over to the ceiling where he stood; another one right on down through the floor where he stood, which lead me to believe he fired two of those shots while I had hold of his hand. He got away from me then, that is when he shot her. She fell; that is all I heard, that shot; that is all I heard. Q. Did you or did you not see him shoot her? A. Oh, no, I did not see him shoot her, no – well, I say I did not see him; I was standing in front of her, or no, in front of him, a little to one side; I did not see him shoot her. I heard the shots, the third shot. Well, there was one shot in the ceiling, one in the floor, one shot her, one shot me, and another one shot her through the leg – five shots – five shells laying right on the floor where he stood. They were picked up by some other people who came there; I did not see that myself; they were picked up. Well, he attempted to shoot at my wife, I guess. They said he did. Q. Don't tell us what anybody said; just what you saw. A. That is all I saw, because I went down and out. Q. What was that school-teacher's name? A. Her name was Taylor; that was her married name. I can't think what her other name was; I always called her Mrs. Taylor and knew her as Mrs. Taylor. Q. What was that man's name? Who was this man you have told us about that shot you and the school-teacher? A. Well, I know him by his name, Tom Coumas; that is all I know."

Darrah then takes Mr. Duval through the photo exhibits which Duval identifies as Tom Coumas, more or less claiming he only saw the man for ten or fifteen seconds, and Duval claimed it was hard to be certain but he thought the photos were of the same man he saw in the classroom that day. Then Darrah continues his examination of Mr. Duval:

> Q. Where did he shoot you, Mr. Duval – where did the bullet that he shot strike you? A. Right there in the face; there is the spot. (Indicates) Q. In the middle of your left cheek? A. You can see it right there. (Indicating) Q. Yes, I see the scar there. A. Well, that is where it struck me; it struck me in the jaw bone and took out a piece of the jaw bone, took out a piece of my ear. Q. Is that why you are deaf? A. Sir? Q. Is that why you are deaf? A. Yes, that is what destroyed that ear, all that side of my face." Darrah then excuses the witness.

Mrs. William J. Duval

Mr. Darrah asks Mrs. Duval her name and if she was present at the school on April 20, 1932. Mrs. Duval responded by stating her name (although she stated it as Mrs. W. J. Duval, and did not give her own given name) and that she was at the school that day. Again nothing about her residency, but Darrah did begin by asking her what she was doing at the school that day, but not the time of day:

> Q. And what, if anything, were you doing? A. I was cleaning blackboards at the time. Q. What happened out there that day? A. You want me to go ahead just exactly as I saw it. Q. Yes. A. Well, the way I saw it, I went in, and I talked for a few minutes

with Mrs. Taylor. She says, "there was a lady here a little while ago that I thought was going to give me a whipping." I said, "what now?" She says – well, she says, " Really, I thought she was going to whip me." I said, "what now?" "Over something silly?" She says, "Yes, I thought sure she was going to give me a whipping." So I went on cleaning blackboards, and all at once I heard a commotion at the door. I was in the farther corner; I looked around and seen this Tom Coumas at the door. I did not know his name then; I founds out afterwards who he was. He was just talking very loud; I suppose he was abusing the teacher. I saw Mr. Duval come in through the door, and I saw him give this man a shove out the door, struck him in the face, and I started to walk down to go around where they were. All at once I heard a shot go off, and I looked and I saw Mrs. Taylor fall. I was looking right at her when she fell. Another shot went off and she fell over on the desk, went on the floor. He throwed the revolver in Mr. Duval's face and shot him. He stooped down, he was standing in the door, he stooped down and shot Mrs. Taylor through the legs; he threw the revolver back to Mr. Duval, and I yelled at him, making all the noise I could to attract his attention to me. He threw the revolver over on me; I throwed myself down behind the desk. He stood there for a second, then went on out the door; he stood there a little while and he left and he went out and went in his car and sat; there was quite a while before he left. The girls had all gone out; they had all gone into the – I can't think of it right now – the theater room; they had gone in there, and the largest girl had closed the door and was peeping out; she was watching all this going on. After he left she run into the room and stood at the door there; after he left I got up and walked over to Mrs. Taylor and Mr. Duval; I saw she was dead, and

> I went to Mr. Duval, he was living. I asked him if he had been hurt; he said "yes"; I said to the girls, "You better run for help." They went up to Mrs. Gustafson's and 'phoned from there up here to the sheriff. Then I – he went, so long before they got back Mr. Duval got so restless and wanted assistance, so I went out to call Mr. – Q. (Intg.) Just a minute, we just want to know what happened in the school-room. A. All right, that is all."

I'm going to interrupt here myself (that is what the court reporter is saying Mr. Darrah did by including the "(Intg)" abbreviation. Why would Darrah limit her testimony to the schoolroom? Well, no matter. I wanted to interrupt her testimony to alert you to the next part of her deposition. What Mrs. Duval says next is astonishing in my opinion. Please remember that Coumas is charged with assault with a deadly weapon with intent to commit murder on Mr. Duval.

You may have already picked up in this and are way ahead of me, but for those that missed it, read on.

Darrah continues:

> "Q. Did Olive Taylor – it was Olive Taylor you spoke of as Mrs. Taylor, the school-teacher? A. Yes, sir. Q. Did she have any weapon of any kind? A. Nothing at all, or Mr. Duval did not either. Q. Did either one of them make any motion to strike Mr. Coumas? A. Mr. Duval hit him in the face when he abused Mrs. Taylor, so he saw the gun in his pocket, I suppose; I don't know that. He jerked the gun out and commenced firing, and I suppose Mr. Duval saw the gun. Q. How do you know that the last shot he fired hit her in the leg, how do you know it might not have hit her in the body? A. The reason why I know

he hit her in the leg, I seen her leg move; I walked down and I could see her from where I was standing; I walked down and I could see. Q. Do you know how many times he fired at her while she was down? A. I don't know, just one time, that was all, in the leg, one time; but there was three shots fired I know, I would not try to tell you how many more. I got excited at the time, I could not tell you. I know there was three; I know Mr. Duval was hit with one of them; I afterwards picked up bullets, the bullet where I was standing, right back of where I was standing; when I went back to the school-house to work, why, I found the bullet there. Q. Did you see the pistol with which Mr. Coumas did the shooting? A. I beg your pardon? Q. Did you see the pistol with which Mr. Coumas shot Mrs. Taylor – did you see it in his hand? A. I have seen it, yes. Q. Where did you see it? A. Where did I see it? I don't know how many times I saw it or where I saw it, I have seen it a number of times. Q. Where? A. Where? Well, I saw it once in one of the Deputy's – I think in one of the Deputy's hands. I am not sure. Q. Did you see it at the time this occurred on the 20th of April, 1932? A. The picture in the paper? Q. No, the pistol? A. Oh, the pistol – I saw it in his hand. Q. At that time? A. Yes, I saw it when he raised it to shoot me; I saw it when he shot Mr. Duval; I saw it when he drew it the second time at Mr. Duval."

Darrah then takes Mrs. Duval through the photographic exhibits where she is able to discern that the photographs are of Tom Coumas. The final question Darrah asks is whether Mrs. Duval had seen Coumas before April 20th, and she replied that she had not seen him before that day.

Do you believe what you are reading here? What must the Grand Jury be thinking when this testimony was given by Mrs. Duval? Was Mrs. Duval wrong? Why didn't Mr. Duval mention that he punched Coumas in the face? More importantly, why didn't Darrah put Mr. Duval back up on the stand and ask him to clarify this aspect of Mrs. Duval's testimony? Did Darrah know this before Mrs. Duval's testimony on the 19th of December 1934? We have heard from all the witnesses giving depositions thus far who were in the classroom on April 20th. Is it possible, is there the slightest chance, is there a shred of doubt, that possibly, maybe William J. Duval caused Coumas to pull that gun out of his pocket <u>after</u> he was punched by Duval, and that by punching Coumas, Duval triggered the act that ultimately led to the death of Olive Taylor?

There are other troubling aspects to this testimony. Aren't bullets evidence at a crime scene? Mr. Duval says he returned to the schoolroom and noticed that the shells he said that were on the floor had been picked up. Did Mrs. Duval when she said "bullets" mean shell casings? Why didn't Darrah clarify this part of her testimony? Why didn't Darrah establish that Mr. Duval was the school janitor? Why didn't Darrah ask Mr. Duval how long he had been employed as a janitor at the Castle School? Why didn't Darrah ask Mr. Duval (or Mrs. Duval for that matter) how and where Mr. Duval received treatment for his injuries, and introduce into evidence a report by the medical practitioner who treated Mr. Duval? Why didn't Darrah ask Mr. Duval at what time and date he returned to the school? If Mrs. Duval found bullets or whatever they were in that classroom does that mean the police did not have proper control of a murder scene? Why didn't Darrah ask Mrs. Duval what she did with the "bullets" she found? Why didn't Darrah pursue the remark by Mrs. Duval about a deputy holding a gun? Was it Coumas' gun? Why this remark is odd is that there is no record of any gun believed to have been used by Coumas in these shootings as having been recovered. Why didn't Darrah ask if Mrs. Duval knew the name of the woman that Mrs. Taylor feared was going to give her a whipping? Is that irrelevant?

Let's reconstruct: Coumas comes to school angry because Mrs. Taylor hit his child; Coumas is verbally abusive to Mrs. Taylor in front of witnesses; Mr. Duval intervenes, hitting Coumas in the face; Coumas pulls a gun from his pocket; Mr. Duval tries to grab the gun; During a struggle between Coumas and Mr. Duval, the gun discharges sending 1) a round into the classroom ceiling, 2) a round into the classroom floor, 3) a round into Mrs. Taylor, 4) a round into Mr. Duval, 5) a round into Mrs. Taylor; Coumas points his gun at Mrs. Duval but does not shoot at her; Coumas leaves the school, apparently alone; Students run to the Gustafson residence to call the authorities at the urging of Mrs. Duval; Mr. Duval went down when he was shot but was conscious after Coumas left the school; Mrs. Taylor is lying on the classroom floor, apparently dead; Mrs. Duval is the only person in the classroom to check whether Mrs. Taylor is living or just wounded; Mr. Duval sees bullet shell casings on the classroom floor where Coumas had been standing when Coumas discharged his gun; The gun was a pistol; The gun was a revolver; Mrs. Duval retrieved at least two bullets (perhaps actually shell casings) from the classroom floor; An unidentified woman came to the classroom just before the arrival of Mrs. Duval at the school; The times of the day for various events are not fixed in testimony by the witnesses.

Mrs. Duval believes Coumas' gun was in the custody of a deputy. Now then, if I have got the essential elements of the testimony covered so far, can anyone tell me beyond a reasonable doubt that Tom Coumas' finger was on the trigger of that gun when all five shots reported were fired?

Has there been any testimony that I have reported here given you reason to believe that Tom Coumas came to the Castle School with the intent of murdering Olive Taylor? That is to say in order to prove malice in one's thinking before committing murder, the prosecution must introduce evidence that the accused actually gave the matter some thought, before the person was killed, and that the thought was malicious.

Has any testimony been reported here that would cause you to believe that Tom Coumas was trying to murder Olive Taylor during the struggle for control of the gun between Coumas and Mr. Duval? Is it even remotely possible that in the struggle for possession of the gun, that Mr. Duval was incidentally, rather than intentionally shot in the face? Take a few minutes with that one. Did anybody testify that Coumas, while having full control of his firearm pointed it at anybody in that classroom and fired a bullet at that person? Yes, Mrs. Duval testified that after the fourth shot, the one that hit Mr. Duval and Mr. Duval was down (presumably on the classroom floor) Coumas pointed his gun at Mrs. Taylor, fired, the bullet striking Mrs. Taylor in her legs. Mrs. Duval also testified that Coumas pointed the gun at her, but did not fire at her. There were no corroborating witnesses that have testified thus far that he/she saw Coumas point his gun at Mrs. Duval. Only Mrs. Duval testified to that.

Is that the reason this Grand Jury did not charge Coumas with assault with a deadly weapon on Mrs. Duval? With five rounds having been discharged, and her husband lying on the floor, while she just witnessed Coumas fire at Mrs. Taylor and strike her legs, did Mrs. Duval not have fear for her life when Coumas then pointed his gun at her?

Is there sufficient testimony here to conclude that when Coumas shot at Mrs. Taylor when she was already down, that such an act constituted malice on the part of Coumas and that by firing at her he was trying to make sure she was dead? Is Mrs. Duval credible on this point?

I think the water is a little murky on this one, but perhaps some of the remaining witnesses can provide some clarity through their testimony. It would really be great to hear from a witness who would testify that he heard Coumas at his house say he was going down to the school and kill that teacher. Perhaps testimony from an investigator who found a note written by Coumas to his housekeeper, saying he was going down to the school to "take care" of that teacher. Some sort of evidence that would indicate Coumas' intent to inflict physical harm on Olive Taylor would surely be beneficial to the case I would think.

When Coumas fled the Castle School, he made many stops and spoke with many people. We will hear from them next.

CHAPTER FOURTEEN
ESCAPE

As I have previously indicated, when Coumas fled the Castle School following the shooting there, he made multiple stops and made contact with multiple individuals in the Manteca area. We continue with the depositions before the San Joaquin County Grand Jury on December 19, 1934. The purpose of these depositions was to assist the government of Greece in their investigation of the charges against Tom Coumas as expressed in the March 14, 1934 amended indictment, handed down by this same Grand Jury. We begin with:

William Pappas

Darrah takes Mr. Pappas through the usual routine of confirming that he is a resident of Manteca, that he was a resident of Manteca on April 20, 1932, and that he saw Coumas on that day, and that he recognizes Coumas from the photos shown the other witnesses. As with other witnesses the photos that show Coumas with a mustache seem to be creating problems of identification as Pappas indicates he has never seen Coumas with a mustache. Darrah:

> "Q. Where did you see him [Coumas on April 20th]?
> A. Well, in 1932, it was about 4:00 o'clock, 4:15 in the afternoon. Why, I went down to his house, to his house, where he was living; there is Mrs. Hickman

there, who is living with Mr. Coumas; she came to my house; it was a little – about twenty minutes after four, and she stopped in the yard, she called me; she says, 'Bill, Bill, come down to the house, Tom killed the school teacher.' So I went up to the house with another person, another fellow, and I didn't have no car; I did not have a car, I told the other man that had a car, I said, 'You better go because you got the car.' And he says, 'Well, all right, I will go.' But he went a half a mile, then he came back again, he wanted me to go in his car, and I went down to Mr. Coumas' house; as I was going to his yard they were driving out. Q. Who was? A. Mr. Coumas, Mrs. Hickman, and the two children. Q. That is Mary and Johnny? A. Yes, sir. They left the little girl over there, Helen, in the yard; I seen the little girl, I picked her up and took her to my home. When I went over there I did not see Mr. Coumas, only I found Mrs. Hickman home. Q. You took Helen over to your house, you say? A. Yes."

I have to interject here that I have never heard of any Coumas child named Mary until this testimony by Mr. Pappas. Newspaper accounts in 1932 held that Coumas took three children, a girl (Helen), and two boys (Johnny and another child) and Mrs. Hickman to the Pappas farm and dropped off Mrs. Hickman and the girl Helen. Darrah doesn't try to clarify this point with Pappas, and I think it is an important one if true, because if a true fact Coumas violated another provision of the California Penal Code by abandoning his child.

Continuing on with Mr. Pappas testimony, Mr. Darrah:

"Q. When did you see him again? A. I seen him the same night at my place. Q. Tell us about that, please. A. Well, it was, I imagine, a little past ten o'clock in the evening, so we were inside, my family, Mrs. Hickman, was there; all of a sudden somebody knocked at the door and Coumas comes in the house; naturally the children, the family, everybody that was there was afraid or nervous and started going in the other rooms. He said, 'Don't be afraid, I am not going to hurt anybody.' And that's all he said to the family, and no further than that, he had a few conversations with Mrs. Hickman, going to the house and getting clothes, and that is all he said. Q. About what time of night was that? A. If I remember correctly I think it was after ten o'clock."

I am having a little difficulty with this testimony. Mrs. Hickman was at the Pappas house when Coumas arrived at around 10:00 p.m. according to what Mr. Pappas just said. When did Mrs. Hickman arrive at the Pappas house and how did she get there? What children were at the Pappas house? Pappas did not say child, he said children. What children? Is Pappas talking about his own children or Coumas' children or both? How did Coumas arrive at the Pappas house? Was he on foot? Was he driving? What was Coumas wearing?

Darrah continues with Mr. Pappas:

"Q. And it was the same night, April 20th, the night Mrs. Olive Taylor was shot in the schoolroom? A. Yes, sir. Q. Did you talk to him about the shooting of Olive Taylor yourself at any time? A. No, sir. Q. Do you know – how long had you known Tom Coumas? A. I knew him for at least fifteen years. Q. Did you also know him by the name of Spyros Smyrnogianis? A. Not at any time. Q. Did you ever know him by that name to be his correct name? A. His correct name is Tom Coumas. Q. What? A. Ever since I knew him, his correct name is Tom Coumas. Q. You did not know him before he had his name changed to Spiro Smyrnogianis from Tom Coumas? A. No."

Pappas testified here that he knew Coumas since 1919. Darrah asked this question of Pappas in 1934. Fifteen from 34 is 19. Tom Coumas changed his name in 1912 <u>from</u> Spiros Smirnagianis <u>to</u> Tom Coumas in Oregon. 1912 is seven years before 1919. I don't really know why Mr. Darrah seems confused on this point, or why he is even pursuing this with Pappas. Perhaps the folks in Greece held the same thoughts on reading this deposition as I've had. Is Darrah reading from his notes or just winging it here?

Darrah continues with Pappas:

"Q. Do you know where Tom Coumas came from in Greece, what part of Greece? A. No, sir, I don't. Q. Did he come from your province? A. No. Q. What part of Greece did you come from? A. I come from Korrinthis, Greece. Q. Do you know what Tom Coumas did in the way of occupation – earn his living? A. What was his occupation – well, it was sometimes vegetables, sometimes farmer, sometimes he was changing around, like peddling fruits and vegetables. Q. How far from him did you live? A. About, I should judge, three quarters of a mile. Q. You knew him quite awhile? A. Yes, sir. Q. And you saw him frequently and visited with him? A. Yes, sir. Q. And prior to the time this occurred, there was no unfriendly feeling between you and Tom Coumas? A. No, sir. Q. You were on good terms? A. Yes, sir. DARRAH: I guess that is all. Thank you."

You have known a man for fifteen years. You have visited with him often and were on friendly terms with him. He shoots and kills the local school teacher, a person whom many people in the community also knew. But you don't discuss the shooting with the man the first time you see him following the shooting? Would you? How long was Coumas in the Pappas home that night? Did Mr. Pappas notify the authorities after Coumas departed his house? Did he still have the Coumas child in his custody? Did Mrs. Hickman go with Coumas or remain at the Pappas house? Did Coumas make any arrangements with Pappas for the care of his child? Did Pappas ask Coumas why he left his child in the yard of his house? Would it not be logical to ask Coumas such a question, considering Pappas brought Coumas abandoned daughter to his home?

Newspapers accounts also reported in 1932 that when Coumas returned to his residence following the shooting at the Castle School, his daughter Helen tried to take Coumas' gun away from him and Coumas threatened to kill his own daughter. Is that why Coumas left her in the yard and drove away with the rest of the family? If this account was true, would that not also constitute assault with a deadly weapon on the daughter? Why didn't Darrah ask Pappas anything about that? In fairness to Mr. Pappas, perhaps he feared for his life if he engaged in conversation about anything with Coumas that night. This gun, as reported by witnesses and the media, seems to be everywhere, and at the same time, nowhere.

Chris Morogiannis

Mr. Morogiannis lived in Manteca and identified Tom Coumas from the photographic exhibits presented to him by Mr. Darrah. Mr. Darrah begins his questioning of Morogiannis:

> "Q. Did you know Tom Coumas during his lifetime, yourself? A. I knew him. Q. During the time he was in the United States? A. A long time. Q. And did you see him on April 20th, 1932? A. Yes. Q. Where? A. He come to my house. Q. What did he tell you? A. He told me, one time six o'clock. Q. The first time, what did he say? A. The first time he says. 'I killed the teacher', he came back at nine o'clock, and he started crying then when he left. Q. What did he say? A. 'I killed people,' he says something like that. Q. He killed some people? A. Yes, he killed the teacher up there. Q. You said he killed some people, did you say that? A. Yes. Q. Did he say anything else about it, as to why he killed them? A. No, he said nothing like that. Q. He didn't tell you why he killed her? A. No, he just killed them, and cry. Q. He did not tell you then he killed her because she spanked his boy? A. No, nothing like that; he just stay a few minutes; then he come back later about nine o'clock. Q. Yes, that same night? A. The same night. Q. And he stayed there all night that night? A. No, no, he go away again. Q. He went away again? A. Yes. Q. Then, when did he come back again? A. He came back the next day; I says to him, 'I give you a cup of coffee, I give you a cup of coffee'; he said, 'All right.' Q. Did he say the officers were looking for him during the time you were talking to him? A. No, he didn't say that. Of course he come the second day, I give him a cup of coffee and he say he was going to see Coniglio. Q. Joe Coniglio, he said he was going to see Joe Coniglio? A. Yes. Q. What else did he say? A. Nothing, he is gone, you know; I just see him go. Q. He didn't say the officers were liable to catch him?

A. Nothing like that. Q. Do you know Mr. Coumas' occupation, was he a vegetable peddler some of the time? A. Yes, sometimes."

Darrah lastly asks Morogiannis where he came from in Greece, "Chryo?" and Morogiannis replies, "Michidina State". There does not appear to be a purpose for this question. The Greek Government wanted to know if the witnesses knew Coumas' country of birth, not where in his country of birth he was born. I'm reasonably certain that the Grand Jury was not acquainted with a finite geography of Greece. If the question is for the benefit of the Greek authorities its relevance is not apparent here unless Darrah was suffering some confusion over the Greek authorities range of questions requested of each witness. Nothing in those questions suggested that Darrah establish where in Greece any other person lived before entry into the United States. Perhaps this went to the question requested as to whether "if the witness had any special connection with Coumas, or business relationship, or only knew him by sight." Of course this particular aspect could have been covered by Darrah simply asking the witnesses who emigrated from Greece if they had known Coumas while living in Greece. Minor point but these are the things that tend to distract jurors and judges when considering witness testimony.

Again, Darrah does not ask how Coumas came and went from his house, whether on foot or by car or did somebody drive him. He doesn't ask Morogiannis whether he notified the authorities that Coumas came to his house the first time, second time or the following morning, or of the time of day on the following morning. He does not ask this witness his occupation or how long he had known Coumas. The only reason I point these inconsistencies out is that Mr. Darrah through eight witnesses thus far does not seem to be functioning from any sort of game plan here, and witnesses keep testifying to things which only beg further questions, the answers for which Mr. Darrah seems to be avoiding. I'm also troubled by this Grand Jury not asking questions of the witnesses themselves. Maybe this is not the protocol when taking depositions before a Grand Jury since an indictment has already been issued in the matter, but if I had been sitting on this jury you can best believe my hand would have been going up repeatedly. People are testifying to crimes being committed but the district attorney is flying right on by them. Hold it, did you say this guy just drove off with his family and left his daughter sitting in the yard? What was Coumas wearing? Don't law enforcement people ask witnesses what various people they observed were wearing? How about, "At those times when Coumas came to your house, was there anybody with him or in the house with you at that time?"

John Soukos

Darrah does not ask Mr. Soukos where he lives, his occupation, or how long he has known Coumas. Soukos does identify Coumas from the photo exhibits presented to him by Darrah. Darrah begins:

> "Q....did you see Tom Coumas on the night of April 20, 1932? A. Yes, sir. Q. Where did you see him? A. I went over the Chrys' house that night, I was there a few times then, the same night Coumas comes around seven or seven-thirty, about, I don't know exactly, and he said, 'Well, I killed the teacher because they did not treat my children right.' Then he asked us to take him to the house, the next house, a neighbor of his, of Chrys, so I took him over there – I think a block or half a block away – he says, 'I am going to leave.' I took him over there, he was there two or three minutes, he got out, I took

him – well, I think he went out on South Avenue, then I went back to Bill Pappas' house; I come back, and found him again in his house; he stayed a minute or two and went out again. Then he came back in the morning and drank a cup of coffee. Q. Did he tell you the officers were after him? A. No, he did not; he just stayed a few minutes. Q. Then, in the morning, he came back and drank a cup of coffee? A. Yes, and he went; I never saw him no more."

Darrah then asked the witness what part of Greece did he come from and the witness replied, "unreadable". That is to say my copy of the transcript is unreadable as to Mr. Soukos response to that question. Darrah then excused the witness.

Who was "Chrys", Mr. Morogiannis? Whose house did Soukos drive Coumas to? Again, why didn't this witness call the authorities? Why did the witness go to Pappas' house? Who was there? What did they discuss? A newspaper account reported that Coumas drove to the home of a friend in Salida after leaving Mrs. Hickman and his daughter at the Pappas house. He then "burned his sweater", the paper said, and forced the friend at gunpoint to drive him to the Kaloutsis home, where he left his two sons and abandoned his vehicle. This 'friend' notified the Manteca police but the police did not know the identity of the friend who made that notification?

How did the police know all of this? Was this man John Soukos? If the news account is true, isn't forcing somebody to drive you somewhere at gunpoint considered kidnapping, a felony?

Aristea Kaloutsis

Let's acknowledge that Darrah had Mrs. Kaloutsis identify Coumas from the photographic exhibits, which he had shown to her, and get right into it. Darrah:

> "Q. Did you know Tom Coumas during the time he was in the United States? A. Yes, I knew him about twelve years. Q. You knew him for twelve years? A. Yes. Q. Do you know what part of Greece he came from? A. No, I don't know. Q. You came from Athens and he came from some other part? A. Yes. Q. You were on friendly terms with him, were you not? A. Yes, until this happened, yes. Q. Did you see him on the 20th of April, 1932? A. Yes. Q. Where did you see him? A. He came to my place and bring the two kids; I saw blood on his lips, he wanted to get a glass of water; I gave him a glass of water. 'What's the matter?' I said, 'What you get in the face?' He said, 'Nothing'. I saw blood on his lips, he was asking for water; I saw he was excited, I said, 'What's the matter, did you do anything?' He said, 'I didn't do nothing.' I said, 'What's the matter, you leave the kids here?' He says, 'I am coming back,' and he said to leave them, so I don't see him no more. Q. He never came back any more? A. No. Q. Have you still got those children? A. The kids, I got one, he was the little adopted boy. Q. You adopted the boy? A. Not yet. Q. Not yet, but you are going to? A. Pete, the little one. Q. What became of Johnny? A. I don't know what became of him, he is some place, I don't know, some place, I don't see him no more. Q. Did he tell you anything about shooting the school teacher? A. No, no, no, but I saw he was pale and had blood on his lips. Q. He was pale and bloody? A. I saw blood here. (Indicating) Q. You saw blood on the cheek? A.

> Yes. I say, 'What's the matter?' He say, 'Just give me water.' Q. The blood was just some that splashed on him?"

This is probably the place, were this at trial that a lawyer would jump up and say, "Objection, lack of foundation, and calls for speculation by the witness." But what comments like this actually do, is cause someone to conclude that Mr. Darrah is wandering about with this witness without a sense for where he is going. The witness testified that Coumas had blood on his lips. Darrah comments that Coumas had blood on his cheek. Now unless the witness pointed to her cheek, how did Darrah make that leap? In any event, he should have clarified her testimony for the record.

Kaloutsis continues:

> "A. Yes. It was cold that day, the kids don't get enough clothes, no shoes, no coat, and I said, 'You can't treat kids like that'; he says, 'I come back, I come back.' That's all, he don't say anything more. The kids had no shoes, it was cold; he says, 'I got three apples in a sack.' Q. Three apples in a paper sack, was that all he had with him? A. Yes."

Darrah then goes into the identification by photograph portion of his presentation, amid much discussion about Coumas' mustache. Darrah asks the witness if she knows Coumas' occupation and she responds that she does not.

Well, we have another witness who is not asked if she notified the authorities. There is nothing from her about Coumas abandoning his car at her home. He doesn't ask her where she lives, or what her occupation is. He doesn't ask who else was in the house when Coumas was there, and did she see anybody arrive with him. Another question that strikes me is why is Coumas' child still in her care 30 months after Coumas left the child there? Would not the authorities take custody of the child? Did Coumas ask the Kaloutsis' to take care of his boys, and did they agree, or did Coumas abandon the boys to them? Under California law, you can get locked up for a year for that. Mrs. Kaloutsis felt she knew Coumas well enough to take care of his children but had no idea what he did for a living? Would that not cause one to conclude that he might have abandoned his sons at the Kaloutsis home? Did Mr. Darrah consider that aspect of this saga? Actually, one would think that Darrah would have been following this case rather closely, which would seem to logically include the status and whereabouts of the Coumas children. The part about the blood on Coumas' face is a little troubling. I mean how is it this was not mentioned by any of the other three witnesses who saw him after the shooting? Why didn't Darrah ask Morogiannis or Soukos about Coumas having blood on him? Why not ask Mrs. Duval if Coumas had blood on him at that time he left the classroom? What of Mr. Kaloutsis? Where was he? Did he see or speak to Coumas?

Joe Coniglio

Darrah establishes that Mr. Coniglio is a vineyardist and grape shipper living in Manteca and has known Tom Coumas since 1928. Mr. Coniglio, after some discussion about Coumas mustache, identifies Coumas from Darrah's photographic exhibits. Darrah:

> "Q. And did you see him [Coumas] on or about the 20th of April, 1932? A. No, I saw him on April 21st, 1932 – on the morning of April 21st, 1932. Q. The next morning after the murder occurred in the Castle

School? A. Yes, sir. Q. And where did you see him then? A. I saw him on my ranch. Q. What occurred, what did he do or say at that time? A. I was just about getting out of the house, between seven-thirty and eight o'clock, he said he wanted to be taken to Modesto, he said he was in trouble about something, he didn't mention anything – he was so nervous and desperate; he told me he was in bad shape and wanted to go to Modesto. Q. And did he have a gun in his pocket that he pointed to you? A. No, I didn't notice the gun, and I went inside the barn; he followed me in, he said, 'I want you to take me to Modesto, I'm in trouble.' When I came out of the barn I noticed he had a gun in his hand; he had a leather jacket on the outside, you know, a leather jacket with a gun – it was an automatic. Q. And he commanded you to take him to Modesto, is that correct? A. Yes, sir. I tried to tell him what was the matter, what was the matter, what happened to you. The way he answer me, he never knew me any more. He was desperate, and I went inside my house, you know; I want to talk to my mother, to tell her it looks like kind of phony, but every time I made a step he was right after me. Then he said, 'I want to go to Modesto, or something is going to happen here.' And I said, 'What's the matter?' He never said what the matter was, he said, 'You will find out what's the matter."

I have to stop here and quote something for your benefit: California Penal Code Section 207 – "Every person who forcibly steals, takes, or arrests any person in this state, and carries him into another country, state or county, or into another part of the same county…….is guilty of kidnapping." Manteca is in San Joaquin County. Modesto is in Stanislaus County. Kidnapping was punishable by imprisonment for 1 to 25 years. Well, maybe

Mr. Darrah didn't see it that way. How about Section 245 – Assault with a deadly weapon? Doing that sort of thing could get you up to ten years in prison. Maybe the problem was that it would have been Conglio's word against Coumas' word. Insufficient witnesses, that sort of thing.

Mr. Coniglio continues:

> "A. That morning I was going to load two cars of (unreadable) I was shipping, representing a fellow back east, two car-loads of (unreadable), and the day before I unloaded two cars, I had two cars more; that morning they had a heavy frost on the 21st of April, 1932, and I couldn't start that truck; I was so anxious to get rid of him, because I had to pay $20.00 demurrage if I didn't unload these two cars, that was the last day, so he said, 'If you don't move something is going to happen to you.' I tried to convince the man what was the matter, but he wouldn't say; so I had a friend of mine happen to come, his name is Steve Souza – he is a dairy farm fellow there and used to live near my place there; he had his car there. I told Steve, 'You want to go to Modesto, take this man?' I did not think of anything; it occurred to me maybe he got in trouble with somebody. I never thought he committed a murder; so I took him to Modesto, and he sat in the car on the center, I did not know anything until I come to Modesto. We took him to Park and Needham; we came from the cannery where we turn through Mr. Anderson's place, a little lane through there, then we went to the Jack Tone road, then we went over that way to McAfee's to Needham; before we got to town we left him at Park Avenue; we left him over there, he told me, he said, that if some officers come that was after him over there, he said, 'Don't say anything or it's going to be too bad for you and your

> family.'; he said, 'If some officer comes and asks for me' – I tried to ask him what is the matter – he said, 'You will find out.' He said, 'Don't repeat anything to the officers or it will be too bad for you and your family,' that is what he said, so that is why I didn't say anything. Q. How far is it where you took him to Modesto from your place to Modesto? A. Well, I think it's about fifteen miles from my place. Q. And Modesto is not in this county, but Stanislaus County, adjacent to this county, is that correct? A. Yes, sir. Q. It's next to this county? A. Yes, sir. Q. In Stanislaus County? A. Yes, sir. Q. And you were fearful that unless you took him as he demanded he might shoot you? A. Yes, sir. He did not act the way he acted with me here, and he told me two or three times not to ask any questions; he said, 'I want you to take me to Modesto in a hurry.' When he got in the car he had his gun. Q. You mean had his hand on the gun like you are showing here? A. Yes, all the time, his right hand, here; I was on the other side, the other fellow was driving, and we had him in the center."

Darrah then takes Mr. Coniglio through the photos as he had with the previous witnesses, with the same results, including commentary about Coumas not having a mustache when he lived in Manteca. Darrah continues:

> "Q. He [Coumas] was a vegetable peddler and sometimes worked on the farm? A. Sometimes he used to farm, and sometimes he used to peddle vegetables. Q. Did you know the people in his household, of Clara Hickman and the children? A. I knew the children, yes, and I knew Clara Hickman; several times they came to my house before that though. Q. How long had she been there, do you know? A. I don't know; they used to live in Stockton

> before. Q. They lived in Stockton before they moved out there – did you know where his wife was? A. His first wife, I think was in the State Hospital. Q. When you say, 'his first wife', you are assuming that Clara was his wife? A. No, sir. Q. Who was his first wife? A. The first wife, the one that was in the hospital. Q You say first wife, which one do you mean? A. I mean that first wife, the one in the State Hospital. Q. When you say 'first', why, there is an inference that there might have been another one? A. The first one, his real wife. Q. The first one is his real wife? A. Yes, his real wife." Darrah then excuses the witness.

I think I read here about a man who was describing a kidnapping and an assault of not only one individual but two individuals, and there appears to be two witnesses to that event, so it's not as if there is nothing to corroborate the event. I think I also read here about a child abandonment of at least three children here. But what we did not read about here is any testimony from Steve Souza, and even more astonishingly, Clara Hickman. We have heard from all of the "civilian" witnesses called by Mr. Darrah, with the exception of the medical examiner. I have not heard from any witness yet who testified as to any evidence that would prove that Tom Coumas "intended" to kill Olive Taylor, or attempt to kill William Duval. I do believe that the testimony given thus far would constitute probable cause to have charged Coumas with a number of additional felonious acts, but oddly he was not. Certainly the statute of limitations was not at issue in 1934, and the Greek Government extended an invitation to San Joaquin County to add whatever to their indictment they thought appropriate to the evidence at hand. The law requires that evidence may only be introduced in the Grand Jury through a witness, so anything Mr. Darrah hoped to accomplish by way of indictment or evidence supporting an indictment had to come from witness testimony. So where are the obvious people who should have been deposed? Why did Darrah allude to Clara Hickman as Coumas wife, when questioning Coniglio? What was the purpose of confirming that a number of these witnesses came to the United States from Greece? Was it to imply that Coumas was a countryman, and their involvement with him was indicative of support for a fellow countryman? Could Darrah have ended that laughable exchange with Coniglio over the "first wife" with the simple question, "Do you know if Tom Coumas had more than one wife?"

Maybe the answers to these questions will flow from the San Joaquin County sheriff's deputies involved in this case.......next!

CHAPTER FIFTEEN
MANHUNT

Following the disappearance of Tom Coumas from the Manteca area in 1932, a number of people working for the San Joaquin County Sheriff's Office were trying to track him down. We are going to hear from the man who was the Manteca City police chief in 1932, who by 1934 was himself a deputy sheriff in San Joaquin County and then Sheriff in 1947, another sheriff's deputy who took the crime scene photographs at the Castle School, and yet another sheriff's deputy who researched Tom Coumas for the purpose of developing any leads that might result in his apprehension. All of these witnesses were shown the same photographic exhibits of Tom Coumas that were shown to all of the previous witnesses and all of these three positively identified the man in the photos as being Tom Coumas, and again, in the interest of time and space have excluded that portion of their depositions. I'm going to leave most of the photographic identification testimony in for those actually connected to these photographs from an evidentiary standpoint. Once again District Attorney Darrah is asking the questions of the witnesses, and it is still December 19, 1934.

Crawford Hitchcock

Mr. Darrah begins:

> "Q. Your name is Crawford Hitchcock? A. Yes. Q. And you were Chief of Police in Manteca in April, 1932, and you are now Deputy Sheriff of San Joaquin County? A. Yes, sir. Q. Did you know Tom Coumas when he was here in the United States? A. I did. Q. Before he escaped to Greece? A. I did. Q. ......did you know this man [Coumas] when you were Chief of Police of Manteca? A. Yes, I did. Q. He lived around Manteca, and as Chief of Police, you came in contact with him at various times, is that correct? A. Yes. Q. I will show you Exhibit 5; do you know what that is? A. Yes. Q. What is it? A. It's an enlargement of the picture that I took out of his house, Coumas' house. Q. That is, after he made his escape to Greece? A. It is. Q. And after he had murdered Olive Taylor? A. Yes. Q. I will show you Exhibit 6, do you know what this is? (witness examines Exhibit 6) A. It's also an enlargement. Q. And do you know where that picture came from? A. It was taken out of the trunk at Coumas' house; it was in the album. Q. At the same time the other picture was taken? A. Yes. Q. Did you take them out of the trunk yourself? A. I did. Q. And would you then recognize them as Tom Coumas, the man you knew in and about Manteca while you were Chief of Police in Manteca? A. I do. Q. And did you or your office cause these enlargements to be made therefrom? A. Yes. Q. Did you get them the same day this murder occurred, April 20, 1932? A. Yes."

Deputy Hitchcock was then shown another series of photographs for identification purposes but was not asked if he was the source of those particular photographs. I'm curious over whether the Chief had a search warrant before he went through Mr. Coumas trunk. You might think that as being a rather odd statement, but I have known many trials that were torpedoed because somebody did not follow the law on search and seizure. It would be reasonable for law enforcement officers to enter the premises looking for Coumas, given that he was alleged to have committed felonies at the Castle School, leaving one dead and one wounded in his wake, and was armed and presumed dangerous. But unless he thought Coumas was hiding in his photo album in his trunk, I think he would have needed to wait until he had a warrant. I also think it interesting that Darrah concludes that Coumas "murdered" Olive Taylor, although no foundation for that conclusion has been established with this witness prior to that remark.

Darrah continues, after having asked Hitchcock if he is positive over the photographic identification of Tom Coumas:

> "Q. And there is no doubt at all in your mind but that those are pictures of Tom Coumas, who murdered [same objection – foundation] Olive Taylor in the school room of the Castle School on the 20th of April, 1932, and thereafter escaped to Greece, is that correct? A. That is correct. Q. Were you called to the scene of this murder immediately after it occurred? A. I was. Q. Did you make an examination of the premises? A. Not very much of the premises; I just saw Mrs. Taylor. Q. Did you see the body of Olive Taylor there at that time? A. I did. Q. I will show you Exhibits Nos. 10 and 14, was that the way the school room and the body of Olive Taylor appeared? A. Yes. Q. At that time? A. It is. Q. And did your office, with the assistance of quite a number of Deputy Sheriffs, make a very thorough search of all the neighborhood in an effort to apprehend and arrest Tom Coumas immediately after this occurred? A. We did, in fact, we left the school immediately; we did not stay there, not over two minutes, I would say. Q. You left the scene

immediately and made an effort to arrest him? A. Yes sir. Q. But he escaped from the officers and went to Greece, is that correct, where he now is? A. Yes." Mr. Darrah then excuses the witness.

There are a couple of things worthy of mention here: first, the time of day he was at the Coumas home is not noted for the record. Who he had with him (he did say "we") at the school and if he had anybody with him at the Coumas house that fact was not noted for the record. I think it is interesting that Mr. Darrah continuously concludes the crime to have been a murder, and leads the witness into agreement when no evidence has yet been presented that a murder in fact took place. Olive Taylor was killed in that classroom, make no mistake about that, but I'm not seeing a murder here. Are you seeing a murder here? The Chief does not share where he looked in the neighborhood when he conducted his "thorough search", and Darrah doesn't ask. No questions are asked about Mr. Duval, what person called the coroner, the nature of Mr. Duval's injuries, how and where was Duval treated, who Chief Hitchcock spoke with in his search efforts for Coumas, and if he was the first arriving officer of the law at the classroom, and did he secure the scene prior to leaving the school?

Darrah did not even establish that Chief Hitchcock had legal jurisdiction over this incident. The Chief does not say if anyone was in the Coumas home at the time he searched it, and does not say if he set up surveillance on the home to watch for Coumas' return to his house. Darrah did not ask how he knew Coumas, or when the Chief had met Coumas. No police report is introduced into evidence here and no statements of any witnesses that may have been interviewed by police or other officials. Darrah does not ask if the Chief at anytime returned to the Castle School and conducted any sort of investigation of the crime scene, or tasked any member of his police department to do so. Perhaps something that a chief of police might look for in the home of a person who just shot some people would be either a weapon or ammunition for a weapon. Darrah did not address that either. Odd.

Rudolph Weber

Mr. Weber is a deputy sheriff working in the Bureau of Identification in San Joaquin County. Weber testifies that he knew Tom Coumas, but Darrah does not ask Weber how he knew Coumas. After the fact, when Weber might have reviewed his statement for errors, there is written onto the deposition in ink the following exchange between Darrah and Weber, Darrah first:

> "Q. Did you know one Tom Coumas, who lived here in San Joaquin County at one time? A. I did. [Writing in ink begins here] Coumas knew my father Otto Weber, for several years. We met him through William Pappas [then the initials in ink] R.W."
>
> Darrah:
>
> "Q. Did you make some, or do some, investigating work in connection with the duties of your office concerning Tom Coumas? A. I did. Q. Concerning his entrance into the United States, and his marriage application, receipt of naturalization, application for and naturalization as an American citizen, and his change of name? A. I did. Q. And his residence while he was in the United States – will you give us what, if anything, you discovered in that respect?"

Weber takes Darrah through pretty much the same history that I gave you in Chapter two, so no use repeating it here. Weber does make an interesting statement regarding Coumas intentions with regard to his allegiance to Greece after immigrating to the United States and making his initial application for naturalization on April 29, 1910, in which Coumas and I quote Weber here,

> "A......at which time he stated it was his bonafide intention to renounce forever all allegiance and fidelity to any foreign Prince, Potentate, State or Sovereignty, and particularly to George I, King of the Greeks, of which he was then a subject...."

Perhaps not a minor point here, but no document was introduced in evidence in support of Weber's contention that Coumas actually made such a statement. Then, later in his testimony, Weber makes reference to a statement Coumas made on April 29, 1910 in which Coumas, and again I am quoting Weber's testimony here,

> "A........and he again renounced absolutely and forever all allegiance and fidelity to any foreign Prince, Potentate, State or Sovereignty, and particularly to Greece and to Constantine, King of the Hellenes, of whom at that time he was subject......."

I'm not making this up. This deputy testifies here that Coumas renounced his allegiance to two different Kings of Greece to which he was subject on the same date. Now each witness is required by law to review their testimony once transcribed for accuracy and I am quoting this to you exactly as it appears in Weber's deposition. We know Weber reviewed this because he changed and initialed other parts of his deposition. Weber then paraphrases the Oath of Allegiance Coumas took on February 25, 1914 in Portland, Oregon Circuit Court.

Weber goes on to testify about Coumas' marriage to Margaret Debauw in 1915, and the names of Coumas' parents in Greece. Finally, Weber closes by stating that this represents the sum total of information about Coumas he was able to uncover. I am going to pick up the testimony here, as Darrah continues:

> "Q. I guess that is all unless you have something further you would like to state. A. I might state that the local sheriff's office was able to trace a letter from - dated New York, New York, June 11, 1932, addressed to Miss Clara Hickman, in care of Bill Pappas, R.F.D. 1, Manteca, California. Q. Now you have a photograph of the envelope in which that letter was received? A. Yes, I have. Q. A photograph of an envelope enclosed within that envelope? A. I have. Q. I will first mark that photograph Exhibit No. 15, and also refer to the Exhibit by number. A. I have in my hand Exhibit 15, which bears a postage stamp, two cents, which had been cancelled at New York, New York, June 11, at 5:30 p.m. 1932, addressed to Miss Clara Hickman, in the care of Bill Pappas, R.F.D. 1, Manteca, and "Manteca" has been crossed out and General Delivery, Stockton, has been written in. On this same Exhibit in Grecian writing, also the words, Piraeus, Greece, written on the same, a five cent postage stamp uncancelled. I hold in my hands Exhibits 16 and 17, photographic copies of the original letter. That letter reads as follows:"

You might think I'm being too picky if I mention that Exhibits 16 and 17 have not been introduced and marked yet, but that is probably just an oversight on the part of somebody in the room generally in charge of such details. I'm also going to quote the letter that Deputy Weber is quoting but I'm going to reformat it so it is easier to read. Deputy Weber reads:

"New York

Dearest Clara –

Each day carries me further from my happiness. As I write to you I can feel tears coming in my eyes. My heart is full of bitterness, bitterness against fate. Last night I cried myself to sleep, yearning for your arms around me and your warm kisses to soothe my bruised spirit. I have missed you more than the kids. I could curse the day I have met the Debauws. Dearest, I can say much when my heart it full. When you get this dear I will be somewhere in Europe. I am not going direct to Greece. But I will be there…..[End of First Page]

[Second page] ….on time to get your letter. Dearest, sell everything and take your time. Don't give things away and save your money so you can come to me. Sell your diamond ring too. I have one five times larger than that for you, and when you come to me I will marry you and you will be mine. Save my good clothes and shoes and some small articles for the house, but not too much because the duty is too heavy on them. Give the kids their clothes, send Chester his shoes and overcoat. It will take about $225.00 to come to me. I will send you instructions when I hear from you. Keep this to yourself. I enclose addressed envelope so you can write to me.

Good bye Dear, Your Loving Husband."

Weber continues with his testimony,

"A comparison of this handwriting with the handwriting of his signature on the papers requesting his application to the United States, also his naturalization papers, and his affidavit of registration in the local office shows them to be identical. The investigation was conducted, tracing the return envelope without results. Tom Coumas did not show at Piraeus, Greece." Darrah: "Q. The place that the return envelope was addressed was kept under surveillance continuously until he was apprehended elsewhere, but never came? A. That is correct. Q. Now, is that all? A. That is all. Q. All right."

And Darrah dismisses this witness.

I'm really not certain what the purpose was for the introduction of the renunciation of allegiance and fidelity to the King of Greece portion of this testimony. It has been made irrelevant by the Greek Court of Appeals at Nauplia in their hearing for the extradition of Coumas from Greece on August 28, 1934. The issue of whatever oath was taken by Coumas, or whatever assertions he might have made on any government applications regarding his Greek citizenship have been rendered moot by that court. The U.S. Government erred in granting him citizenship without proof before the act of naturalization that he had permission from the Greek Government to divest himself of his Greek citizenship.

The introduction of the Hickman letter is troubling in that there is no testimony of its purpose of being introduced into evidence. There is no statement on the record of where this letter was obtained, under what circumstances, and when it was obtained. One could conclude that the purpose might have been to show Coumas' intentions with regard to fleeing to Greece and when he might have left the

U.S. to go there. I really do not think it helpful to the case to introduce evidence without establishing the purpose of the evidence. Otherwise, everyone is left to come to their own conclusion of purpose, and that could just as easily sink a case as support it. The authentication of the letter as being written by Coumas is somewhat troubling in that there is no identification of who certified or authenticated the handwriting, and what were the qualifications of that individual to make such an authentication. Remember that under California law of that era, all evidence had to be introduced through witness testimony before a Grand Jury and Weber did not testify as to how the sheriff's office came into possession of this letter, and no certification as to the source of the photographs of the letter, and most certainly no testimony from Weber in that regard. Darrah also did not establish Weber as any sort of expert or attempt to qualify him on the grounds of experience in terms of the length of his employment in the Bureau of Identification.

Another aspect of the case that is raised with the introduction of this letter into evidence is Ellis Parker. Chief Parker held a theory that Coumas escaped to Greece via Mexico and Brazil. Were that the case, how did Coumas mail a letter to Hickman from New York on June 11, 1932? Did Darrah advise Parker of this letter? From the public record, it would appear that Parker was not aware of it as late as perhaps July 1934, when newspapers were trumpeting the news that Coumas had been found in Greece, and were reporting the Brazil angle.

Darrah also did not capitalize on a potential character issue with regard to Coumas based on the fact that the man had a wife to whom he was probably still lawfully married in the Stockton State Hospital, and it would appear he was having a relationship with Clara Hickman well beyond her being his housekeeper. If this letter does anything, it serves as evidence that Coumas intended to abandon his wife, which is yet another violation of the California Penal Code for which a person convicted could spend up to two years in the lockup and a $1,000 fine. Did anybody take a statement from Clara Hickman as part of this "investigation", and if so, where is it?

Did Coumas give Mrs. Hickman a ring? For what purpose? What sort of an investigation is this? Could Darrah have just asked Weber, "Do you know the whereabouts of Clara Hickman at this time?"

Ivan E. Hitt

Ivan Hitt is also a San Joaquin County sheriff's deputy assigned to the Bureau of Identification. Deputy Hitt was responsible to taking crime scene photographs at the Castle School, and of the body of Olive Taylor. Deputy Hitt testifies as to the various views of the school in his photographs, and of Mrs. Taylor lying on the schoolroom floor. Mr. Darrah begins:

> "Q. Are you a qualified expert photographer? A. Yes, sir. Q. What experience and training have you had qualifying you as such? A. I have been employed in the Bureau for the past thirteen years doing that kind of work. Q. Doing photographic work? A. Criminal photographic and identification work. Q. Were you called out to the Castle School – you were, during that period of time – have you taken photographs which were taken for the purpose of adducing evidence in Court? A. Many times, yes, sir. Q. And which were subsequently adduced and received in evidence in Court? A. I have. Q. And you have qualified, on many occasions, as an expert photographer, and testified as such in Court here in

> the United States, is that not correct? A. I have. Q. You were called out of the Sheriff's office on the 20th of April, 1932? A. Yes, sir, I was. Q. Where were you called to? A. I received a call a little after five o'clock to go to the Castle School in this county to photograph the body of a victim that had been slain by pistol shots."

Well, you might object to that on the grounds that there has been no foundation established here for this witness as to the manner of death, only that he took various photographs of the victim and has only been qualified as an expert with regard to photography not the victim's death, but there is no judge to appeal to in this session, and no legal representation present for Coumas.

Darrah then takes Hitt through the various school photographs taken by Hitt showing the back entrance to the classroom, several views of Mrs. Taylor lying face down on the classroom floor near a folding room divider at what would be the front of the room, and a stain on the classroom floor that Deputy Hitt testifies is blood. Of course again he has not been qualified as a medical or forensic expert for the purpose of this testimony. Perhaps more troubling is that Darrah does not bother to establish with Hitt whose blood is on the classroom floor or how the conclusion was reached that the stain was actually blood. There also appears in one of the photographs what seems to be a large cloth with some sort of stains on it, which might be blood. Mrs. Duval did not testify as to the blood on the classroom floor or on the cloth lying on the same floor in the vicinity as the stain. I suppose it could be reasonable to conclude that this blood came from Mr. Duval's head wound, and quite possibly Mrs. Duval used the cloth on Mr. Duval in an attempt to stop loss of blood from that wound, but the point is not clarified in testimony or evidence presented before the Grand Jury. The cloth should have been collected in evidence and accounted for, but if these investigators didn't think shell casings or bullets were important evidence, a bloody cloth could hardly be expected to snag their attention.

Darrah then asks if Hitt later took photographs of Mrs. Taylor at the San Joaquin County morgue, and Hitt confirms that he did. Darrah:

> "Q. Did you later take pictures of the same body in the San Joaquin County Morgue? A. Yes, after the body had been moved from the school to the morgue by the Coroner I then proceeded to the morgue, and there I made three photographs of the body."

Darrah then asks Hitt to identify those photos for the record, which Hitt does. Darrah asks Hitt to confirm that he took the photographs, developed, and printed them himself, and Hitt replies that he did. Darrah then dismisses this witness.

What Darrah does not do is confirm with Hitt that he took the photographs of the Hickman letter. There are larger questions however. Why wasn't Hitt or somebody from the Bureau of Identification dispatched to photograph Mr. Duval's injuries? Did somebody gather samples of the blood on the schoolroom floor and type that blood to any of the victims? Did somebody retrieve the shell casings referenced by both Duval's that were on the classroom floor? There was testimony from Mr. Duval that one bullet went into the ceiling and one bullet into the floor. Did somebody retrieve them just in case you might want to use them to establish the caliber and just maybe the gun they were fired from? Mrs. Duval testified that she picked up "bullets" off that schoolroom floor. Did anybody retrieve them from her?

We have had two deputies from the same division testify here as to 1) a background check on Coumas, and 2) photographs of the school and Olive Taylor. Also in *The Stockton-Record* on April 21, 1932 there appeared a news story about these shootings and it was accompanied by a photograph of Coumas that does not match any of the photographs introduced into evidence at the December 19, 1934 depositions session before this Grand Jury. This is the same news story mentioned earlier where the newspaper also published a line drawing of the school, showing where Mrs. Taylor fell to the classroom floor. I think it is important to mention that drawing again at this point as it was the sort of diagram one would expect to accompany a crime scene investigation, yet this diagram was not introduced into evidence in these depositions. This begs the question, who drew this diagram? The reporter? Who supplied the photograph of Coumas to the newspaper, and where did that person obtain that photograph?

Perhaps even more telling about the "manhunt" for Coumas is that the residences for the Pappas, Morogiannis, Coniglio, Souza, and Kaloutsis families were all within a three-mile zone, which included Coumas residence and the Castle School. Coumas was in that zone for at least twelve hours following the shooting yet no law enforcement person was able to find him. Where did Coumas spend the night of April 20th, from the time he left the Pappas residence until he surfaced at the Soukos residence the following morning? No one seems to know.

Nothing has been introduced into evidence here regarding the weapon used by Coumas to kill Olive Taylor and wound William Duval. When Coumas showed up at the Coniglio ranch on the morning of April 21, 1932, Coniglio testified that the gun Coumas exhibited was an automatic, others said it was a revolver. Which was it? Did Coumas own more than one firearm? Why hasn't the coroner been called to testify in these depositions? The only witness left is the medical examiner. Maybe he has the answers to these questions.

CHAPTER SIXTEEN
AUTOPSY

The medical examiner for San Joaquin County in 1932 was Dr. William P.J. Lynch, M.D. In referring to his testimony, I am going to eliminate the exhibit numbers for the photographs taken by Deputy Hitt of Mrs. Taylor's remains at the county morgue. Out of respect for Olive Taylor, I am not going to publish those photographs. But I am going to replicate Dr. Lynchs' description of her wounds and the cause of her death. Mr. Darrah:

> "Q. What is your name, Doctor? A. William P. J. Lynch. Q. You are residing here in Stockton? A. Yes, sir. Q. You were the autopsy surgeon who performed the autopsy on the body of Olive Taylor? A. Yes, sir. Q. On or about April the 20th, 1932, was it? A. Yes, sir. Q. Will you tell us what your examination revealed? A. I was called to the Coroner's office and performed the autopsy on the body of Mrs. Olive Taylor; when I arrived there the body was lying on one of the examining tables of the examining room, and before I did the autopsy I examined the body for any wounds that might be present. There were four wounds on the body. One was – the point of entrance was at the left side of the chest, just at the level of the sixth rib and slightly in back; there was a wound of exit on the right shoulder; and there was a wound of entrance in the calf of the left leg, about six inches below the knee, and there was a wound of exit on the calf of the

> same leg about two inches below the wound of the entrance on that leg. The body was that of a rather large woman, approximately, I would say, fifty years of age; and during the autopsy I found that a bullet which entered the left chest had passed through both lobes of the left lung, had passed on through the large vessel; that is, the aorta, the vessel leaving the heart, passed on out through the chest, out the chest wall, and on out through the right shoulder. Q. Now, Doctor, I show you [photograph] and will ask you whether or that shows the wound which you have described? A. Yes, that is the wound of [word exit crossed out in ink and correction in ink entered] entrance."

There is some confusion here between Darrah and Dr. Lynch over which photograph they are each referring to. Darrah has shown Dr. Lynch a photograph of the upper body bullet entry wound. Lynch is having difficulty determining the orientation of the body from the photograph he is looking at. Darrah:

> "Q. This is the head, here is the shoulder, and this is the – A. Arm. This is the arm, yes; there is the wound of entrance just back here at the level of about the sixth rib. That is [names the photograph]. Q. And [names another photograph] is that a photograph of the body of this same person you examined? A. Yes, sir. Q. And is that wound that shows on the arm of this body the would [typographical error – should be "wound"] of – A. Exit. Q. Exit that you just described? A. Yes, sir. Q. Now, I show you [another photograph]; is that one of the wounds you described – if so, which one? A. That is both wounds on the leg; this is the upper one, the left leg, upper one, the wound of entrance; the lower one is the wound of exit. The bullet went

in there and out here. Q. That is [names photograph]? A. Yes, sir. Both the plural cavities were entirely filled with blood, and the aorta was punctured in two places where the bullet went in and went on out. Q. What is the aorta, which you described? A. It's the large vessel which comes out of the heart and pumps blood out through that into the body. Q. That wound was sufficient to cause her death? A. Oh, instantly. Q. You are a regularly licensed physician and surgeon, are you not, doctor? A. Yes, sir. Q. And you have had considerable experience in performing autopsies? A. Yes, sir. Q. And you are licensed by the State of California to practice medicine in the State of California? A. Yes, sir. Q. And practice surgery? A. Yes, sir. Q. For what period of time have you been so licensed? A. Fifteen years. Q. And you have been in practice in the City of Stockton a good portion of that time, is that correct? A. All of it. Q. What medical school are you a graduate of? A. The University of California. Q. The Medical Department of the University of California, is that correct? A. Yes, sir. Q. And you took your Medical Degree from the University of California? A. Yes, sir. Q. I think that is all, thank you, Doctor."

What is somewhat interesting to me is that Olive Taylor received the leg wound when she was laying face down on the classroom floor, but Deputy Hitt took the picture of that same leg in the morgue with Mrs. Taylor facing upward. Hitt should have photographed the wound in the morgue with the body in the same position it was in the classroom. Also, if the leg wound was visible while the body was still on the floor of the classroom, Deputy Hitt should have photographed that leg before the body was moved to the morgue. To alleviate any further confusion the reader might have regarding the leg wound, the bullet caused both wounds to be on the same side of her left calf. The round entered her leg almost parallel to it, went through the muscle, and exited perhaps 2 ½ inches from the point of entry. This is significant because if she was on the floor in the position Deputy Hitt's photographs depicted, then the shooter fired at her leg from floor level and to the side of her head. The bullet would have traveled past her left side and struck her in the outer part of her left calf, just past her left knee. The bullet trajectory would had to have been from low to high, because the entrance wound is lower on her calf than the exit wound. Mrs. Duval testified that Coumas stooped down and fired the shot at Mrs. Taylor, after she was already down on the floor, hitting her leg. Coumas gun would have had to have been mere inches off the classroom floor, and angled upward to strike her in that orientation. This is hardly where you would have expected his gun hand to be even if he was in a stooped position. And why would Coumas be trying to shoot Mrs. Taylor in the leg? Unless when Mr. Duval went down, Coumas went with him and another round was discharged and the bullet strike was random rather than intentional. Mrs. Duval also testified that Coumas was stooped down in the <u>doorway</u> when he shot Mrs. Taylor in the legs (yes, Mrs. Duval did say 'legs'). From the angle of her body on the floor, and although Mrs. Duval does not identify which door, and Darrah did not ask her which door, there is no way the bullet could have struck Mrs. Taylor's left leg in the manner in which Deputy Hitt's photographs show, if Coumas was stooped down in any doorway in that classroom. Not knowing the surface of the schoolroom floor, it is also possible that the bullet that struck Mrs. Taylor's leg was the result of a ricochet during the struggle between Coumas and Mr. Duval. All of these irregularities in testimony and circumstance of the evidence thus far introduced could surely call reasonable doubt into question regarding the conclusions reached by the district attorney. Mr. Darrah did not explore this with Dr. Lynch, and of course, since the coroner was not called to testify, that particular theory could not be corroborated. This is why some evidence of the bullet strike locations within the classroom would have been helpful. Darrah did not ask Dr. Lynch from what direction either bullet that hit Olive Taylor might have been fired. We know the wounds were through and through, so no bullets were in the body, but Darrah did not ask Dr. Lynch for his opinion of the caliber and type of bullet from the nature of the wounds he examined. Oddly, there was at least one newspaper account that claimed the weapon was a .32 caliber firearm. However this factoid was not supported in any testimony I have reviewed as being placed before this Grand Jury. Darrah did not ask Dr. Lynch the sequence of the bullet strikes to Mrs. Taylor. This is significant because if Coumas intentionally fired a round into Mrs. Taylor after she was dead, then we have another crime having been committed by Mr. Coumas, that of unlawful mutilation of a dead body, which was also a felony.

Odd that Mr. Darrah did not have somebody attempt to create a diagram of the classroom and show the positions of the witnesses relative to Coumas' acts while in that room. No exhibit was introduced that shows the door through which Coumas entered and exited the classroom. Well, Deputy Hitt did photograph the exterior view of two of the doors into the building but Darrah didn't have any of the witnesses testify as to which door Coumas used coming and going from the school. Darrah had no diagram to refer the witnesses to during his questioning of them. Deputy Hitt did not show all elevations of the room photographically, so that their relative points could be established in evidence. For example, there was a folding partition between the room in which Mrs. Taylor was shot, and the room next to it, also a classroom. Opposite the folding partition on the side of the room where Mrs. Taylor fell is the stage that two of the students referenced in their testimony. Had Deputy Hitt stood with his back to the folding partition, he could have photographed that side of the room for orientation purposes. He could have also photographed the view at least one student had of the classroom from the stage area. Hitt took no photographs of the left side of Mrs. Taylor's body in the school classroom. Even if he didn't think to photograph the entire room in 1932, Darrah should have sent him to the school in 1934 to photograph the exterior and the relevant interior rooms for the benefit of the Greek authorities. I doubt that the rooms or the school had changed all that much in the time past since the shooting.

Be that as it may, the description of the wounds suffered by Olive Taylor by Dr. Lynch in this deposition is in much greater detail than that presented in the Coroner's Record by Mr. DeYoung. Can you think of a rational reason why that would be? The coroner, in his "official" report, noted that Coumas fired three shots at Olive Taylor. That conclusion was not supported by a single witness giving depositions on December 19, 1934.

Nobody testified here as to the seizure of Mrs. Taylor's personal property, under what circumstances and why were they seized. Mr. Duval testified that Mrs. Taylor's vehicle was at the school. Was that processed for evidence? Coumas' vehicle was said in newspaper accounts to have been abandoned at the Kaloutsis home. There is no testimony here regarding that. Why else would Coumas have to force Joe Coniglio and Steve Souza to drive him at gunpoint to Modesto? Why is there no information about Coumas' vehicle, which was used in the commission of several crimes here? And what of Steve Souza? Why was he not brought forward as a witness to kidnapping and assault with a deadly weapon?

Not one single witness of the fifteen deposed has testified that Tom Coumas tried to murder William Duval. Of the four students in the classroom at the time of the shooting, none testified that they saw Mr. Duval shot by Tom Coumas. No evidence of Mr. Duval's injuries was introduced, with the exception of Mr. and Mrs. Duval's individual testimonies. The bullet that struck Duval went through him. No evidence was introduced that this bullet was recovered. Is it at all possible that the bullet that struck Mr. Duval, also struck Mrs. Taylor in the leg? There can be no doubt that Mr. Duval and even Mrs. Duval suffered assault with a deadly weapon, a crime that carries a prison sentence of up to ten years for each count. The same could be said for Joe Coniglio and Steve Souza. We have testimony here that Coumas abandoned at least one child, and possibly two others, but no charges for child abandonment were filed. At least two people were kidnapped by Coumas, and possibly a third, but nothing came forth from Mr. Darrah regarding that. I guess Margaret Coumas might not have been capable of testimony regarding her husband and Clara Hickman, but in reading Tom Coumas' letter, can there be any doubt Coumas intended to abandon Margaret Coumas? Again, silence from the District Attorney.

Witnesses testified as to Coumas having been seen at the homes of various persons on six separate occasions on April 21st following the shooting at Castle School, yet no law enforcement person could locate him. He was seen at two separate places in Manteca on the morning of April 22nd, yet no law enforcement person could find him. I find all of this just astonishing.

You may be amazed to learn that in 1932 it was not a crime in California to wander about with a loaded and concealed firearm. It was also apparently not a crime then to take flight to avoid prosecution, because Coumas was never charged with that conduct either. I'm also not sure about harboring a fugitive from justice, or aiding and abetting. After all Coumas spent the night somewhere on April 20th and it was cold in the San Joaquin Valley that particular April. I find it very hard to believe that the entire community was not aware of what happened at Castle School and that Tom Coumas was involved in it.

The Greek authorities have already decided that Coumas is legally their citizen, and they have the legal right under Greek law to hold him accountable for the violation of any laws while he was in the United States that would also violate any Greek laws. The Greek Government had asked San Joaquin County to revisit their evidence and bring forward whatever they have in support of their amended indictment of Coumas as expressed by this Grand Jury on March 14, 1934. They had also invited San Joaquin County to bring forward any evidence that was not expressed in that indictment, or any previous indictment, for that matter. How do you lose a transcript from an indictment for murder and attempted murder? That would of course be the documentation in support of the original indictment in 1932. And I also find it not helpful in any legal proceeding for a lawyer throwing $100 words about, adducing this and that, which only tends to confuse people, and not conclude that the lawyer is not particularly bright, and only serves to provide unwarranted and unnecessary distractions from the matters at hand. What did Wilbur S. Worcester witness originally in this case, and why was he not called to testify again? Could not a Greek jury wonder that point as well?

We have heard from all fifteen witnesses to the crimes of murder and attempted murder that Mr. Darrah cared to bring forward. You be the jury: would you find Coumas guilty of those charges based on this evidence?

What questions would you have asked that were not answered here?

CHAPTER SEVENTEEN
THE TRIAL IN GREECE

On December 29, 1934 in Department 1 of the San Joaquin County Superior Court, at the court house in Stockton, California with acting Judge Daniel McLeod Young presiding, Darrah caused all of the fifteen witnesses to appear, with the exception of Joe Coniglio, for the purpose of certifying the correctness and accuracy of their depositions as given on December 19, 1934, which all did before Judge Young. The court reporter for this hearing was Herman G. Spalinger. The depositions were certified as having been taken before Henry F. Ellis, Foreman of the San Joaquin County Grand Jury. Representing the People was District Attorney Darrah. Others certified to the proceedings were R. E. Graham, Chief Deputy Clerk of the Superior Court, that Bea Scantlebury was an acting Clerk of the Superior Court, and Eugene D. Graham, Clerk of the Superior Court certified Judge Young, and Judge Young certified R. E. Graham, and Herman Spalinger certified that he took the notes during the giving of the depositions and in what manner and how transcribed and that the witnesses were duly sworn, that they would tell the truth and that Spalinger was a disinterested party to the proceedings, and so forth.

Guard Darrah brought forward the fourteen witnesses present, after all of the swearing and certifying had been concluded. They were asked to certify that their depositions were true and correct, which they all individually did. These witnesses were listed in a separate certification that certified that Henry F. Ellis was qualified to take depositions, and administer oaths, and that the Judge was a disinterested person who actually took the depositions as taken by Henry F. Ellis and other interesting factoids which tend to keep legions of lawyers gainfully employed in this country. Not the least of which was Mr. Darrah who supplied his own certification regarding the laws governing the functions of grand juries in California, for the benefit of the authorities in Greece. Joe Coniglio appeared on his own behalf to certify his own deposition on January 5, 1935 - maybe before the same judge and other people mentioned here or maybe not. The document I am quoting from is not all that clear. Judge Young signs this "Certificate of The Presiding Judge of the Superior Court" on January 7, 1935.

All of these depositions, statements and certifications, along with the various photographic exhibits were then transmitted to the authorities in Greece. If there were any other evidentiary instruments or exhibits sent to the Greek Government, I have not been able to find any copies of them in the public record.

Tripolis, Greece

Coumas had been locked up in the Tripolis jail since September 1934. It took some considerable time for the San Joaquin County documents to be translated into Greek and reviewed by the investigating authorities in Greece. The result of that review caused Tom Coumas to be summoned for trial on the following charges, all violations of Greek law:

1st - Murder of Olive Taylor
2nd - Attempted Murder of William J. Duval
3rd - Attack with a firearm on Mrs. William J. Duval
4th - Unlawful use of a firearm

The firearm charge was levied under Greek law, not U.S. or California law, and although the other charges were violations of California law, Coumas only stood trial in Greece for allegedly violating Greek laws. A jury trial was held on October 16, 1935 before the Corinth Assize Court. Coumas was represented by counsel, and the government of Greece by the Attorney General, and the Assistant Secretary of the local Court of Common Pleas. Writs dated June 13, 1935 and July 3, 1935 had been conveyed to Coumas giving notice of the particulars of the actions of the Tripolis Court of Common Pleas. These writs probably conveyed the charges against him and may have been similar to the preliminary hearing process in criminal matters in the U.S. Courts.

Here is what the jury decided on the charges before the court:

> "Honestly, and with the utmost conscientiousness it is stated, that the Verdict of the Jury, compiled by virtue of the lawful majority of vote required, is as follows: Yes, the accused, Spryidon Dem. Smyrnoyannis, born and residing in Roino of Mantinia County, aged 45, a grocer by occupation, of the Christian Orthodox faith, is guilty, so far as the charge: - that on April 20th of the year 1932, in the City of Manteca, San Joachim County, State of California, U.S.A., unintentionally and at a moment of great anger, decided and committed murder with as a victim Olivia Taylor, teacher, having fired against her from a very short distance with his firearm loaded with gun-powder and bullets, i.e. with his revolver-pistol, having wounded her in different parts of the body, from which wounds her death occurred, is concerned. Yes, at the time he perpetrated the said act, the victim excited and

irritated the accused. Yes, this irritation and excitement was caused to him by the victim by great insults and for serious reasons. No, it was not proved that the said accused perpetrated the said act of murder while not the master of himself owing to idiocy, in which state of mind he was not able to judge clearly the consequences of his act or to understand his liability to penalty on account of such act. Yes, it clearly and undoubtedly results from all circumstances that the said accused perpetrated the above act while not the master of himself but not in a mood so, or substantially, far from normal as to render impossible the application of the penalty foreseen by the law in such cases. Yes, the said as above accused is guilty that the time said and place, intending unpremeditatively and in an unsettled state of mind to perpetrate murder against William Duval, decided and in this connection attempted an act – bearing in it at least the characteristic of the commencement – that is to say, he fired against him with the automatic pistol he carried on him, but by chance and quite independently of his will he missed his object of committing murder and only wounded him in different places of the body. No, at the time the said act was perpetrated, the victim did not excite or irritate the accused. Yes, it is proved that the above accused perpetrated the said act of attempt to murder while not the master of his judgment owing to idiocy, in which state of mind he could not, of course, judge the consequences of his act or understand the liability of his penalty for such an act. No, he is not guilty that at the same time and place, he unjustifiably attacked by fire-arm Rosiana, wife of William Duval. Yes, said above accused is guilty that at the same time and place and at the time he perpetrated the said act of murder, and

> attempt to murder, he made use of a forbidden firearm, i.e., of an automatic pistol."

There you have it, guilty of unpremeditated murder of Olive Taylor, not guilty of attempted murder of William Duval by reason of insanity, not guilty of assault with a deadly weapon on Mrs. Duval, and guilty of making use of a forbidden firearm. I have to wonder, where did the testimony come from that Olive Taylor "excited and irritated" Coumas? There was nothing about anything of that, or anything about "insults" of Coumas by anybody in the statements of the San Joaquin County witnesses. The only comment that was included in those depositions was that Olive Taylor said to Coumas, "Now, listen here" which was all she managed to say. Unless, the jury heard at trial and agreed that when Olive Taylor disciplined the Coumas child by hitting him on the hand with her ruler was sufficient to meet the test of "exciting and irritating" under Greek Law. Perhaps striking a child in Olive Taylor's manner of schoolhouse discipline was considered an insulting act in Greek society. Unfortunately I have not found a copy of the translated version of the trial transcript, so I don't know what defense was made on Coumas' behalf. Here is the section of Greek law that was applied in these circumstances:

> Greek Criminal Code Section 293 – "Whoever without premeditation in the excitement of passion, decided and committed homicide is guilty of involuntary manslaughter and is punishable: (1) With imprisonment for from 15 to 20 years if none of the cases enumerated in sub-sections two and three are present. (2) With imprisonment to the most of 15 years if the party killed provoked and aggravated the killer. (3) With prison term if this aggravation was made by grave slanders and malice.

I can't possibly conceive that any of the testimony taken in depositions on December 19th in San Joaquin County mentioned anything that could have remotely concluded that Olive Taylor committed any act that could have been judged as gravely slanderous or malicious.

The insanity (idiocy) finding is interesting, because that is also contrary to the testimony of the witnesses. That Duval did nothing to excite and irritate Coumas is somewhat odd, given that Mrs. Duval testified that Mr. Duval punched Coumas in the face. If Mr. Duval did nothing to "excite and irritate" Coumas in the jury's view, where does the insanity part come into play? I wonder how the court came to consider an assault with a firearm on Mrs. Duval, since that was not charged in either the San Joaquin County 1932 or 1934 Grand Jury indictment? Perhaps threatening by pointing a deadly weapon is not considered an assault under Greek law. I find it curious that the jury found the weapon to be both an automatic and a revolver. Obviously a translation issue I would think, rather than any confusion on the part of the jury.

For the record, what I have quoted here was translated from Greek to English by the official translator of the Ministry of Foreign Affairs of Greece. The local Court of Common Pleas heard from the Attorney General who asked for a sentence of 6 and 1/2 years on the charge of unpremeditated murder of Olive Taylor and a sentence of 4 months on the firearm charge. Coumas' attorney asked for the lowest prison penalty. In considering the sentence to be imposed, credit was given to Coumas for already having spent 13 months and 8 days in the Tripolis jail. The sentence handed down by the Court was 4 years 10 months for the involuntary manslaughter of Olive Taylor, and four months for the use of a forbidden firearm, less time already served, caused Coumas to be returned to prison for three years, eight months and twenty-two days.

He would be required to serve the four month term at the conclusion of his manslaughter conviction term. The Court also ordered Coumas to pay judicial charges and expenses. Tom Coumas was now a convicted felon.

The California equivalent of unpremeditated murder would have been involuntary manslaughter, which would have carried a maximum sentence of ten years in prison. Being a first time offender with no criminal record, I think the Court would have probably given him less than the full term. I do not think that he could have been convicted of premeditated murder in San Joaquin County on the evidence I have reviewed. I do think that he might have been convicted of assault with a deadly weapon on a number of people, not the least of which was William Duval, but as we know, Coumas was not charged with that crime. I do not believe he would have been convicted of attempted murder of William Duval in San Joaquin County on the Darrah's evidence. In particular, I believe that Mr. Duval provoked Coumas if he indeed punched Coumas in the face before Coumas drew his firearm. I really think that Duval was the trigger for this entire event, if the witnesses' statements are accurate and represent the facts. I also believe that had Coumas been properly charged by Mr. Darrah, and a jury concurred, Tom Coumas could have been locked up for over 60 years in a California prison, less any reduction below the statutory maximums by a judge passing sentence on conviction and not counting any reduced sentence for good behavior while in a California prison. It is not uncommon to receive less than the maximum term in prison at sentencing for a first time offender, but the record suggests that Coumas committed multiple crimes against multiple people. Convictions could have added up to an impressive prison term, served concurrently, even for a first time offender.

Yes, you can achieve a reduction in sentence for good behavior, even from a Greek prison. With a good conduct credit of seven months and twenty-nine days, Coumas was released from the Tripolis prison on June 26, 1937.

CHAPTER EIGHTEEN
THE NEXT TEN YEARS

When Tom Coumas was released from the Tripolis Prison in Greece, he was not exactly a free man. The Greek government had levied a three-year parole condition on his release from prison. I did not find a copy of any parole order, but surely there must have been one and surely it must have placed some post-prison restrictions on Coumas. After his release Coumas traveled to Athens in 1937 and sought out Ambassador Lincoln MacVeagh at the U.S. Embassy. Once there, Coumas made application for a U.S. passport so that he could return to the United States. I don't know if he also made application for his wife Gregoria Yaitros, whom Coumas married in Greece on April 29, 1934 or his daughter who was born from this union on April 6, 1934. This child has not been identified by name in any official record I have uncovered thus far. Gregoria and her mother ran the grocery store in Roino while Coumas was serving his prison sentence in Tripolis. But the grocery business in Roino was not his main objective, as it would turn out - getting back to the United States was.

When Coumas consulted Ambassador MacVeagh regarding the passport, MacVeagh told Coumas to return after his parole term had been served, as MacVeagh could not grant Coumas a passport while he was still subject to the oversight of the Greek authorities. Coumas went back to his grocery store in Roino.

Coumas claimed that he tried to learn the fate of his children and had repeatedly written to friends and family members in California, but none would answer his letters, including a sister living in San Diego.

Coumas returned to Athens to make application again for the passport in 1940. He was again asked to take an oath of allegiance to the United States, which Coumas claimed he did. However, the U.S. State Department did not issue Coumas a U.S. passport, and Coumas would return to Athens every month or so making inquiry as to the status of his application.

Unknown to Coumas at the time, his son John, the boy who had his hand slapped by Olive Taylor in her classroom in Manteca, died in Sonoma County in March 1940. He was only sixteen years of age.

Then Germany invaded Greece in 1941. With that invasion, also went the American embassy in Athens. Coumas attempted to board one of the last ships leaving Greece with Americans bound for the United States but was denied passage because he did not have the proper documents in his possession. Coumas had to wait for the war to end.

I would imagine that either Coumas kept his plans to return to the U.S. a secret from Gregoria and her family, or he had managed to convince her he had important business back in the United States and would send for her once he reestablished himself there. It probably would be reasonable to conclude that Coumas did not fulfill his promise in having Mrs. Hickman join him in Greece, as he did in his letter to her in June of 1932. In fact, I have no idea what became of Clara Hickman. She was last known, through all records reviewed, as having been at the William

Pappas home in Manteca, California on the evening of April 20, 1932.

With the end of the war with Germany, came the return to Athens of Lincoln MacVeagh and the U.S. embassy. Coumas returned again to Athens in yet another attempt to obtain a U.S. passport. Coumas claimed that an unidentified embassy official told him early in 1947 that the U.S. State Department in Washington D.C. had concluded that Coumas had expatriated himself to Greece and was therefore no longer considered a U.S. citizen. As Coumas tells his version of the story, embassy personnel in Athens acted as if the State Department was a separate decision making authority rather that both being part of the same organization. Regardless, what this meant for Coumas was that the United States Government was not going to issue him a U.S. passport. Coumas would stew on that revelation for a while, but not for very long. By August 1947, Tom Coumas was on his way back to the United States.

CHAPTER NINETEEN
COUMAS RETURNS

By early 1947, Coumas was getting restless and running out of patience with the American embassy in Athens. Quite frankly, I really don't think the embassy was all that much interested in accommodating any request that Coumas might bring. I do find that somewhat ironic, given that the Unites States was originally trying to get Coumas back because he was wanted in the U.S. for murder and attempted murder, and now here is Coumas trying to return on his own initiative, and the American embassy in Greece is doing nothing to facilitate his return. I mean how easy would it have been to nab him? Issue him a passport, then put out an alert for him traveling under that name and arrest him once he was back inside the United States. Each time Coumas would inquire about the status of his passport application, he would be told that Washington (D.C.) had not as yet responded to the request. After several unsuccessful trips to obtain a U.S. passport, and having been eventually told by embassy personnel that Coumas was essentially no longer considered a U.S. citizen, Coumas did what Coumas generally did when it came to his various travels. He found somebody who could craft false papers under an assumed name.

Hard to say what he told his new wife or his daughter in Greece, but Coumas seemed determined to return to San Joaquin County, no matter what it took to get him there.

Sometime in July 1947, Coumas armed with false papers that identified him as a seaman by the name of Christos Mermingos, left Greece by ship and journeyed to Marseilles, France where Coumas believed he had employment on another ship there. When Coumas arrived in Marseilles he learned there was no ship by the name he had been given in Greece and thus no job aboard that vessel. After a week or so trying unsuccessfully to find work on a ship bound for the United States, Coumas tried his luck in Rouen, France.

After hanging around Rouen for about a month, Coumas found a man who was the captain of the SS Ameriki. The captain offered Coumas a job as a cook on the ship, a circumstance much to the delight of Coumas; the ship was bound for Norfolk, Virginia. Coumas would later claim he did not know the Ameriki was bound for the U.S. until three days out of Norfolk, but quite frankly I find that hard to believe given Coumas' known history. On August 16, 1947, Tom Coumas once again stood upon American soil. Immigration officials at Norfolk checked Coumas' papers, found them in order and allowed him to walk off the ship and into America. The captain of the Ameriki had just lost a cook.

Coumas made his way first to Newark, New Jersey in search of his eldest son Chester. The record does not reflect whether Coumas ever found him, but the next sighting put Coumas right back in Manteca, California, and he headed straight for the home of the Kaloutsis family.

In 1947, a man by the name of Tom Brockman was Chief of Police of the City of Manteca Police Department. He was born in Arizona in 1885, and when he was 25 he was punching cows there. Not literally, just an old term for a cattle herder. Ten years later, he was a chauffer for a lumber company in Manteca. Ten years following that he was working as a salesman for a lumber company also in Manteca. Somewhere between 1930 and 1947 he became Police Chief. At age 62, Chief Brockman, acting on a tip as to Coumas presence, arrived at the Kaloutsis home in Manteca on September 26, 1947 and placed Tom Coumas under arrest for the murder of Olive Luella Taylor and the attempted murder of William Duval.

In 1932, following Coumas' flight from San Joaquin County and the United States, a hearing was held in Stockton, California on the adoption petition of Mr. and Mrs. Kaloutsis regarding Coumas' son, Peter, and the adoption was granted. Peter had just graduated from Manteca High School the year previous to his father's return. Manteca was a relatively small community. Can you imagine the embarrassment to this young man, who had last seen or heard from his father when he was just three years old, that his father is arrested 15 years later at his new home for murder? What of the impact to Peter and Aristea Kaloutsis? Peter Kaloutsis would have been 71 and Aristea 61 in 1947. Coumas did not seem to care a whole lot about his kids if you can believe Aristea's assessment given in her deposition in 1934. That pretty much was corroborated by Coumas' own comments in his letter to Clara Hickman from New York in 1932. Plus the fact that there exists nothing on the record that shows Coumas did anything to provide for the care of his children in the fifteen years he was living in Greece. The daughter Helen might have ended up with Coumas' sister who was living in southern California in 1932. Custody of son John could have been awarded to Coumas' cousin Sam Stavros also living in California at the time, but that theory has not been independently proven. Coumas knew before he fled California in 1932 that the relatives of his wife Margaret had traveled to Stockton in an attempt to gain custody of the Coumas children, and it was Coumas' understanding that his sister and Stavros had been awarded custody of two of the children.

Chief Brockman escorted Tom Coumas to the San Joaquin County Jail. Guard Darrah was no longer the district attorney for San Joaquin County, having left office sometime in 1936. A man by the name of Chester Watson, the district attorney in office at the time was more than happy to pick up the torch and press forward to bring Coumas to trial. Interestingly, Watson would pick up where Darrah left off in 1934, even though there probably existed in 1947 a statute of limitations issue on the 1934 charge of attempted murder of William Duval. Under the California Penal Code, a person had to be charged and tried within three years for felonies and one year for misdemeanors. There is no limitation on the charge of murder. So, even with evidence of a number of crimes committed by Coumas in 1932, but for which he wasn't indicted then, it was too late to bring those charges against Coumas in 1947. So, Watson apparently had nothing left but the original March 14, 1934 indictment charging Coumas with committing murder upon Olive Taylor. Not so in the mind of Mr. Watson who pressed forward on all charges originally brought in 1932 and amended in 1934.

A preliminary hearing was set and Coumas appeared before San Joaquin County Superior Court Judge Marion G. Woodward on October 22, 1947. An attorney by the name of Stanley P. Mamalakis appeared before Judge Woodward to argue that Coumas had already faced trial in Greece on these charges and could not be tried on them again. The Judge was apparently not impressed, as he continued the matter until October 29, 1947 at which time Coumas pled not guilty and not guilty by reason of insanity and trial was set for November 25, 1947. No bail was agreed upon, and a young public defender by the name of Anthony (Tony) J. Chargin was additionally assigned to represent Coumas. Trial was later rescheduled for January 5, 1948 (later rescheduled again to February 16, 1948) before Superior Court Judge Raymond M. Dunne. Of course bail would not have been at issue in a crime for which the penalty could be death.

I don't know who arranged it, but Mamalakis was the legal counsel for the Greek Consulate in San Francisco, California and initially a genuine gift to Tom Coumas. Tony Chargin and Stan Mamalakis formed a partnership that would result in a petition being filed with the California Supreme Court, requesting that San Joaquin County be barred from trying Tom Coumas for murder and attempted murder again, but in their jurisdiction.

Yes, you read it right: again. I was not able to find, nor was the San Joaquin County Superior Court, a copy of the preliminary hearing transcript from that event in Judge Woodward's court in 1947. Therefore I can't relate to you the points and authorities that might have surfaced in the hearing or the nature of the case made on behalf of the People by District Attorney Watson or defenses raised by anybody in that hearing on Coumas' behalf other than he had already been tried in Greece, but I do find troubling a number of things that often transpire in our courts in the name of justice. I make these observations not as someone thirsting for justice regardless of the law, but out of interest that everybody play by the same rules so that equal treatment under the law is the gold standard of legal practice in this county, no matter who stands before the court. It is reasonable to presume that people who wear those black robes and sit upon high benches understand and are knowledgeable of the laws that govern the various matters for which their various courts have jurisdiction. But for some inexplicable reason, Judge Woodward saw fit to ignore all of that and hold Coumas for trial anyway.

The purpose of a preliminary hearing is to hear evidence sufficient that a person be held for trial on the charges. This concept, one would think, also holds that if someone raises certain legal reasons that somebody should not be held to answer to whatever the charge or charges might be, that they be set free and excused from further legal process. Murder is a charge that is about as serious as charges generally get, with some few exceptions, so it would seem to me that a judge would have to be assured that there exists probable cause to believe that the person in custody is likely the person who is guilty, and therefore liable under the law to be held accountable to answer to those charges.

Actually it falls to the district attorney to make a determination over which cases are moved forward to trial long before the matter ever shows up before a judge. One would assume, since a district attorney is considered an officer of the court, that awareness of the provisions of law is a foregone conclusion. In reality, Chester Earl Watson had no case against Coumas, but he plowed ahead anyway. Judge Woodward should have agreed with Mamalakis that Watson had no case against Coumas, but he also plowed ahead and set trial on the murder charge anyway. I don't want to oversimplify what must have been a highly charged atmosphere in San Joaquin County following the eventual arrest of Coumas there in 1947, and all of the emotion on the part of many people as a result of it. But it just astonishes me the number of people in our society holding positions of responsibility who just do not seem to measure up to the requirements of the job.

All things being somewhat lopsided in this case, Mr. Mamalakis was about to give the San Joaquin County legal community one whale of a lesson on the protections guaranteed under the California Constitution.

CHAPTER TWENTY
CALIFORNIA SUPREME COURT

I would imagine the history books and law schools everywhere are replete with examples of how a bunch of lawyers and judges can tie up the courts with meaningless legal challenges when all they had to do is read the law. Now I recognize having had to enforce a law or two over the years, that there are some laws that defy determination as to their intent and meaning, but in this particular case, there are so many prohibitions that existed against the legal folks in San Joaquin County as to qualify holding Tom Coumas for trial a real "head scratcher".

Stan Mamalakis and Tony Chargin filed a petition with the California Supreme Court against the San Joaquin County Superior Court, asking that the county be prohibited from holding Tom Coumas for trial on the March 14, 1934 Grand Jury indictment. District Attorney Chester Watson, along with San Joaquin County Deputy District Attorney Brad Crittenden, the California State Attorney General Fred N. Howser, California Deputy Attorney General Clarence A. Linn, not to mention two San Joaquin County Superior Court judges Marion G. Woodward and Raymond M Dunne, that would be by my count six lawyers, did not appear to have familiarity with the provisions of the California Penal Code or the California State Constitution, or the United States Constitution on the subject of double jeopardy. If this were not serious, it would be hilarious. Perhaps even worse, San Joaquin County's own legal counsel Fred Feldon threw his ante on the table betting that all these lawyers and judges were right, and the county had every legal right to hold Tom Coumas for trial on the March 14, 1934 indictment.

What this matter amounted to, is that San Joaquin County was violating the law and had no basis for the arrest of Tom Coumas let alone holding him for trial and got the California Attorney General to agree to violate the law with them. When Chester Watson called on the Attorney General for help with the Coumas Supreme Court petition, Frank Howser should have had Clarence Linn read Mr. Watson Article 1, Section 13 of the California Constitution, which says in part "...No person shall be twice put in jeopardy for the same offense". Watson could have then read it to Woodward and Dunne, after calling a staff meeting and reading it to the entire district attorney's office. After all, all of these guys take oaths themselves where they swear to uphold the law, the Constitution and so forth. What? Oh, you're saying that this provision in the Constitution does not apply because Coumas was tried in a Greek court, not an American court, as he should have been because the crimes were committed here in the United States?

Let's take a look at the historical perspective of this situation again. Coumas was born in Greece. Under Greek law, Coumas was not permitted to renounce his Greek citizenship without permission of the Greek Government, which Coumas had never received. The United States and Greece entered into a treaty that says that neither country can be compelled to extradite their own citizens to the country of the other. That is a two way street: If the United States has an American citizen who committed crimes in Greece, under that treaty, if the American is in the United States, then the American Government is under no legal obligation to deliver that citizen to the Greek Government for trial. It works the same way in reverse. Coumas was in Greece. He was a Greek citizen under Greek law. Greece tried him, and convicted him. Under the treaty, Greece could not be compelled to deliver Coumas to U.S. custody. Treaties between the United States and other countries are ratified by the United States Congress and have the full weight and effect of law. Well, a trial in Greece is hardly the same as a trial in the United States, you say? That's what the six lawyers in California in 1948 seemed to be saying as well. I assume that lawyers who work for the government are provided with law books. If the lawyers in class are ready, let's all turn together to Section 793 of the California Penal Code.

> "When an act charged as a public offense is within the jurisdiction of another state or country, as well as this state, a conviction or acquittal thereof in the former is a bar to the prosecution or indictment therefore in this state."

Perhaps you might be hung up over the word "is" in this citation, but it reads crystal clear to me. Still not convinced?

Section 1 of the Fifth Amendment of the Constitution of the United States; "...nor shall any person be subject for the same offense to be twice put in jeopardy of life or limb". Seems pretty clear to me. Nothing in that civil right exempting when a trial takes place in another country.

The United States has legions of laws for which its citizens are held accountable no matter where they might be in this universe. Other countries such as Greece have laws that hold their citizens accountable no matter where they might be in this universe. Section 656 of the California Penal Code,

> "Whenever on the trial of an accused person it appears that upon a criminal prosecution under the laws of another state, government, or country, founded upon the act or omission in respect to which he is on trial, he has been acquitted or convicted, it is a sufficient defense."

Sufficient defense of what you ask? Why a defense of not guilty, of course.

And also, of course, I cannot take credit here for these points of legal brilliance, those being the work of Mamalakis and Chargin. Here is a quote from the Petitioner's Brief filed on behalf of Tom Coumas, last paragraph:

> "The petitioner stands on the application in this matter of the laws of the United States as well as of the laws of California and not in particularly in the application of the principle of international comity. He has suffered a more severe and costly punishment for the acts that he allegedly committed than the case would have warranted. He has lost the greatest and most important part of his life in paying for these acts and now respectfully requests that the flimsy balance of his miserable existence be spared by the proper application and construction of the rules of law, justice and fairness. Therefore, petitioner respectfully requests that the Alternative Writ of Prohibition hitherto issued out of this court may be made permanent and that the respondent court be forever restrained from proceeding any further with his prosecution or trial."

This brief was filed with the California Supreme Court on March 5, 1948. Tom Coumas was still locked up in the San Joaquin County Jail. That is to say, he had been locked up in the San Joaquin County Jail for a matter of five months and some change by the time March 5th rolled around, illegally. The Pledge of Allegiance ends with, "...with liberty and justice for all." Not for some, or a few. Not, for these people over here, but not for those people over there. Yes, even those people who cause the life of another to be extinguished do not forfeit their legal rights just because we are outraged at their conduct, stupidity and wanton disregard for the rights of others. The law applies equally to all of the people. I would have thought that district attorneys and judges in 1947 would have been aware of that.

The lawyers representing the People responded with the argument that expatriation of all peoples of the world is an inherent right under U.S. law. The Greek Government did not pass a law that said that their citizens could not become citizens of other countries, but they did pass a law that said their citizens could not renounce their Greek citizenship unless with permission of the Greek Government. The People's lawyers claimed that the Greek Government had no jurisdiction over Coumas, and therefore the judgment of their court is not recognized. In order to accept this concept one would have to accept that the laws of the United States are universal laws, binding on all other countries on this earth. How incredibly arrogant is that?

I'm certainly no expert on the matter of International Law, but I do have a problem with the concept that one country can declare another country's laws invalid simply by passing laws that make such declarations. What is really interesting in the arguments presented by the People in this case is quoting the Nationality Act of 1940, when all of the various acts regarding nationality on the part of Tom Coumas occurred <u>before</u> 1940. I find it equally interesting that the People are trying to put forward their best legal arguments that Coumas was not a Greek citizen, but a naturalized American citizen at the time he caused the death of Olive Taylor in Manteca and the wounding of William Duval. That is the basis for the declaration that the Greek court had no jurisdiction over Coumas. The real problem here is that the U.S. oath of allegiance taken by foreign nationals who want to become U.S. citizens requires the renunciation of that individuals' allegiance to their native country. Coumas did not have the legal authority under Greek law, as a Greek national to make that oath of renunciation, and the U.S. government should not have naturalized Coumas in absence of the required approval of the Greek Government. I mean it's not like the U.S. Department of State could have been in the dark on that point. Could they?

What is even more amazing to me than that is that Greece also had a law that said the Greek Government could not give its permission to divest citizenship to any Greek citizen who had not completed their military service obligations to Greece, which at the time of his naturalization Coumas had not. One would think the State Department was up on that one as well. What occurred here is that the U.S. Government naturalized a Greek citizen who could not be naturalized by the U.S. Government under Greek law, if the United States claimed that by such naturalization Coumas was no longer a citizen of Greece. U.S. law on this subject was not binding on the Greek Government under any legal standard jointly recognized by both countries.

The California Supreme Court in 1948 consisted of Chief Justice Phil S. Gibson and Justices Homer R. Spence, John W. Shenk, Douglas L. Edmonds, Jesse W. Carter, Roger J. Traynor, and Benjamin R. Schauer. On April 23, 1948, the Court issued a Preemptory Writ of Prohibition restraining San Joaquin County from any further proceeding (trial) against Coumas. On May 7th, the Court received filing of a Petition for Rehearing (presumably authored by Mr. Linn), and the Court denied that petition on May 20th. The Court made the Preemptory Writ of Prohibition permanent on May 24, 1948. The decision of the Court was unanimous.

The essential points presented by Mamalakis and Chargin were considered by the court to be correct, while the government's argument was mostly a lot of hot air and gaseous releases, combined with multiple pages of legal nonsense and flights of philosophical fantasy. Justice Spence wrote the opinion. Here are some highlights:

> "Section 793 of the Penal Code provides as follows: "When an act charged as a public offense is within the jurisdiction of another state or country, as well as of this state, a conviction or acquittal thereof in the former is a bar to the prosecution or indictment therefor in this state." Petitioner's pleas come precisely within the contemplated scope of this penal statute, and "prohibition is an appropriate remedy to prevent [his] retrial" on the offenses in question."

> "There is no dispute as to the facts. Petitioner, a native of Greece, emigrated on January 4, 1907, to the United States. He was then 17 years of age. On February 25, 1914, he became a naturalized citizen of this country, at which time he took the required oath in renouncement of "allegiance ... to any ... state or sovereignty of ... which [he] was before a subject or citizen" and in pledge of "true faith and allegiance" to the United States."

> "The taking of the oath of allegiance to the United States and the accompanying renunciation of national ties to any foreign state upon petitioner's

naturalization in this country would not automatically divest him of his Greek citizenship, for the matter of denationalization is one for domestic regulation by the government concerned under its particular laws of expatriation."

"The so-called American doctrine of "voluntary expatriation" as a matter of absolute right cannot postulate loss of original nationality on naturalization in this country as a principle of international law, for that would be tantamount to interference with the exclusive jurisdiction of a nation within its own domain."

"The qualification of the right of expatriation prescribed by the Greek law, conditioned upon the national's fulfillment of his military obligations in the country of his origin and his procurement of the consent of the government, does not involve abandonment of the fundamental principle but simply accords with recognized distinctions in the nationality concept as followed in different countries."

"The matter of extradition is a proper subject for treaty negotiation between sovereign nations, and any point of controversy with regard thereto will be governed by the prevailing stipulations of the contracting powers."

"In the present case, the Treaty of Extradition with Greece expressly provided that "the State appealed to shall decide whether the person claimed is its own citizen," an explicit stipulation according full recognition to any variance in the laws of expatriation existing between the two signatory powers and indicating their mutual intent that the citizenship status of the person seeking refuge in either's territorial limits should be determined in a manner consistent with its standards. Such stipulation in the treaty, signed May 6, 1931, effectively countervails any argument that the United States nevertheless intended that its long prior established position on the "absolute right of expatriation" should prevail in an extradition demand upon the Greek government and would permit disregard of the latter's law under which its national, irrespective of his American naturalization, might still be deemed its citizen. So here, according to Greek law, petitioner on April 20, 1932, the date of his alleged commission of the crimes in Manteca, was still a citizen of Greece by reason of his failure to procure the necessary consent to his foreign naturalization and, upon return to its territorial jurisdiction, he was amenable to prosecution under its penal statutes."

"There is no force to the argument that petitioner may not effectively plead the defenses of "prior conviction" and "former jeopardy" before the respondent court because the Greek trial proceedings and judgment were procured by "fraud or collusion". There is no evidence in the record indicating any fraud, collusion, trickery or subterfuge on the part of petitioner in procuring, according to Greek law, the determination of his guilt on the criminal charges in question. Rather, it appears that petitioner's trial in the Felony Court of Corinth, Greece, was fair and impartial; that depositions of witnesses before the grand jury of San Joaquin County were duly submitted along with the oral testimony of petitioner for the consideration of the jury in reaching its verdict; and that substantial terms of imprisonment were imposed on petitioner--four years and four months--and served by him....."

That last part is particularly illuminating since the Greek Government charged and tried Coumas on two additional violations of law he wasn't charged with by Guard Darrah. Of course in fairness to Mr. Darrah, as I have pointed out previously, that use of a forbidden firearm in the commission of a felony was not a crime in California in 1932, but Mr. Darrah could, and should have charged Coumas with assault with a deadly weapon on Mrs. Duval. Greece got the majority of the charges right, Mr. Darrah didn't.

Here now are some clues that the United States Government knew the Greek Government was within its rights in the handling of the Coumas situation. First, the U.S. Government made no legal attempt to fight the Greek government over their assertions of sovereignty over Coumas. Second, the American embassy in Athens in its initial dealings with Coumas treated him as a U.S. citizen in his application for the U.S. passport, accepting documents from him on that application and administering an oath of allegiance to him while he was still in Greece. Now we have lawyers for San Joaquin County and the California Attorney General trying to claim he is an American citizen and not a Greek citizen when all of that had long since been resolved between the U.S. and Greek governments.

I wonder how many nights in jail were served by Tom Brockman, Chester Watson, Judge Woodward, Judge Dunne, Brad Crittenden, Fred Howser, and Clarence Linn for violating Tom Coumas civil rights.

Make no mistake; I am not defending Tom Coumas here. I am defending the <u>concept</u> of everybody being held accountable under the same laws as everybody else and that public officials cannot be allowed go about willy-nilly violating the rights of people and violating the law under color of authority. That is abuse of power in its worst form. I have always felt that if law enforcement people can't read and understand the law they ought to go into a different line of work.

Eight months after Chief Brockman arrested him in Manteca, Coumas was now a free man. Or was he?

CHAPTER TWENTY-ONE
DEPORTATION

The ruling of the California Supreme Court did not set well with Chester Watson. A newspaper account of the ruling indicated that Watson intended to travel to San Francisco to confer with immigration officials and to consult further with the California Attorney General as to the possibility of appealing the decision to the U.S. Supreme Court. Exhibiting grace in defeat seemed to be a concept foreign to Mr. Watson. Immigration officials were quoted in news accounts following the ruling as claiming that Coumas had "automatically" renounced his American citizenship when he fled to Greece to escape prosecution in San Joaquin County.

This is quite amazing stuff. First the government claims the man is an American citizen and therefore is subject to trial in the United States and after that theory did not fly, now the claim is made that he is no longer an American citizen because he fled to Greece to escape prosecution in the United States.

Coumas was not immediately released from San Joaquin County custody, since the immigration authorities had placed a "hold" on him, no doubt unsure of the outcome of the Supreme Court case. I can't imagine what possible justification might have existed in the mind of Chester Watson for taking this case before the U.S. Supreme Court. Apparently the California Attorney

General took a different view, because the case never made it there.

The "hold" that was placed by immigration authorities consisted of a federal arrest warrant issued by the District Director of the Immigration and Naturalization Service (INS) at San Francisco and served on Coumas while still locked up in the San Joaquin County Jail on February 18, 1948.

When the California Supreme Court ruled that San Joaquin County could not press forward with its trial of Coumas, the sheriff was compelled to release him. And release him he did, right into the open arms of the INS, who then transported Coumas to federal detention quarters in San Francisco. The record is not clear on how long Coumas spent in INS custody. Coumas was probably not released to the INS until sometime in June of 1948. Coumas would later recall that he spent a total of 14 months in jail following his arrest in Manteca in 1947. Enter once again longtime Coumas friend George Laurentzos. A bond hearing was eventually held and Coumas was advised that he could be released from INS custody by posting a $1,500 bond. Just to give you some perspective on the size of this bond in 1948, the 2008 equivalent amount of money would have been $13,275 dollars. Laurentzos not only paid the bond on Coumas behalf, he got him a job as a waiter at the famed Fairmont Hotel on Knob Hill in San Francisco.

There were several hearings held on the matter of Coumas' deportation by the INS San Francisco District. One such seemed particularly significant on the subject of the "impartiality" of the district staff regarding Coumas. On January 24, 1950 Tom Coumas, along with attorney Stan Mamalakis appeared before a man by the name of Robert S. DeMoulin, Presiding Inspector for the U.S. Department of Justice, Immigration and Naturalization Service in San Francisco, California. The purpose of this meeting was for DeMoulin to continue a previously adjourned hearing into the matter of the deportation of Tom Coumas. There is no possible way that a deck could have stacked higher against Tom Coumas, and that no public official ever acted with such undisguised bias and contempt and abuse of authority than DeMoulin exhibited at this particular hearing. If deportation hearings in this time period were intended to be fair and impartial, DeMoulin slept through that part of the training. The transcript of this hearing is absolutely dripping with venom in DeMoulin's conduct. I have no idea what authorities are held by an INS presiding inspector, but the outcome of this hearing was ordained before anybodies' bottoms met the chairs in the hearing room. First of all, DeMoulin does not open the hearing with a statement of what laws, if any, Coumas is accused of having violated. He just launches into questioning Coumas on a broad range of subject matter. However, I was able to locate the charges on which he was arrested in other documents, so for the sake of clarity here is what this deportation hearing is all about:

> "Violation of the Immigration Act of May 26, 1924, in that, at the time of entry, he was an immigrant not in possession of a valid immigration visa and not exempt from the presentation thereof by said Act or regulations made thereunder."

Now I'm assuming that "at the time of entry" the reference is to Coumas' disembarkation of the S.S. Ameriki at Norfolk, Virginia on August 16, 1947 as Christos Mermingos, and not as Tom Coumas without benefit of a valid U.S. passport. Regardless of any of that, this hearing did not open with any statement from the presiding officer as to the purpose of this particular hearing session. Just to give you a little taste for the "neutrality" of Mr. DeMoulin, during the course of this hearing Mamalakis objected 9 times to questions DeMoulin was asking of Coumas and was overruled by DeMoulin 9 times. After reading hundreds of pages of documents in which Mamalakis has objected at one time or another in various legal proceedings regarding Tom Coumas, he struck me as not a man who objected just to hear the sound of his voice. If this guy DeMoulin was tilted any further in favor of the Department of Justice he would have fallen out of his chair.

There were essentially two issues on the table from a "legal" standpoint that caused the U.S. Government to conclude that Coumas was an immigrant and not a U.S. citizen in this thing, if you read between the lines of the transcript. First the government claimed that Coumas, when he was conscripted into service for four months in the Greek Army, he took an oath of allegiance to Greece. Second, when he fled to Greece to avoid prosecution in San Joaquin County, he remained in Greece longer than two years before he returned to the United States. It was the position of the INS, acting on behalf of the U.S. Government, that when Coumas did these things he forfeited his American citizenship, thus he was an immigrant when he arrived in Norfolk in 1947, and not a U.S. citizen. Coumas, on the other hand, claimed that he never took an oath when he entered the Greek Army, and he never intended to remain in Greece, and that he was prevented from returning to the United States by circumstances and events beyond his control. Here now is a little slice of this hearing so that you can witness yourself the flavor of the moment:

> "DeMoulin: Now, Mr. Coumas, have you any comment to make regarding the nature of the oath to the Government of Greece which is stated to be compulsory to all recruits into the Greek Army?
> Coumas: That's wrong in my case as I went in later

than the regular recruits. They never asked me to take the oath. I made that statement in Athens to our Consul when I took the oath again to the United States. DeMoulin: Now, isn't it a fact, Mr. Coumas, that you did subscribe to this oath in connection with your service in the Greek Army? Mamalakis: I object to the form of the question. DeMoulin: Your objection is overruled. I think the question can be answered by the respondent [Coumas]. Coumas: Will you say that again? DeMoulin: Isn't it a fact that you did subscribe to the oath of the common soldier in connection with your service in the Greek Army in 1932 and 1933? Mamalakis: May I interpose an instruction to my client as how to answer? DeMoulin: Yes. Mamalakis: Mr. Coumas, no one is compelled to remember what he cannot remember. If you do remember, certainly you have to testify to it. However, if you have any doubt as to the fact to subscribing or not subscribing, you so state. Do you understand? Coumas: I am going to tell it just as I had it in my mind. I had it in my mind that if they asked me to take an oath I would refuse. They didn't ask me so I didn't have to. I always had it in my mind if they asked me to take an oath I would refuse. I never even voted – never even registered. DeMoulin: Now, from what you have said, Mr. Coumas, if I understand you correctly, and I want you to correct me if this is not correct, you are, I believe, categorically denying that you ever took any oath in connection with your service in the Greek Army. Is that right? Coumas: Yes. D. You do deny that you ever took any such oath? Coumas: Yes, that's right."

This hearing more than less takes this kind of a course throughout the entire process. This was a major shift from the previous position of the INS that Coumas lost citizenship by fleeing the country to avoid prosecution. Keep in mind that flight to avoid prosecution was not unlawful in the United States in 1932, and Coumas has never been charged with this conduct by any government as being unlawful, including the INS:

> "DeMoulin: Mr. Coumas, at the time that you left the United States during the summer of 1932, you testified that you went to Greece. Is that correct? Coumas: Yes. D: Just what was your purpose in going to Greece in the summer of 1932? Coumas: Well, I was wanted for a crime in the United States and just made a dive for Greece. DeMoulin: Do I understand correctly then that your primary purpose in going to Greece in the summer of 1932 was to avoid arrest and prosecution for the crime for which you were wanted in the United States? Coumas: I could avoid it altogether, that wasn't the purpose. Just advice of friends. DeMoulin: You say you could avoid it but that wasn't your purpose. What do you mean? Coumas: Yes, I could avoid paying for the crime by staying away altogether. DeMoulin: First you said you were wanted for a crime and for that reason you left the United States and as you say 'took a dive for Greece'. It isn't clear to me how you connect those two. Coumas: Well, a person who is in trouble and out of his head – a few friends advise you and that's what you do. When I got there I could have avoided paying. DeMoulin: If you had remained in the United States you would have been arrested here in the United States, would you not? Coumas: Yes. DeMoulin: Then actually your primary objective in leaving the United States was to avoid that arrest and prosecution. Was it not? Coumas: No, not to me. I had no ideas to avoid it. DeMoulin: What were you running from when you went to Greece? Coumas: What do you mean? DeMoulin:

What were you running from? Coumas: Something terrible happened to me and I didn't know what to do. DeMoulin: How can you say it wasn't your purpose to avoid prosecution for the crime in the United States when as a matter of fact....Mamalakis: [Interrupting] I object to the question as incompetent, irrelevant and immaterial and particularly argumentative and not a proper examination. DeMoulin: Your objection is overruled, Counsel. This line of questioning is definitely competent and relevant to the issue. Mamalakis: Not the argument. You can get facts about it but not argue the position of the respondent at the time he fled the United States. DeMoulin: Your objection has been overruled. DeMoulin: (To Respondent) Do you care to state further for the record, Mr. Coumas, in answer to my question, the purpose of your leaving the United States in 1932 immediately following the crime for which you were wanted? Coumas: Well, as I said before, I was out of my head – where to turn – advice of friends told me to leave so that's what I done because I never had in my mind to avoid paying for the crime because I knew I was right. Just as soon as Uncle Sam reached for me I was tickled to come back."

Well, I rather doubt that Coumas was tickled to come back to the United States a wanted man, since clearly he left the United States because he was a wanted man. My purpose in relating this portion of the hearing to you is not to belabor the issue of why Coumas fled or what he had in mind by going to Greece. My purpose is to show you that the majority of this hearing covered ground that was irrelevant to U.S. immigration law, and is attempting to hold trial on the crimes Coumas committed in San Joaquin County all over again. Central to this entire hearing is the crimes for which Coumas was charged, and his attempt to avoid prosecution. I grant you that is exactly what Coumas did, but it has no bearing on this hearing, which has at its center to determine if Coumas renounced his American citizenship by the acts he committed <u>after</u> he fled to Greece, not before he fled to Greece, or the fact that he fled to Greece or even <u>why</u> he fled to Greece. DeMoulin even tries to get Coumas to admit that he gave up his U.S. citizenship by "resisting" extradition from Greece. This results in an "apples and oranges" debate between DeMoulin and Mamalakis:

> DeMoulin: Isn't it a fact that you resisted extradition to the United States? Coumas: I don't know whether I resisted. They took me in court, after they had me three months locked up then brought me to the Supreme Court. DeMoulin: Didn't they have a hearing after your arrest and ask whether there was any reason why you shouldn't be sent back to the United States? Mamalakis: I will stipulate [agree] that he resisted the attempted extradition on the basis of his rights of his original Greek citizenship. DeMoulin: In other words, Mr. Mamalakis, Mr. Coumas at the time he resisted extradition to the United States, did then and there assert his right to protection by the Greek Government as a Greek national? Mamalakis: Yes, that is true.

Well, not exactly true. Coumas was arrested based on a claim by U.S. authorities that he be returned to the U.S. to stand trial on the San Joaquin County indictments, and the Greek Government decided to hold an extradition hearing to determine if he was legally subject to extradition under the circumstances of the extradition request. Coumas took no action to "resist" the extradition attempt other than to have legal counsel represent him at that hearing, which was his legal right. DeMoulin continues:

DeMoulin: In other words, from the legal point of view, he gave up his American citizenship and called himself a Greek? Mamalakis: Not on that basis, on the basis of his original Greek nationality, because he was still entitled to this. DeMoulin: Mr. Mamalakis, how can you reconcile his attitude at the time of the extradition proceedings with his statements before me today and previously that all the time he only wanted to pay the penalty and clear himself and the only reason why he didn't return was because he didn't have money enough, whereas the United States was ready to pay his way, all the way back to Fresno, California, and he resisted the efforts of the Government? It is hard to reconcile. Mamalakis: This man believed he could have more opportunity to defend himself in Greece than in the United States because he knew everyone in the community where the crime was committed would be hostile but he said under the provisions of the laws at the time it was as though he committed the crime abroad. DeMoulin: What you are trying to tell me is that he sought and obtained what amounted to a change in venue? Mamalakis: Punishment by the courts of Greece or the United States not by any authority but the treaty between Greece and the United States at that time. Rights were based on the law and he did not attempt to violate any law. His conduct in jail gave him the privilege of being released prior to the completion of his penalty.

DeMoulin drops this line of questioning at this point, since he was completely on a fishing expedition anyway. In fact most of what occurred in these various hearings has DeMoulin straying repeatedly from immigration law into science fiction. I do disagree with Mamalakis' claim that Coumas would have more opportunity to defend himself in Greece as unsupported by the records I have reviewed in this case. I also do not believe seeking a decidedly friendlier trial venue was what Coumas had in mind when he fled the U.S. for Greece in 1932.

Even though he married another woman in Greece, Coumas was never charged with bigamy either in Greece or the United States, and most certainly was never convicted of bigamy in either country, and even if he were guilty it is irrelevant to his intentions regarding his American citizenship. DeMoulin even goes into the fact that Coumas had a child with Gregoria, when the child was born, and of course the circumstances of his arrest and subsequent trial in Greece. DeMoulin eventually concludes that Coumas never paid for crimes he committed in the United States.

> "DeMoulin: In any case, it appears that it took the American authorities approximately two years from the summer of 1932 to the summer of 1934 to determine your whereabouts because in June of 1934 the warrant was issued for your arrest. Now, you had by that time completed your service with the Greek Army; on the basis of the information furnished by your friend, Lorentzos [spelled Lourentzos], you had married again and you had a child. Did you have any intention under those circumstances of ever returning to the United States Again? Coumas: I always had that on my mind. DeMoulin: Why? Coumas: I couldn't see the reason why not if I paid for my debt. DeMoulin: But you hadn't paid. Coumas: I was expecting to pay. I had that in my mind that I wanted to clear myself. DeMoulin: Why didn't you come back to the United States to pay for your crime? Mamalakis: I object to the question as incompetent, irrelevant, and immaterial. DeMoulin: Objection overruled. Why didn't you come back? Coumas: I had no choice. It wasn't up to me. DeMoulin: The choice was up to

you. Mamalakis: I object. DeMoulin: Objection overruled."

I could go on but I think you get a sense for the flavor or this hearing. Or perhaps the odor. If you can't find the bias in this last exchange, perhaps you might read it again. What is crystal clear here is even in this hearing is that a representative of our government is ignoring the conviction in Greece and time served on that conviction as meaningless because the trial, conviction, and prison term did not take place in the United States. This is arrogance in its worst form from a public official.

During the course of the California Supreme Court case regarding Coumas, and the attempt by San Joaquin County to try Coumas for murder in 1947, the California Attorney General floated a theory that Coumas' trial in Greece should not be recognized because it was acquired through fraud and collusion. The legal argument presented was that such a trial and its verdict could be set aside if fraud and collusion could be proven. The legal "theory" advanced in this regard was that Coumas intentionally fled to Greece to avoid prosecution in the U.S. and sought a more favorable justice climate in Greece and in particular because he successfully "fought" extradition in Greece.

The California Supreme Court did not buy this argument and pretty much tossed that theory right out the courthouse window. I have to assume here that Mr. DeMoulin was aware of the Court's position on this particular point, but he obviously does not think Coumas paid for his crimes by trial and incarceration in Greece. What any of this has to do with immigration law escapes me.

Nobody appeared for the U.S. Government at this hearing. Well, if you don't count the presiding inspector that is. The U.S. Government has never introduced any evidence that showed Coumas did anything with the intent of renouncing his American citizenship. In fact, the U.S. Government has never introduced any evidence that supports the allegation that Coumas in fact did take an oath of allegiance upon entering the Greek Army. The Governments' entire argument regarding this oath rested on a letter, dated September 22, 1948 and authored by Dimitri Sophianos, Consul General of Greece in San Francisco, which related a mandatory oath for conscriptors inducted into the Greek Armed Forces. Mamalakis objected to that letter being introduced into evidence on the basis that;

> "This letter does not make reference to the date when the respondent was inducted into the Greek Army and it is necessary to mention in this connection that at the time the [transcription error here and context lost – I think Mamalakis was saying that on the date of Coumas' service Greece was not a Kingdom, to which this particular letter applies] Date of Greece was a Republic and not even a kingdom, whether or not an oath was necessary or counseled at the time the respondent was inducted into the military service in Greece is another question. I object to the admission of this document in evidence as not being the best evidence and as not pertaining to the facts and circumstances surrounding the induction of the respondent into the Greek Army in the year 1933."

Of course DeMoulin overruled Mamalakis' objection and entered the letter into evidence anyway, claiming that the letter was merely "corroborative" evidence which was doubtful on the merits. I think it is important here to take a minute or three on this particular point regarding evidence, and the practice of accepting certain instruments in evidence as being actual evidence of something the instrument really does not prove. A memorandum from the county Sheriff to the jail commander that all detainees shall be allowed a telephone call within three hours of their detention is evidence that the Sheriff has in force a policy regarding the right of a detainee to a telephone call within specified time limits. The memorandum is not evidence of compliance with that policy on the part of the jail staff. For the purpose of this deportation hearing, the government wanted to use a letter that confirmed a policy as evidence of compliance with the policy. In my view, there is a significant difference.

Immigration law implies you must "intend" to give up your citizenship, by some voluntary act in order to lose it. DeMoulin was trying very hard to use Coumas having fled to Greece to avoid prosecution in California as an act intending to give up his U.S. citizenship. That "intent" has never been proven in any tribunal regarding Coumas, including this one.

However, intent on preserving fairness and impartiality, Mr. DeMoulin tries to attack Coumas' credibility and character, which I agree is a much easier road to travel than violations of U.S. immigration laws. The issue of Coumas having married a woman in Greece, while his lawful wife was locked up in the Stockton State Mental Institution, is repeatedly brought into play, with DeMoulin claiming that Coumas is a bigamist. Mamalakis attempts to defend by introducing a divorce decree Coumas obtained in the State of Nevada in December of 1949, and explanations that Coumas had reason to believe that Margaret had died based on the letter his parents received in Greece from the Laurentzos family in Manteca in 1932. DeMoulin asks whether Coumas is providing for his daughter (the child he had with Gregoria) in Greece, spends a great deal of time regarding Coumas' flight from the U.S. to Greece and his conviction in Greece for crimes committed in the United States, all of which by the way are NOT violations of U.S. immigration laws. DeMoulin wants to learn all about Coumas' various activities while in Greece. What the rationale for such questions might be is not clarified by the transcript or DeMoulin. Then DeMoulin does a rather odd thing - he charges Coumas with a third violation of immigration law, and I have to quote it here for the purpose of "clarity":

> DeMoulin: "You are informed [speaking to Coumas] that I will now lodge against you an additional charge, as follows: The Act of February 5, 1917, in that he has been convicted of a felony, or other crime or misdemeanor involving moral turpitude prior to entry into the United States, to wit: murder."

I may be reaching on the interpretation here, but I really believe that this section of U.S. immigration law was intended to address a circumstance where a person committed a crime as an alien in another country and was convicted of it before they entered the U.S. At the time Coumas committed his crimes against Olive Taylor and William Duval he was already in the United States, and was considered an American citizen. Maybe the application of the immigration law here is that the conviction came prior to his entry into the United States in 1947, but the point is not well explained in the transcript I am reading at the moment. First the government says they don't recognize the Greek Court as a legitimate court of law and reject their verdict, and now they are embracing it. Well, if at first you don't succeed, you can always reach a little further down into the "magic hat". A small point, but Coumas was not convicted of "murder" he was convicted of involuntary manslaughter - Big difference when considering whether a particular act involves moral turpitude. I'm not certain of the U.S. Governments' definition of the term when adopted into law, but one dictionary at my disposal defines it as conduct that is regarded as immoral or depraved. The Greek Court made no finding of fact as to the immorality or depravity of the crimes for which Coumas was convicted in Greece. Seems like a hair splitting exercise to me, based on my reading of the documentary evidence on the public record.

Stan Mamalakis did a masterful job of defending Coumas before the California Supreme Court, essentially because the law was on Coumas' side in the matter. At this hearing the majority of evidence presented on behalf of Coumas was only Coumas himself. Mamalakis did not have documentation to back up Coumas' oral testimony, and Coumas himself did not have in his possession the majority of documentation he testified about. He should have waived the ruling of the California Supreme Court under DeMoulin's nose but I doubt it would have gained him anything. The government did not offer much documentation of its own, except somewhat vaguely, but what DeMoulin did manage to do was to get Coumas on the record as wandering about and contradicting himself, and looking pretty sleazy as human beings sometimes tend to be. Coumas' entire record on his conduct just about everywhere he went makes him look sleazy. Unfortunately for the government, being sleazy is not one of the criteria one must meet to lose one's American citizenship. Unfortunately for Coumas, none of that mattered to Mr. DeMoulin.

DeMoulin winds up the hearing by asking if Coumas will be represented before the Board of Immigration Appeals. This statement came before DeMoulin indicates he will prepare his findings of fact, and his proposed conclusions of law, and proposed order in the matter. That message seems to be clear; that Coumas will likely appeal those findings and conclusions and order is a foregone conclusion in and of itself.

True to expectation, Mr. DeMoulin on June 8, 1950 made his Proposed Findings of Fact, Conclusions of Law, and Recommended Order, which here are endorsed and affirmed by the INS district hearing examiner Harold D. DeMello. We shall take them here in that order:

> "Upon the basis of all of the evidence presented, it is found:
>
> (1) That the respondent [Coumas] is an alien, a native and citizen of Greece;
> (2) That the respondent first entered the United States at New York, New York on January 4, 1907;
> (3) That the respondent became a naturalized citizen of the United States at Portland, Oregon, on February 25, 1914;
> (4) That the respondent committed the crime of Murder at Manteca, California on April 20, 1932;
> (5) That the respondent fled to Greece in mid-summer, 1932;
> (6) That the respondent was inducted into the Greek Army and served therein from November 1, 1932, to February 28, 1933;
> (7) That the respondent denies taking an oath of allegiance to Greece;
> (8) That taking an oath of allegiance to Greece was compulsory in 1932 and 1933 for all Greek Army inductees;
> (9) That the respondent resisted extradition proceedings to the United States, in Greece, as a Greek citizen entitled by treaty to trial in Greece for the crime committed in the United States;
> (10) That the respondent was tried in the Corinth Assize Court, Corinth, Greece, on October 16, 1935, and convicted of the crime of Murder, in

accordance with the International Treaty between Greece and the United States, and sentenced to prison for a term of four years and ten months;

(11) That the respondent last entered the United States at Norfolk, Virginia, on August 16, 1947, as a seaman ex SS Ameriki under the assumed name, Christos Mermingos;

(12) That the respondent intended to remain permanently in the United States;

(13) That the respondent was not in possession of an immigration visa at the time of his last entry.

Upon the basis of the foregoing Findings of Fact, it is concluded:

(1) That under Section 2 of the Act of March 2, 1907, the respondent became expatriated by taking an oath of allegiance to the Greek Government in connection with his service in the Greek Army from November 1, 1932 to February 28, 1933;

(2) That under Sections 13 and 14 of the Immigration Act of May 26, 1924, the respondent is subject to deportation, that at the time of entry, he was an immigrant not in possession of a valid immigration visa and not exempted from the presentation thereof by said Act or regulations made thereunder;

(3) That under Sections 19 and 20 of the Act of February 5, 1917, the respondent is subject to deportation on the ground that he has been convicted of a felony or other crime or misdemeanor involving moral turpitude prior to entry into the United States, to wit: Murder;

(4) That under Section 20 of the Immigration Act of 1917, the respondent is deportable to Greece at Government expense.

Recommended Order

> It is recommended that the alien be deported to Greece at Government expense on the charge contained in the Warrant of Arrest, to wit: "The Immigration Act of May 26, 1924, in that, at the time of entry, he was an immigrant not in possession of a valid immigration visa and not exempted from the presentation thereof by said Act or regulations made thereunder," and also on the lodged charge, to wit: "The Act of February 5, 1917, in that he has been convicted of a felony or other crime or misdemeanor involving moral turpitude prior to entry into the United States, to wit: Murder."
>
> Dated: June 8, 1950 /s/ HAROLD D. DeMELLO, Hearing Examiner"

A couple of points on all of this: The matter of the oath seems to ignore the provision in the Act cited that such an oath must be taken with the <u>intent</u> of renouncing one's U.S. citizenship which was not proven in this hearing, in fact there was no finding of fact in that regard; being inducted into someone's armed forces is an involuntary act. Evidence existed that service in the Greek military was mandatory for all Greek citizens who could not pay their way out of that obligation; if he had an invalid (false) immigration visa at Norfolk, why was he admitted into the country? I think they are picking at nits with the criminal conviction for the reasons I have suggested here earlier. He was ordered into service in the Greek Army, and even if he was lying and in fact did take the oath, he would have had to do so under threat of prison and therefore such an oath would have been coerced. I think what is really going on here is that somebody in the government decided that this guy was going to be booted out of the country and the "hearing" involved no actual hearing on the part of anybody connected with the INS. Some in history have referred to such tribunals as "Kangaroo Courts" where the outcome has been pre-ordained, and therefore largely an exercise in futility for the person attempting any sort of defense.

Coumas took exception to the district level ruling and appealed to the Commissioner of the INS in Washington, D.C. who promptly agreed with the ruling of the San Francisco Office. The Commissioner was Watson B. Miller, himself a lawyer, a former lobbyist for the American Legion, and an executive level official with the Federal Security Agency prior to the INS appointment. Taking full advantage of his "administrative" remedies, Coumas then appealed to the Board of Immigration Appeals (where Robert DeMoulin had concluded Coumas would go, before DeMoulin reached his own findings and conclusions, etc.), which functions under the Attorney General of the United States. Of course the Board upheld not only the folks in the San Francisco Office, but the Commissioner as well.

The results of the "appeals" process are not all that surprising. Within any governmental body, the hierarchy seldom ever reverses subordinates. Were one to actually do that at a higher level, it would make the higher level look bad, by conveying the message that the people in the field office did not know what they were doing. Everybody would take a pounding all the way down the organization chart. Then there might have been certain "political considerations" associated with all of this that needed considering. After all, Coumas was getting a free ride back to Greece, and the United States was ridding itself of a weasel that killed a school teacher in her own classroom full of kids and tried to bail out of the country to avoid being held accountable for it. Mr. Duval was not a factor since the Greek Court was not credible in the eyes of multiple U.S. legal representatives and law enforcement officials, with the minor exception of all nine justices of the California Supreme Court.

Coumas only had one choice left to him, and he took it. On March 20, 1952 Tom Coumas sued the United States Government.

CHAPTER TWENTY-TWO
UNITED STATES DISTRICT COURT

Stan Mamalakis asked for a jury trial, but didn't get one. I wish I could tell you why, but the record is silent on that point. The docket indicates that the jury petition was filed, and I have a copy of the petition, but the record falls silent on the matter of why a jury was not impaneled in this case. The docket does not reflect a hearing on the matter of the jury request. A docket is sort of a log of events related to a case and keeps track of significant actions that take place regarding a particular case. Perhaps there was agreement to waive trial by jury by the parties to the lawsuit. I certainly hope so, because otherwise this lack of a jury business could have been a denial of rights under the Seventh Amendment of the U.S. Constitution. I can tell you that although the lawsuit was filed in March of 1952, the actual trial was not convened until May 4, 1953. The trial took place in the District Court for the Northern District of California, Southern Division in San Francisco. The judge assigned to the case was the Honorable George B. Harris. Like the INS, Judge Harris was not impressed with Tom Coumas. Representing the Attorney General of the United States was a government lawyer by the name of Charles Elmer Collett, whose essential talent seemed to be objecting. If one were going to try to use the box score method to gauge the fairness of this trial, which even I admit is somewhat non-scientific in its approach, but consider this: when Collett objected to something, Judge Harris agreed with Collett 70% of the time; When Mamalakis objected to something, Judge Harris overruled

Mamalakis 80% of the time. I also recognize that this is probably not a good measure of the quality or validity of the objections raised, but I point it out only because at face value it tends to tilt the Judge heavily in favor of Mr. Collett and the U.S. Government.

The basis for the lawsuit is that the United States Attorney General, who oversees the Immigration and Naturalization Service, wants to toss Coumas out of the U.S., and Coumas, who is claiming he is a U.S. citizen, wants to prevent the toss.

Mamalakis, with the exception of several documents representing ground that has already been well plowed by the San Joaquin County authorities, the authorities in Greece, the INS and other U.S. Government officials, only has at his disposal one essential witness in favor of the lawsuit - Tom Coumas. Now, going in this is not a good thing for either Mamalakis or Coumas. The trial consists largely of Coumas taking the stand and giving testimony in response to questions posed by Mamalakis, while Collett takes every opportunity to object. The Judge seems to get lost in the minutia of it all, and Mamalakis has no effective documentation to corroborate Coumas' testimony. Without such corroboration, one is more or less left with believing or not believing Coumas, whose track record, on and off the record is one strewn mostly with lies, deception, and self-serving opportunism. The chances that a judge is going to believe a guy in those circumstances are fairly slim. Even worse, drawing a judge who is clearly biased against the person bringing suit stands no chance whatsoever.

A great deal of time was spent in this trial on Coumas' domestic circumstances, his use of aliases, his comings and goings under dubious circumstances, and of course the criminal conduct, the trial in Greece and his subsequent prison sentence. Playing a large role was the rehashing of the service in the Greek Army. Mamalakis made some excellent legal points in that precedent existed that when military service was involuntary that expatriation due to such service was not at issue. Also, that while the U.S. Government continued to insist that evidence existed that plainly proved that an oath of allegiance to Greece is mandatory by all persons entering the Greek Army, evidence had never been introduced proving that Coumas had actually taken such an oath. Personally, after reviewing all of these documents I don't believe Coumas. I think he probably had to take an oath, and probably had to sign some paperwork that reflected that he had taken the oath. I also think all of that is immaterial because his service was forced, and was involuntary including any oath that might have been taken. In fairness, Coumas did have three choices under Greek law with regard to his military service obligation to Greece: 1) He could have served his time as required by Greek law. 2) He could have paid a fee and avoided serving in the military altogether. 3) He could have gone to jail until he either paid or served. Coumas claimed he didn't have the money to pay the Greek Government. The U.S. Government took the position that he did in fact have an alternative to serving in the Greek Army and he chose not to take it. Whatever!

The U.S. Government then tried to take the course that Coumas had renounced his U.S. citizenship by remaining in Greece longer than two years. I thought Mamalakis did a decent job of presenting a good case for exemptions existing in U.S. immigration law, and that some circumstances were beyond Coumas' control such as the German invasion of Greece. Coumas did make application for a U.S. passport as early as 1937, but he claims he was told to come back after he had served his parole. Coumas claims he did return after that and was required to provide several documents in order to obtain the passport, and at that time an embassy official administered the oath of allegiance in conjunction with that application. Coumas claims he later provided the requested documents, and when he checked back several times on the status of his passport was told the embassy was waiting on Washington (D.C), then in early 1947 he was advised by the embassy that Washington had sent him a letter declaring that he was no longer considered a U.S. citizen. Hard to say what the details of that particular conclusion might have rested on, or whether due process in that determination was provided to Coumas. I very much doubt that a U.S. citizen can be stripped of their citizenship without due process, and perhaps the letter to Coumas from the State Department reflected his right to challenge the determination, and perhaps he did not understand his options, if any, in the matter. It would have been helpful to Coumas' testimony in this court to have in hand documents that supported his contentions on the subject, and his attempts at repatriation through the U.S. embassy in Greece. If Collett knew of the State Department ruling letter, he did not attempt to introduce it in evidence in this trial. In fact there was no statement from Ambassador MacVeigh on the subject of Coumas' contacts with the embassy submitted on behalf of the U.S. Government in this matter. Nor was there any statement from the U.S. State Department on the subject either. I find that rather odd, given the findings and conclusions previously reached by the INS and the Department of Justice regarding Coumas' American citizenship status. What I find even odder still, is that it took the U.S. State Department from 1940 to 1947 to resolve Coumas' application for a U.S. passport. At least so Coumas claimed in his testimony in District Court. I am surprised that Mamalakis would have thought his client would have been viewed as believable, given Coumas' history, no matter whether Mamalakis believed his client or not. There did not appear to have been any investigation conducted to find documentation that would bolster Coumas' testimony and accusations against the U.S.

Government here. Mamalakis managed to get a concession from the judge that Coumas domestic circumstances were not relevant to the case at hand. The judge later reversed himself when Collett out maneuvered Judge Harris on the issue, and plunged right into it, even suggesting Coumas was guilty of bigamy. There were moments when you had to wonder who had custody of the gavel.

The U.S. Government kept trying to paint Coumas as a fugitive of justice and that his sole intent in fleeing the U.S. was to avoid prosecution for murder. No legal citation was offered in evidence that such conduct was illegal in the United States, reprehensible as such conduct might be, but this allegation keeps surfacing throughout this story without regard to statuatory reference. The court on the other hand didn't require the government to prove its theory on the subject. Mamalakis did not bring up the California Supreme Court decision, nor introduce the findings into this trial which I find very odd, since it largely laid to rest several points in law on the subject of the flight, trial and conviction in Greece. Mamalakis did not point out that Coumas had been acquitted on the charge of attempted murder of Mr. Duval, although I have no idea what the theory of the moment was in the Greek trial that could have caused the Greek jury to conclude that. They were working largely off the depositions taken in San Joaquin County in December of 1934, and as you have read, those depositions introduce some doubt due to conflicts between witnesses to the events of April 20, 1932.

What didn't help Coumas all that much was Collett bringing up the fact that Coumas attempted to obtain a copy of his naturalization papers while in San Francisco after returning from Greece in 1947. Collett came up with an application that Coumas had filled out and submitted claiming that the original papers were lost when he fell ill on the streets of San Francisco on May 24, 1932. Coumas claimed that when he awakened, he had been moved to the house of a friend and his papers were missing. On this application, Coumas certifies that he had not been out of the United States since he became a U.S. citizen in 1914. Well, we know that is certainly untrue. This revelation completely blindsided Mamalakis, who clearly had not previously seen the document or was aware of its existence. Tip: Might not be a good idea to let your lawyer get blindsided in a court of law. Coumas' credibility has always been on shaky ground, but Collett succeeded in destroying what little was left of it. An interesting point falls out of this testimony that has little relevance to the trial at hand and that is an admission that Coumas was in San Francisco in May of 1932. In fact, Coumas provides a lot of details of his movements following the shootings in Manteca and his flight to Greece.

From the testimony of various persons with whom Coumas had contact following the wounding of Duval and the death of Olive Taylor, we know that he was in Manteca the afternoon and evening of the day of the shootings, April 20th. We also know that he was still in Manteca on the following morning, April 21st. We believe, from news accounts, that Coumas may have spent the night of April 21st in the Mill Valley, California jail and was released on the morning of April 22nd. There the trail went cold. We now know that Coumas was in San Francisco on May 24th, and that there was physical evidence that Coumas mailed a letter from New York to Clara Hickman in Manteca on June 11, 1932. So where was Coumas between May and June of 1932? How did he get to Greece? Did Ellis Parker have it wrong? Could Coumas have made his way to Mexico, then to New York instead of Brazil?

Here is how he did it. In addition to the month he spent in the San Francisco Bay Area, he would remain there another week, while a friend of his from his days in Portland, Oregon drove down from Oregon to California, and agreed to take Coumas to New York. The journey would take the two of them three weeks by automobile. They went by way of Arizona, but that is as close to Mexico that the two ever got. The name of the friend from Oregon was Sam Jaskon.

Sam turned out to be a pretty good friend, considering he drove from Oregon to California and then hauled Coumas all the way to New York. Coumas claimed that Jaskon had read about the shootings in Manteca in the Oregon newspapers and drove down to California to search for Coumas. Coumas and Jaskon were friends while Coumas was living in Oregon after Coumas came to the U.S. in 1907. After arriving in New York, Sam looked up some folks who were in the business of providing fake documents and credentials and furnished Coumas with an Albanian passport in the name of George Vares. Jaskon paid $120 for the fake passport on Coumas' behalf. Coumas then boarded a ship of Italian registry, which took him to Italy, then to Piraeus, Greece. From Piraeus, Coumas made his way to Roino and his parents' farm, where he awaited eventual discovery by the Greek Army.

Not that Coumas expected the Greek Army to come looking for him. He was more concerned about the authorities in San Joaquin County. However, all Greek men were expected to serve and it was only a matter of time until Coumas came to the attention of the Greek Government.

One of the more interesting points of this two-day trial is the manner in which Coumas served as his own worst enemy through his testimony in court. Mamalakis apparently did not do a very good job of briefing Coumas on how to testify because Coumas kept volunteering more information than the questions warranted, or for that matter asked. Coumas actually brought out a lot of information to his detriment, the nature of which only served as fodder for Collett. Often, even when his own lawyer objected, rather than wait for the judge to rule on the objection, Coumas kept right on talking. Even when the judge agreed with Mamalakis, which in this trial was exceptionally rare, Coumas still answered the question anyway. It was sort of like Coumas sitting on the witness stand and continuously firing bullets into his own foot.

I did mention earlier that Collett in particular seemed to be constantly objecting. Here's one – Mamalakis has the witness:

> "Mamalakis: Since you came to the United States did you get married? Coumas: In 1915 I get married. Mamalakis: Did you have any children from this marriage? Coumas: Two dead and four living – six. Mamalakis: Six children? What was the citizenship of your wife? Coumas: She was born here in Oswego, Oregon. Judge Harris: What was her nativity? Mamalakis: She was born in Oswego, Oregon, Your Honor. Coumas: She was born in Oswego, Oregon, outside Portland, Your Honor. Mamalakis: She was an American born citizen? Coumas: Yes. Collett: Of course it is all hearsay as far as he is concerned. It would be objectionable on that basis. Judge Harris: Well, the materiality is open to question. However, it merely gives me a little background."

I suppose there exists a law school someplace that advocates that a witness giving testimony as to their knowledge of a given subject with which they might be intimately acquainted might be considered hearsay, and therefore one would be prudent to object. Hard to say exactly what aspect of that particular testimony Collett finds objectionable, and Judge Harris does not ask Collett to clarify his objection.

At another part of the trial Mamalakis asks Coumas about the circumstances in which he came to be required to serve in the Greek Army. Coumas testified that the Roino police came to see him at his parents' farm and told Coumas that he should report for military service. Coumas claimed that he told the police that he was an American citizen and the police said to him, "Once a Greek, always a Greek." Later in the trial, Collett would bring up the provision in Greek law that allows paying a fee to avoid service, and Coumas testifies that he didn't have the required amount of money. Collett then reads into the record a section of law that allows such payments to be made in three installments. Coumas claimed that he did not know he could make the payment in three installments. Whether he did know of that provision or not, what Collett seems to be trying to establish is that Coumas had options available to him to avoid serving in the Greek Army, and by choosing to serve, essentially did so voluntarily. This whole line of reasoning of course requires one to ignore the fact that as a Greek citizen, Coumas had an obligation to Greece and could not refuse the obligation, no matter how it might be fulfilled. Whether he served or paid a fee to avoid service, it still was coerced, and many a court has found that something coerced is not voluntary. This particular Court did not seem to follow that line of reasoning and Mamalakis did not make an issue of this point for the benefit of this judge.

I had indicated earlier that Judge Harris had ruled early in the trial that Coumas' domestic history was irrelevant to this trial. Yet, when Collett stuck his toe in that stream, this encounter came up. Collett had been asking a series of questions of Coumas about his children and wife

Margaret. He asked the children's ages, and about his wife being committed to the mental hospital. Then he asked this question:

> "Collett: Did you contribute to her support in the State Hospital during any of the period up to April, 1932? Mamalakis: I object to the question as incompetent, irrelevant, and immaterial. The Court even stated we are not going to go into the domestic affairs of the Petitioner. Judge Harris: sustained. Collett: Well, where were the children in June, 1932? Mamalakis: I object to this.... Coumas: I suppose they were here. Mamalakis: Just a minute. The witness testified he had no knowledge of where they were in June. He has already testified to that. Collett: If the Court please, I think we have here a situation in which a pattern of behavior is involved. The man is naturalized. This is a different situation from the ordinary case, perhaps, in which you have dual citizenship. That is, a person may be born in the United States of foreign parents, or born in a foreign country of American parents and has dual citizenship, whereby he assumes one of the other. This is a case in which the individual has taken an oath and disavowed any allegiance. The circumstances surrounding the leaving of the United States, part of which has come out whereby we find he obtained a passport under a fictitious name and left the country in a sequence of approximately a month and a half or two months, whatever it may have been. I simply was going to ask this question...... Judge Harris: (Interposing) The circumstances surrounding his departure, insofar as his family life, I will allow that...... Collett: (Interposing) I assume that arrangements were made with regard to the children at the time he left. Mamalakis: I believe we were the ones trying to

show morals in this case and the Court said the Court wasn't concerned with that; and Counsel was one who started objections as to our bringing in any testimony that would tend to support his moral conduct. I believe that since that was the attitude of the Court and Counsel for the Government, it isn't fair...... Judge Harris: No, in terms of accuracy, Counsel, I said I wasn't so much concerned with the matter of the background of the judgment of conviction, that I would have to stand on the judgment, that we could not go behind the judgment and either attack collaterally or explain it collaterally because otherwise I would have to try the criminal case. And as it may appear, I might well have to try the domestic case. [There is no domestic case before this Court] But this man claims he left the jurisdiction by reason of circumstances surrounding the death of an unfortunate school teacher who was killed at his hands. If in fact he left for a purpose other than that, in addition thereto, I think we should know it. Mamalakis: If the Government..... Judge Harris: (Interposing) Let's assume, without stating the fact to be, that he left here as a result of the unfortunate incident as well as desiring to rid himself of a family, I think that would be a circumstance that might be considered. Mamalakis: I do not believe, Your Honor, the testimony that Counsel wants to adduce tends to establish anything of the kind. Judge Harris: All right. Mamalakis: And the Government in the Immigration proceedings never contended it because they knew they didn't have a scintilla of evidence that this man had any idea when he fled to Greece that.... Judge Harris: (Interposing) All right, I will sustain the objection. Collett: If I may have one more word before Your Honor rules? [Never mind that the Judge has already ruled, and this Judge doesn't seem to understand that he has already ruled] There is no attempt to inject at this time any matter of consideration of the morals of the man, as to whether or not by marrying the second time he committed bigamy [Coumas has never been charged with bigamy let alone convicted of having committed bigamy] or what it was, or what moral judgment the Court might take [The Court exists to make judgments about the law, not morals]. It simply relates to the growing record of objective facts of what the man does, trying to get at his intention. The sequence of factual events is what the Court must have in mind to see what the pattern of this man's behavior is after he leaves the Country and continues on after attempt is made at extradition. The facts pertaining to his family, wherever these several children were, his wife is in an institution, he goes to Greece, and within the period of a year he remarries. He lives there for a period up to the end of 1934 or 1935, when an attempt is made to extradite him – facts necessary to check into the pattern and course of behavior. [You might want to read that last part again and see if it makes any more sense to you the second time around before you give up on trying to make any sense of it at all] Mamalakis: Your Honor, this is not a criminal prosecution by the Government against the petitioner. The petitioner wants to establish that he hasn't lost his citizenship, and the only way we can establish, all the evidence we can introduce is what was the intention. Was it intended to abandon American citizenship and leave the country, abiding by the loss. I don't believe this evidence has anything to do with that, and up to this time no one ever tried to allege otherwise. That this was a loss of American citizenship – certainly, as the Court has intimated, we will have to confine the case within those issues. Counsel himself – We wanted to show the entire case and show the morals, and Counsel objected strenuously. And now that the Petitioner is punished, and showing the vindictiveness of the prosecution, this man was released and relieved by the authorities of the State of California from serving another sentence since he was punish[ed], and they want to find another way of punishing him again. I believe that is contravening the laws, and I believe that the Government has [no] right to another and new prosecution against the petitioner now. Collett: This is not a prosecution. Mamalakis: It is nothing else but that, Your Honor. Collett: Look at [cites case law]. There is no prosecution of this man other than the endeavor to get before the Court the factual situation surrounding his departure from the United States after having become a naturalized citizen. Certainly the record should be before the Court. Nobody is going to prosecute him for having possibly failed to support his children, if he didn't do that for which he might have been liable at the time. I don't know. But the fact that he did leave, the fact that he did go to Greece, the fact that he served in the Army shortly thereafter, the fact that he married very shortly after he got there....... Judge Harris: I think the Government is entitled to show in a general way the circumstances surrounding his leaving. Mamalakis: We do understand that, Your Honor, but whether he supported his children, whether he left them with one person or another, I do not believe that has anything to do with the circumstances. Judge Harris: That is the question, I suppose, of moral turpitude [The question of moral turpitude has nothing to do with Coumas' domestic circumstances – it has to do with the INS claiming Coumas committed murder in San Joaquin County]. And conceivably we might go into the many factors that might have a persuasive effect on the matter that the

> broad vistas of the situation might be lost sight of. But it seems to me generally I should know how he left the country. He left here in flight. He has testified to that. Mamalakis: That is true, Your Honor. Judge Harris: I assume when a person leaves in flight they are [not] too much concerned about obligations. I would infer that. Unless a person has considered the matter, considered leaving cash or the like for the relatives. He left in flight, that is about it. He did marry in Greece. I suppose hereafter the Government Counsel will argue as to the callous indifference, not only toward the country, but his relatives as well. I suppose that in a case of this character and at the very core is the man himself. There is the nub. You can't get into a man's heart without knowing some of the externals. Mamalakis: That is correct. Judge Harris: As I have said before, I can't pry open a persons brain and look into the recesses of his mind without knowing how he acts. I think a little latitude should be allowed. I can't decide this case in capsule form. I am not a clairvoyant. I am just a human being, a Federal Judge, and I think I will allow it."

Did you understand the rationale behind any of that? I think the argument was to limit the testimony to those facts relevant to the loss of citizenship, which is the issue central to the lawsuit. The Government did not decide any violation of Federal Immigration Law based on anything having to do with Coumas' domestic circumstances, nor did the Government conclude loss of citizenship on any "moral" grounds other than conviction of a felony <u>prior</u> to entry into the United States, which was a stretch in the first place. The felony was alleged by the INS to involve moral turpitude, not his conduct with regard to his marriages or his family. But there is more incredible stuff yet to witness here, so, Mamalakis responds to the judge just having reversed his previous ruling on the matter:

> “Mamalakis: That is true. That is what I tried to say to begin with. When one decides to take a course of action, that doesn't mean he is reckless of any other obligations. If this man was killed, what protection his children would have..... Judge Harris: (Interposing) Counsel, I sometimes wonder what protection the family of the school teacher had, speaking of protection. He doesn't even recall the school teacher's name. Collett: No. Judge Harris: Rather callous, I take it.”

Got to stop the tape here yet once again. Look, I don't think for one minute that this guy Coumas is anything more than an opportunist, who is reckless, and irresponsible with regard to his life and the life of others, but a Federal Judge sitting in a Court of law cannot, I repeat, cannot show any bias whatsoever sitting in judgment on a matter involving federal law. For a judge to do this, no matter what his personal beliefs or conclusions might be, is to exhibit behavior no better than the person he faults. In particular the fault he finds has no bearing on the case before his court. Mamalakis did his client a huge disservice by not immediately moving for a mistrial, or at the minimum asking that the judge recuse himself for cause.

> “Mamalakis: That is true. When a man's future is at stake, his mind is confused. Judge Harris: That may be. Mamalakis: Even us attorneys forget the details we go over. It isn't callous, but this man is not as young as he looks, and there are so many details in this case no one could retain every part of them. Judge Harris: Counsel, I would not wonder that the events be lost sign of. Probably he would

> like to black them out of his memory. I am not reflecting on the unfortunate man here. Had he remained here and entered a plea of not guilty by reason of insanity, I don't know what might have prevailed. I sometimes wonder whether a man under those conditions could be in his right mind, if the events are as disclosed before the Court. I am not pre-judging the matter. The man undertakes wreak vengeance on the school teacher because the school teacher wreaks punishment on the children, and wounds the janitor. It seems to me the acts themselves per se might indicate some impaired mentality. But I am not defending the man in a criminal case. What I would have done had I been in San Joaquin valley, I might have acquitted him on the ground of insanity. He might have wound up in a mental institution for the rest of his natural life. He might be mental now for all I know."

This judge is going into matters that are not before the court, and even worse does not even have the facts straight in the matter. I think that this judge commenting on a case that was not before him is doing just what he previously said he wasn't doing, trying the criminal case. If the statement regarding Coumas' mental condition without benefit of expert testimony is any indication this trial was ruled in favor of the Government from the outset. Hold on, it gets worse:

> "Collett: This is at the point of the argument, and I am going to make a further argument. The man has succeeded in escaping from standing trial in the jurisdiction in which the crime was committed, he endeavored to avoid it by going back to the country from which he had come, and he stays in that country and takes advantage.... Judge Harris: (Interposing) He gave the answer, maybe, when he

said, "Once a Greek always a Greek." He said he sought the companionship, the solace and companionship of his own people. Maybe that is the answer to that. Mamalakis: If I am not mistaken, when the witness testified about that, he said the officials told him he had to serve in the Greek Army and he was told, "Once a Greek, always a Greek." Judge Harris: That is what the situation was. Mamalakis: But this witness did not testify, "Once a Greek, always a Greek." So far as he was concerned. Judge Harris: [I think Mamalakis was getting a little hot, since he was himself a Greek] Some of the greatest citizens we have in this Country are Greek. Some of the greatest pals I had in my career are Greek. Mamalakis: I am glad to hear that, Your Honor. Judge Harris: That is true. In my early career they were more or less shoulder to shoulder with me. I have gone back many years in Greek San Francisco. When I was studying law I had my dinner every night over here at the Imperial Grill. The man's name was Peter – I don't recall, but he was a Greek. Collett: But American Citizenship is not a cloak one puts on and takes off to sui[t] one's convenience. Mamalakis: I object to the argument. I don't believe this is the time for Counsel to make an argument. Judge Harris: I agree. Collett: Argument has been made by you? Mamalakis: You are making the argument. You want things to go in the way that will suit you, Counsel, and I believe that is not fair, and I believe on redirect examination we will elicit..... Judge Harris: (Interposing) Counsel, if you desire to offer the moral aspects of it, as I feel I have gone to far in response, I will allow you considerable latitude and allow you ample time. I have the whole week to try this case, and I know Mr. Collett has nothing else to do but try this case, and I will hear you out.

Mamalakis: Very well. That is all we want to do, present all the facts. Judge Harris: We will hear you out. We will open both barrels and take the full import. Mr. Bonsall knows that [Assistant U.S. Attorney Edgar R. Bonsall, who authored the Government's response to the case before this Court, but is not a participant in the trial]. Mr. Bonsall, your colleague is in the back of the room. This is a serious case to this man. When I spoke of the events and experiences you have had, Mr. Coumas, I am not reflecting on you. [Huh?] I have nothing but sympathy for a man situated like him. But at the same time, we have a definite principle of law, whether they want this man back, and that is what we are trying."

What? He is trying whether the Government wants Coumas back? I thought what was being tried was that the Government is trying to throw the man out of the country by claiming he gave up his U.S. citizenship by serving in the Greek Army and other associated grievances, and Coumas is claiming he didn't violate any of the laws cited by the INS. I think this judge knew he was in trouble for his demonstrated prejudice on the record and has been trying to do damage control on the issue by making nice. How on earth could Mamalakis think that no matter what evidence he presented at this Court that this judge was going to give it a fair and impartial consideration? That would be the stuff of Easter Bunnies and Tooth Fairies.

This sort of nonsense goes on all throughout this so-called trial. Collett takes up the business of Coumas marrying Gregoria in Greece again, and Mamalakis doesn't even bother to object. The whole line of questioning is totally out of the area of what the judge agreed to explore and the judge isn't even reining Collett in. I think you get a sense for how this trial is going to resolve, but I can't resist offering up one additional snippet of this nonsense. Collett is trying to get on the record that Coumas did not try to validate the letter from the Lourentzos family that his wife Margaret was in fact dead. We pick up the trial transcript there.

> "Collett: Now, you told us yesterday that after you heard or saw this alleged letter that was sent by Mr. Lourentzos to your father and mother, which relied upon as disclosing to you that your wife was dead, that you made no effort thereafter to find out whether or not it was true that she was dead. Coumas: I did, sir, but I never got no answers. Collett: You did? Coumas: I never got no answers. I wrote to people. Collett: To whom did you write? Coumas: I wrote to my sister. I wrote to my friends. I wrote to Sam Jaskon and others. Collett: What did the letter say with regard to your wife's death? Coumas: I remember it saying that she was in bad shape. I knew she was in bad shape when I left here. She had TB and she looked awful bad. I wasn't surprised to hear it. But she said that she was sorry to announce that the daughter-in-law was dead. Collett: Sorry to announce that the daughter-in-law – whose daughter-in-law? Coumas: My father and mother. My wife. Collett: I don't understand. Mamalakis: The letter was addressed to the father, and he was the father-in-law of his wife. Collett: I see. Collett: Did it make a positive statement that she was dead? Coumas: Yes, sir. Collett: And did it disclose from where the information was obtained? Coumas: No. Supposed to know, my folks, living there together know all of us, took it as a fact. Collett: Did you write to the Lourentzos and ask them..... Coumas: No, sir. Collett: ....what the basis of the information was? Coumas: No, sir. Collett: Why didn't you write to them? Coumas: I

wrote to several people. I don't want to incriminate them. I want to pay for my own sins. I don't want to drag people in and tell what...... Collett: (Interposing) What do you mean, "incriminate"? It was simply a matter of information. Coumas: Anybody helps you out, it is against the law. You are a fugitive from the law, and they help you out, that's the way I understand it, and I go ahead and give you a bunch of names of different people, that would incriminate them. Collett: Did the Lourentzos help you become a fugitive from the law? Coumas: No, sir. Collett: Isn't that what you are saying? Judge Harris: Mr. Collett, in the final analysis what evidentiary value would the fact that any of these persons aided or assisted this man as a fugitive have in aiding the Court in determining the issues involved? Collett: [Here we go] Well, if the court please, this is simply a situation in which I am pursuing one but of information, and the answers I receive are of such a nature that they prompt further explanation in order to substantiate that they have any materiality as a matter of an answer. If I ask him why he didn't write to the person who had written disclosing certain information to find out from those people, it seems to me it should render a simple answer to the question. That question is definite. I am simply endeavoring to probe as to whether or not the answer is a proper answer and consistent with truth or simply an endeavor to avoid giving an answer in light of the possibility that the original answer might not be true."

I think what is sometimes interesting about lawyers is that when they have no rational reason for what they are attempting to do they spout a bunch of gibberish, not unlike a chaff discharge to distract a missile from its intended target. I could quote more of the argument that ensued here, but I think you get the idea. Eventually Judge Harris gets worn down by Collett's rhetoric and orders Collett to continue, never mind that the course Collett is attempting to follow with Coumas has no relevancy to the reasons the Government wants to throw Coumas out of the United States. The trial is just strewn with questions like this from Collett. On one occasion, Collett asks Coumas if he remembers the building his extradition hearing was held in. Mamalakis objects on the grounds that the question is immaterial to the matter before the Court. The judge overrules him. I can't think of a single reason this judge needs to know the name of the building in which the extradition hearing was held as critical to the judge deciding if the Government is acting properly in deporting Coumas from the United States.

Mamalakis called only two witnesses, Coumas and George Lourentzos. Collett called none. Lourentzos was called to corroborate Coumas' claims regarding the content of the letter to Coumas' parent's regarding the death of wife Margaret, which George Lourentzos wrote. Lourentzos claimed he only wrote what his (Lourentzos) parents in Manteca told him to write in the letter, that he had no personal knowledge of Margaret Coumas' death. This witness was not helpful all that much to Coumas, because Lourentzos own character was called into question by Collett. Mamalakis was really in over his head in this trial. Perhaps his trial experience was limited, or maybe he was fearful he would anger Judge Harris if he asserted misconduct. He made a critical mistake in not calling for a mistrial, and an even further critical mistake in making Coumas the essential evidence, and Coumas was not credible due to his own testimony. Mamalakis might have been able to get documents from the Greek government in support of Coumas' testimony, but it would seem that he did not. Under discovery I would think he could have demanded the records of the American embassy in

Greece, regarding Coumas' repatriation attempts, but it would appear that he did not. Mamalakis called no expert witnesses to testify counter to the conclusions reached by the INS or on matters of Greek, U.S. or international law. He called no representatives of the federal government even though he was suing them on behalf of his client.

The trial winds down with final arguments and the usual assertions of the parties pro and con. Mamalakis argues that the United States is at fault for not processing Coumas' requests for repatriation to the United States not Coumas, that the military service was involuntary, that the length of stay in Greece was not an issue until Coumas appealed his deportation hearing, and that the immigration law was changed in 1945 (due to the war) to allow repatriation within six years of enactment of the amendment, which Coumas attempted to do, but was not accommodated by the American embassy in Greece.

On July 2, 1953 the Honorable George (Some of my greatest pals are Greeks) Harris found in favor of the U.S. Government. Here are the man's very words:

> "This matter having been tried, briefed, and submitted for ruling, The Court finds that plaintiff expatriated himself under the law of March 2, 1907, by taking an oath of allegiance to a foreign state [case law citations]; the Court further finds that the plaintiff expatriated himself by remaining in the country of his birth for more than two years during which time he married bigamously in Greece and asserted his Greek nationality in opposing extradition to the United States. Accordingly, it is ordered that judgment be entered in favor of the defendant upon preparation of findings of fact and conclusions of law."

Judge Harris ignored the fact that the military service was not voluntary, therefore the oath, if indeed Coumas actually was "required" to take one, was also involuntary, and the Judge ignored the October 11, 1945 amendment to Section 409 of the Nationality Act of 1940, which gave American citizens six years from enactment of the amendment to repatriate themselves to the United States. Coumas essentially did that when he went to the American embassy in Greece to file the necessary paperwork to obtain a U.S. passport to return to the United States. Clearly, the Government was hugely annoyed that this man escaped trial in the United States, and regardless of the decision and findings of the California Supreme Court wanted badly to be able to have San Joaquin County take a run at him in Superior Court. But having been legally barred from doing that, decided to ignore the law and found a judge who would ignore it with them. There existed in federal law remedies for naturalized citizens against whom the presumption of expatriation had arisen. Coumas made the test of those remedies by making application to return to the U.S. at the American embassy in Athens. It's one thing to hold a person accountable under a law that makes certain conduct illegal, but quite another when the authorities themselves deprive a person of the protection of law out of resentment, revenge, or just plain old bias.

Perhaps some small measure of victory for Mamalakis and his client is that Judge Harris did not affirm the INS contention that Coumas violated "The Act of February 5, 1917, in that he was convicted of a felony, or other crime or misdemeanor involving moral turpitude prior to entry into the United States, to wit: murder." The part about the "bigamy", as was the whole foray into Coumas' moral conduct was rather interesting, and implied that immoral conduct on the part of naturalized citizens is of great legal concern to the U.S. Government. That the Government would seek to toss out of the country a naturalized citizen on moral grounds, but not a native born citizen for the same conduct sort of doesn't square with the equal protection clause of the U.S. Constitution, but who could expect a federal judge to concern himself with nitpicky stuff such as that. Bigamy is criminal conduct. This was not a criminal trial. How a Judge concludes a person guilty of bigamy without due process escapes me.

So, Tom Coumas alias more people than we can hardly list is going back to Greece at last. You think?

"In the United States District Court for the Northern District of California, Southern Division

COMPLAINT FOR DECLATORY JUDGMENT TO ESTABLISH CITIZENSHIP UNDER SECTION 503 OF THE NATIONALITY ACT OF 1940
NOTICE OF APPEAL

To the Clerk of the Above-Entitled Court, To Herbert Brownell, Jr. Attorney General of the United States, and Lloyd H. Burke, Esq., United States Attorney, His Attorney:
You and each of you will please take notice that Tom Coumas, the plaintiff in the above-entitled action, hereby appeals to the United States Circuit Court of Appeals from the judgment rendered, made and entered on the 4th day of August, 1953 for the defendant and against the plaintiff, and from the whole of said judgment.
Dated: October 23, 1953:

/s/ STANLEY P. MAMALAKIS
Attorney for Plaintiff
(Endorsed): Filed October 23, 1953"

CHAPTER TWENTY-THREE
UNITED STATES COURT OF APPEALS

I think Stan Mamalakis was exhausted with this entire Coumas thing. Maybe he had other obligations, or simply felt he gave it his best shot. Perhaps he thought the Court of Appeals was above his level of rational expertise and decided to hand the baton off to another team. Maybe it was all of the above. I do know he made a flight from Paris, France to New York on August 15, 1953 so he may have been out of the country when the final order of the District Court was filed.

Enter Andrew J. Eyman, and Bernard B. Glickfield, both of San Francisco, California. I don't know how these two became counsel on behalf of Tom Coumas, but I would imagine they were both brought in by Mamalakis. Mr. Eyman was the more experienced of the pair, having been first licensed to practice law in California in 1936. Mr. Glickfeld was licensed in 1941. I'm not really certain what Mamalakis hoped to accomplish by filing this appeal, but here is the statement filed by Andrew Eyman that covers the seven points that serve as the basis for the appeal:

1. The Judgment of the Trial Court is contrary to the Law in the case.
2. The Judgment of the Trial Court is contrary to the evidence in the case.
3. The Findings of the Trial Court are contrary to the evidence of the case.

4. The Conclusions of Law of the Trial Court are erroneous in Law.
5. The Conclusions of Law of the Trial Court is not warranted or supported either by any evidence in the record or by any proper finding.
6. Finding No. III [Service in the Greek Military and taking an oath of allegiance to Greece] is unsupported by the evidence and is contrary to the evidence in that the record is absent of evidence to show Appellant took a voluntary oath of allegiance to Greece.
7. Finding No. VI [Lived in Greece from 1932 to 1947 and returned to the U.S. as an alien seaman] is unsupported by evidence and presumes the question of Appellant's status as an alien seaman, and in and of itself does not support the Conclusions of Law.

This was dated December 29, 1953. Having read several times the 180 page District Court trial transcript, I would lean toward Mr. Eyman having captured nicely the essence of the situation.

In Finding No. III, Judge Harris stated, "Plaintiff served in the Greek Army from November 1, 1932, Until February 28, 1933, during which time he took an oath of allegiance to Greece." The only "evidence" that the Judge relied on was a statement on Greek Law, communicated by the Greek Ministry of Foreign Affairs through its Greek Consulate in San Francisco, that all inductees into the Greek Army are required to take an oath of allegiance to Greece. There never was any evidence that Tom Coumas took such an oath at the time of his conscription into the Greek Army in November 1932. Remember that Stan Mamalakis objected to this letter in Coumas' deportation hearing, but was overruled on the matter. In that particular hearing, Mamalakis could have asked for directions to the nearest restroom and been overruled. Everybody is somewhat splitting hairs here, because saying that something is "required" under law is not prima facie evidence that a particular law has been complied with by a particular person. For example, that the U.S. Park Service may have a rule that all visitors to U.S. Parks must dispose of trash in approved containers does not support a conclusion that all trash actually ends up in such containers. If you don't believe that, just check the sides of any road running through a U.S. Park.

In Finding No. VI, Judge Harris stated, "Plaintiff remained in Greece from mid-summer of 1932, until August 16, 1947, when he returned to the United States as an alien seaman under the assumed name of Christos Mermingos." Simply put, Judge Harris did not believe Coumas' testimony regarding his attempts to return to the Unites States by his application for a U.S. passport at the American embassy in Athens, and essentially ignored the provisions of the October 11, 1945 amendment to the Nationality Act of 1940. Other than Coumas' own admission on the subject, no other evidence was introduced that proved he entered the United States as Christos Mermingos, a seaman, on August 16, 1947. That is to say, if Coumas had not made that admission, there did not seem to exist any independent evidence that he was actually the person who walked off that ship posing as Mermingos. Where he entered the U.S. is irrelevant since the INS would surely have found a way to declare him an alien and still charged him with not being in possession of a valid visa.

I wish I had a transcript of the hearing before this Appellate Court, but I have not been able to find one. I would have imagined that the arguments presented were pretty much along the lines of what was presented and argued in the District Court by both sides of the issues.

The Appeals Court for the Ninth Circuit consisted of three judges: Chief Judge William Denman, Circuit Judge William E. Orr, and District Judge James M. Carter. Judge Denman was the senior of the three, having been born in 1872. Orr followed in 1881, and Carter in 1904. All of these men were well experienced in matters of the law. It didn't take the court long to reach the conclusion that Judge Harris was 100% correct in his ruling on Coumas. The decision was more an indictment of what Mamalakis was not able to do in District Court, rather than anything Coumas did or did not do in his somewhat convoluted and imaginative testimony. The Court made no comment on the conduct of the trial by Judge Harris, and I can't say that the conduct of Judge Harris was brought up or not by either Eyman or Glickfeld.

What the Appeals Court found was that Coumas was a liar, deceptive, and reprehensible in his conduct. Those are my words, not the words of the Court, but that pretty much captures their take on it. Because of Coumas testimony in District Court, and his various admitted deeds and contradictory statements before Judge Harris, the Court held that Coumas was not credible and that his testimony as evidentiary was worthless. I can't quarrel with that. The Court also held that a declaration of a requirement in law, the Oath, carries with it a presumption that the Greek Army required Coumas to take it, and it is up to Coumas to provide evidence to the contrary. The Court believed that Coumas knew if he went back to Greece it was likely he would be required to serve in the Greek Army and yet he went there anyway, which was a voluntary act on his part. I don't believe that was proven at trial, but I have pretty much concluded that every time a judge gets a look at this whole thing all that falls out is yet another way to justify the action taken by the INS. Coumas left Greece in 1907 at age 17 and did not return until 1932. I think it somewhat presumptuous to find probable cause to believe a person would be familiar with his native country's laws when he had not lived there in 25 years. The same logic might be found in a person who was born in California, moved to Texas and lived there for 25 years to be knowledgeable of both Texas and California law. Coumas could hardly be expected to be familiar with a law passed in Greece in 1914, in the same year he was naturalized as an American citizen in Portland, Oregon. It was that 1914 law that gave Greece retained sovereignty over Coumas, and served as the basis for his induction into the Greek Army as a citizen of Greece, at the same time he was also a citizen of the United States.

If Congress passes a law in 1945 that gives somebody six years to do something from the date of passage that means to me it must be done by 1951. Coumas testified in District Court that he went to the American embassy in Athens in 1946 to apply yet again for a U.S. passport and was administered an oath of allegiance to the United States at that time. I guess there is no burden on the U.S. Government to show that he was never there, and never did what he claimed that he did there. Given the nature of the man, I can well see that the Court would disbelieve his testimony. That is why I said previously that I think Mamalakis erred when he didn't have valid documentation to backup Coumas' testimony. A lie Coumas made in his District Court appearance that everybody missed and nobody took issue with is a statement by Coumas that on the day of April 20th was the first time he had ever met Olive Taylor. If the newspaper accounts of the day were accurate, that statement was simply not true. Coumas was known to have had encounters with Olive Taylor previous to the day his conduct ultimately contributed to her death.

On the business of living in Greece in excess of two years meaning automatic loss of U.S. Citizenship, I can't follow the Courts' reasoning in trying to reconcile the length of his residency in Greece and the six year extension provided for in the referenced amendment. In fact this Appeals Court made no mention of the amendment at all. The Court sees no evidence that Coumas protested his induction into the Greek Army. What would constitute evidence of protest; being arrested and thrown in prison by the Greek Government? This is one of the reasons I take no comfort from laws that are all gray and fuzzy around the edges, and invite many different interpretations, and points of view as to their meaning. The Government can make its accusations, but it is up to the accused to prove them wrong? I always thought the burden of proof was on the Government in such circumstances. Where along the way did Coumas become responsible for the U.S. Government violating his civil rights?

The Court seems consumed by the fact that Coumas fled the U.S. to avoid prosecution, an act he was never charged with as a violation of law. Another obsession of this Court is that Coumas successfully "resisted" extradition. The U.S. Government made a demand that Coumas be delivered into U.S. custody. San Joaquin County even sent two detectives to Greece to escort Coumas back to this country. The Greek Government made the decision to hold an extradition hearing, in accordance with a valid treaty I might add, not Tom Coumas. It was the Greek Government that ruled that Coumas was a Greek citizen and not subject to extradition under that same treaty, not Tom Coumas. Tom Coumas did not petition the Greek Government to do any of those things. He was locked up by the Greek authorities until those same authorities could straighten it all out: the authorities, not Tom Coumas. So, how does that translate into Coumas having "resisted" anything having to do with the U.S. request of the Greek Government to cough him up?

Another circumstance critical to the Government attempt to jettison Coumas from the U.S. is the business of his landing at Norfolk on August 16th under an assumed name, and not in possession of a valid immigration visa. Not valid because he used a false name or not valid because the papers were false, or both? He was charged with some of those things, by the INS, but not until his deportation hearing in San Francisco in 1950. Oddly, no evidence in that regard was introduced by the federal government prior to that hearing, and the charge seems to have been levied solely on the basis of Coumas' own testimony at that same hearing.

Coumas was indeed not credible. Nothing that he said could be rightfully believed because very little existed by way of evidence supporting his allegations and contentions, except when it suited the government's purpose to believe him. In this country, every person is entitled to his day in court, but if there ever was a story that illustrates that the ability of your lawyer is the most critical aspect of how that day will turn out, it has got to be this one. I don't believe the matter of guilt or innocence should rest on the skill of one's legal counsel. I don't know to what extent Mamalakis searched for evidence to corroborate Coumas' version of the facts in this case, but clearly such evidence went glaringly lacking in both the INS deportation hearing and the District Court trial. For evidence that did exist I don't believe proper argument was presented by counsel on Coumas' behalf, particularly the lack of independent witnesses to shore up Coumas' testimony.

I don't know when the INS took Coumas back into custody, but I feel certain that they did. Nothing on the record supports any belief that this case was appealed to a higher level. Was Tom Coumas going home to Greece for the last time?

CHAPTER TWENTY-FOUR
JUSTICE SERVED

The U.S. Court of Appeals handed down their ruling on May 9, 1955. It had come 23 years after Olive Taylor's death, and the wound suffered by William Duval in that classroom in Manteca. I have no doubt that Tom Coumas was destined to be deported to Greece following the May 9th ruling. It took eight years from the date he last entered the United States in 1947 to get a final ruling on whether he would stay or be booted out of this country. I would not be willing to bet it was his last trip to the United States. Coumas was too skilled at moving about as other people and fooling the immigration authorities as to his comings and goings.

The number of people associated with this case is just downright astonishing. I do believe had many of them been more diligent, more qualified and more dedicated to their jobs this story might have had a completely different outcome. Guard Darrah fumbled the ball many times over in this case. The law enforcement authorities associated with the case exhibited such a total lack of knowledge of fundamental investigation practices as to be laughable. It was widely reported in newspaper accounts that Tom Coumas had quarreled previously with Olive Taylor over his children's behavior problems in school. What investigator looked into that? Does that not go to motive? Wouldn't motive be essential to a murder trial? Even the Master Detective himself got it wrong. If indeed Coumas was actually in New York and indeed if while in New York he actually mailed that letter to Clara Hickman? Or was that letter mailed by someone else on Coumas' behalf? Another deception?

The county coroner was inept, and the medical examiner marginal. The coroner reported that his "investigation" concluded that three rounds had been fired at Olive Taylor, with no evidence to support the conclusion or even naming the source of the information on which the conclusion was based. I think Olive Taylor, William Duval and their families deserved better.

I'm troubled by the number of lawyers and judges involved in this thing who seemed unaware, unfamiliar or just downright blind to the laws of this country. Maybe there existed legitimate reasons why Coumas was not charged with a myriad of crimes that the evidence on the record seems to support. I stand for the rule of law. I am repelled by law that is twisted, distorted, and convoluted by public officials in order to serve some individual concept of justice and ego. I can't abide any human being sitting in a robe with a gavel in any court of law that is not fully, completely and unconditionally impartial, and who doesn't pay attention to what is going on in the courtroom. Assistant U.S. Attorney Collett did not win the case in District Court in my opinion. I found him juvenile, arrogant, unfamiliar with the particulars of the case, combative, and insulting. Judge Harris was deferential in his attitude toward Collett, not unlike a proud papa watching his boy in his first soccer game. To Collett's credit, he led Judge Harris around by the nose from beginning to end in that trial. Not that it took a whole lot to do that, given that Collett spent considerable court time finding clouds in a clear blue sky, much to the confusion of Judge Harris.

So many lives have been adversely impacted by the decisions made after John Coumas threw his lunch to that classroom floor on April 20th. You can point to parents who believe their children to be angels when in fact they are the enemy of angels. If the Greek Court believed that Olive Taylor excited and irritated Coumas to the extent that her death was justified at his hands, I have an enormous problem with that. Perhaps it is the custom in Greece to not allow public teachers to discipline their students through corporal punishment. I would imagine had anybody bothered to take her statement, and from the "authorities" leaking details of the circumstances to the press, that Clara Hickman probably did a fairly good job of exciting and irritating Coumas before he left his home and went to the Castle School to confront Olive Taylor. Corporal punishment meted out to deserving pupils in public schools was fairly commonplace in the United States in 1932. I can remember an indiscretion of my own that sent me as a young man to the school principal who had a good arm and a keen eye with a very effective wood paddle. I got the message, loud and clear. No, neither of my parents shot the principal. They probably would have thanked the man, had the opportunity presented itself. I am astonished over the ruling of the Greek Court regarding William Duval. Coumas was in possession of a loaded firearm in a school classroom. Did that not have any meaning to that jury? Clearly there was not a lot of testimony as to what exactly took place between Duval and Coumas, but pulling out a gun is hardly a justifiable defense, even if Duval did punch Coumas in the mouth. What was Duval doing to Coumas that could have been judged to have caused Coumas insanity? Or was the insanity caused at the moment Duval punched Coumas in the face? The problem with those depositions as directed by Darrah is that it would not have taken a whole lot to introduce all manner of theories and doubt as to exactly what did happen in that classroom. The lack of direct evidence in support of the witnesses' statements was appalling. Astonishing given the time lapsed between 1932 and 1934. One would think that would have been ample time to prepare a proper case against Coumas on multiple fronts.

Perhaps Darrah didn't believe that Greece would take the case seriously, so why bother going all out on a full prosecutorial presentation. Perhaps Darrah thought he would eventually get Coumas returned to San Joaquin County, and did not want to show all of his "evidence" prematurely.

I was surprised that the Greek Government charged Coumas with assault with a deadly weapon on Mrs. Duval. I was very surprised when the jury acquitted him on the charge. True, the evidence was not all that solid, but I really think that pointing the same gun that has wounded your husband and killed a human being right in front of you could give one pause when that gun was turned toward you. Of course there were other charges that Greece could have brought, that Mr. Darrah for whatever his reasons passed on by, but they didn't. The Greek trial transcript was not translated, so I have no idea what the testimony was, what witnesses were heard, what arguments were presented, or how the judge handled the trial in Corinth.

I think the American embassy in Athens lost a fantastic opportunity to have Coumas back on U.S. soil when the passport was denied to him. If one can believe Coumas, which I admit requires a lot of faith, if what he said of his contacts with the embassy are true, then the officials there only doubled his resolve to return by any means by denying him the documents he sought. Clearly embassy staff knew all about Coumas from the extradition hearing and the subsequent trial in Greece. If he was not welcome back in the U.S. they should have had the honesty to tell him so, instead of jerking him around. If you can truly believe Coumas' version of it, and that is one really big "if". That there was never introduced any record of his calling on the embassy for the purpose of repatriation is troubling to me. Either government officials buried the paperwork or Coumas was lying. If the embassy was in contact with Washington regarding Coumas, there should have been a record of it, and Mamalakis should have demanded the records under discovery. It just might be that Mamalakis did that very thing and what information he was able to obtain did not shore up his client. I rather think not because if Mamalakis knew something that would look negatively on Coumas, you can bet that Collett would have known and would have used that information against Coumas at trial. There is no record of any hearing having been conducted by the U.S. State Department regarding the "finding" that Coumas had lost his U.S. Citizenship by serving in the Greek army. To make such a finding without due process would have violated Coumas' Constitutional rights under the 14th Amendment.

Tom Coumas as a human being was morally corrupt, which might explain to some degree his children's behavior problems. I think there is ample evidence of that on the record, some of which by his own hand. The record alleges that Coumas had an illegitimate child in San Joaquin County. The record is unclear as to which Coumas child that might have been. Coumas' son, Chester, was in the state reform school at the time of the shootings in Manteca. Chester died in Las Vegas in 1996. I don't know when he was released from state custody, but Coumas tells us he was in Newark, New Jersey in 1947. Chester would have been 28 years of age in 1947. Coumas mentioned another child in his District Court testimony. According to Coumas, the child was named Cornelius, probably named after wife Margaret's father. Cornelius would have been five years old in 1932, but there is no mention of him anywhere else in any public record or investigation. Cornelius died in California in 2004. Guard

Darrah asked William Pappas about a child named Mary in his deposition in 1934, but I have not found any record thus far of a child by that name as being a child of Tom Coumas. Coumas also said that the Debauw family traveled from Oregon to Stockton in 1932 for a hearing into the disposition of Coumas' children Helen, John and Peter. I don't believe the Debauw's prevailed at that hearing. Custody of Peter went to the Kaloutsis family in Manteca. Helen and John probably ended up with Coumas' relatives: a sister living in Southern California and his first cousin Sam Stavros. Sam Stavros died in California in 1985 at age 88 years. As I mentioned earlier Coumas' son, John, died in Sonoma County in 1940, a few days prior to what would have been his 16th birthday. I have reason to believe that he was in the care of the Sonoma County Hospital at Santa Rosa, California at the time of his death. It is also possible that he was in foster care in San Joaquin County, prior to becoming ill and being hospitalized in Sonoma County. Helen was living in California in the same part of the state in 2004, where Coumas' sister was living in 1932. Peter died in California at age 77 in 2004. Aristea (more commonly known as Esther) Kaloutsis died in Manteca in 1970 at age 85. Her husband, also named Peter, died in Manteca in 1952 at age 78. Imagine their reaction when Coumas walked into their home in Manteca in 1947. Coumas' wife, Margaret, first committed to the State Mental Hospital at Stockton, in 1928 died there in 1979 at age 86. Obviously, Coumas' expectation of her "imminent" death in 1932 was somewhat premature.

The record is clear, by his own admission, again if he can ever be believed, that Coumas was something of a ladies' man. While Margaret was locked up, Coumas was writing promises of love, passion, diamond rings, and a future life together to Clara Hickman. When Coumas got out of the Greek Army he married Gregoria in Greece because he needed her money. She carried and delivered his daughter in April 1934. He may have abandoned them in Greece when he left for the U.S. in 1947, amid promises that he would send for them. Maybe the same way he abandoned his wife and four (perhaps five) children when he fled Manteca for Greece in 1932, and promising Clara Hickman he would send for her. In his deportation hearing, Coumas brought up the subject of his having obtained an annulment to his marriage with Gregoria after he obtained a divorce from Margaret. In his trial in District Court, Coumas mentioned that his relationship with Gregoria was strained, and that they were not speaking. Maybe the new Mrs. Coumas finally got the whole story on the man she married.

And what of Clara Hickman? Why was she off limits as a central witness for the authorities in Manteca? What became of her? Was she still there when Coumas returned in 1947? What line did he give her then? Did she simply disappear and no one could find her? How did the San Joaquin County authorities come into possession of that letter from Coumas? Why wasn't William Pappas questioned about Clara Hickman? After all, she was initially staying at his home the evening of April 20th, and that letter from Coumas was addressed to Hickman in care of Mr. Pappas.

How could you have an assignment to photograph a crime scene and only take five photographs? How could you photograph anything and not photograph the wounds to Olive Taylor's left calf while she was still on the floor of her classroom? The photographer was an expert in criminal photographic and identification work of some thirteen years experience? How could you have numerous reports of gunfire in a school classroom, one dead on the floor, another receiving treatment in the county hospital and not look for bullets or shell casings in the room where they were fired? Ivan Hitt photographed Olive Taylor but not

William Duval? Would not a report by the medical doctor treating Mr. Duval tend to corroborate Mr. Duval's testimony as to his injuries? Why wasn't a deputy sent to the hospital to obtain that information? Surely Mr. Duval's wound required treatment on some level.

Who was talking to the press? I have printed here a report from the San Francisco Chronicle that held that Coumas shot Olive Taylor twice at point black range in the heart and then shot her again in the head. Where did that come from? When a newspaper includes a banner "Special to" it usually means that the source of the story is a local reporter. That could have been anybody in Stockton or Manteca or even some other place. Who told the press that the police had cornered Coumas in a home in Manteca on the evening of the shootings? Coumas managed to remain one step ahead of the authorities at every turn, and nobody managed to even come close to him. There was a lot of misinformation in the press. Some of it was downright outrageous as to its lacking in fact. The news stories I have reviewed suggest to me that the various reporters were speaking with government authorities that were very close to certain details of the story, but even sources such as official reports had misinformation in them.

William Duval died in Manteca in 1943 at the age of 85. Yes, Duval was 74 years of age when he got into the wrestling match with Coumas, age 43 in 1932. I strongly believe, based on the records I have reviewed, that if Mrs. Duval's testimony is the truth, that William Duval may have triggered his own injuries and Olive Taylor's death.

I think the handling of this entire matter was so sloppy I would be truly astonished if any reasonably competent defense attorney, had Coumas stood trial in San Joaquin County, could have not blasted the prosecution out of the courthouse on this evidence. Surely Darrah must have had more evidence against Coumas than I was able to find. But if so, who has it?

Olive Taylor's mother, Nancy Hite Bailey, was living with the Taylor's in Stockton in April of 1932. Thirteen days after her daughter's death, Nancy died of heart failure in Santa Rosa. Many in the family believed that Nancy just gave up living after her daughter was killed. Ethan Taylor never remarried. He died in California a widower in 1957 at the age of 84. He was buried alongside his wife in Stockton. The Taylor's daughter, Mildred, joined her parents in that same plot in 1957. She was only 51. Mildred and Sam Cohn (not Cohen as the Chronicle reported) divorced sometime after her mother died in Manteca. Sam's father was California State Senator Philip C. Cohn.

While not directly related to this story, the fate of Ellis Parker deserves mention here. The master detective ran afoul of the law himself and wound up in the Federal Penitentiary at Lewisburg, Pennsylvania where he died in 1940 halfway through a 6-year prison sentence for abduction. Parker held his own theory regarding the Lindbergh baby kidnapping, decided to kidnap the man Parker believed responsible and attempted to extort a confession out of the man. The whole deal came unraveled and Parker was found guilty in 1937. Yet another example that good judgment can erode in the most competent and highly regarded of public servants.

Anybody that has been paying even the most casual attention certainly has discovered that we often demonstrate that we are a nation of contradictions, double entendres, and convoluted meanings in our language and our laws. Bad law, law that defies interpretation, and people in law enforcement who do not list reading comprehension among their skill sets all manage to keep our courts and legions of lawyers saddled with work as far as the eye can see. Ninety-five years after Tom Coumas spoke his oath of allegiance to the United States in Portland, Oregon, the U.S. Government still requires newly naturalized citizens to "absolutely and entirely renounce and abjure all allegiance to any foreign prince, potentate, state or sovereignty", even though the U.S. Government accepts more dual citizenships from more countries than ever in its history. The legal curiosity that arises out of this entire Coumas naturalization oath of allegiance issue is the implication by the U.S. Government that a foreigner by taking such an oath results in the provisions of the oath being legally binding on another sovereign country. Certainly U.S. officials were not receptive to Greek law being mandated upon the United States. Nothing new about the U.S. trying to have a particular matter viewed as applicable in one sense, but not in another. Stan Mamalakis made a very effective argument before the California Supreme Court that there exists ample legal precedent for the United States having legal authority over its citizens who commit crimes in foreign countries. I really do not believe that had an American citizen killed somebody in Greece and fled to the United States that there would have been a trial in Greece on the matter.

And speaking of matters regarding justice served, consider that there existed in California law in 1932 the right for a defendant to be represented by counsel in a matter of criminal law. There seems to be implied, in certain sections of the California Penal Code, that the accused counsel has the right to be present during the taking of depositions of witnesses in a homicide. Guard Darrah, in remarks before deposing the first witness on December 19th, invited counsel for Coumas to participate in the deposition taking session. His exact words, taken from the transcript were as follows:

> "Mr. Darrah: May I say at this time, if anyone is present in Court authorized to represent the defendant, Tom Coumas, also known at Spiros Smyrnogianis, he is invited to come forth and take a seat at the counsel table and propound [to put forward for consideration; propose] such interrogatories [expressing a question] on cross-examination of the witness as he deems proper." The court reporter notes in the transcript: "(No one appeared to represent the defendant, Tom Coumas)".

I don't know if there existed in 1934 in California the legal requirement to appoint counsel if a defendant was not capable of such appointment or was not able to afford counsel. Clearly, Coumas was under arrest in Greece and not able to appear himself in the Stockton County Court House on December 19th. It is reasonable to conclude that any counsel that might have been appointed on his behalf by the Greek Government may or may not have been appointed on December 19th, since the Greek Government was only conducting an investigation into the allegations made regarding Coumas' criminal conduct in San Joaquin County through the Grand Jury indictment. It is also reasonable to conclude that if such counsel had been appointed in Greece to represent Coumas that such counsel was probably not going to travel to San Joaquin County to represent Coumas for these depositions. I have no idea if the Greek authorities were even notified of the date and time of the intended taking of these depositions and that counsel for Coumas would be welcome to attend.

Surely, Coumas had the right to have counsel on his own behalf present and to question the witnesses to be deposed, because Darrah implied as much in his statement on the record. So, the question that is begged is what if any obligation did San Joaquin County have to appoint counsel to represent Coumas in this proceeding? Given that this entire matter was unique in the first place, and given that the purpose of these depositions was evidence in keeping with another provision in the California Penal Code that requires that witnesses be deposed in a homicide case, which this certainly was, and given that the purpose of these depositions was to be used at trial of Coumas on the San Joaquin County criminal charges in Greece. My point being, if the defendant had the right to be represented by counsel at these depositions, were these to be used as evidence against him at trial in San Joaquin County, why then was he not entitled to the same counsel for a proceeding in San Joaquin County as part of a criminal trial in Greece?

Here is what Darrah also said, in his own words, about the purpose of these depositions:

> "Mr. Darrah: May it please the Grand Jury, at this time we are assembled for the purpose of taking the depositions to be used in the trial of Tom Coumas, alias Spiros Smyrnogianis, and I would ask that first the Foreman appoint Herman Spalinger, a competent shorthand Reporter, to take down and transcribe the testimony of witnesses to be taken in here."

That seems rather clear to me. Did Darrah have any sort of communication with the San Joaquin County Judge who received the indictment regarding the appointment of counsel for Coumas at these deposition proceedings? What of Judge Young who received and certified the depositions? Did Judge Young wonder about Darrah's statement regarding lack of counsel representing Coumas? Did Judge Young have any obligation to ensure that

Coumas rights were protected with regard to the taking of these depositions?

If Judge Young did, or Darrah did or anybody did, I have not found any record of any comment on the record about the matter, or any concern raised about the matter. If Coumas had the right to challenge the witnesses at the time of these depositions and was not afforded that opportunity, was that a violation of his civil rights? Was this another violation of his 5th and 14th Amendment Constitutional right to due process? Is that "justice served"? All too often verdicts are tossed out on appeal due to some procedural error on the part of some individual somewhere in the legal process. Pilots use checklists to avoid forgetting something critically important to successful flight. Did Darrah have a checklist or was he flying mostly by the seat of his pants?

Regardless of how that might appear, everything you have read thus far is based on the records and information publicly available to me prior to July 2009. In June 2008, I sent a Freedom of Information Act (FOIA) request to the U.S. Citizenship and Immigration Services branch of the U.S. Department of Homeland Security. My request was for all public records associated with Tom Coumas for which they had oversight. It took them awhile to gather it all up, but in August 2009 I received 1,012 pages of information and a declaration that I was receiving all materials I had requested except for a few pages that in their view constituted attorney-client privilege and some redactions as required by law. The redactions turned out to be nothing more than blanking out dates and places in reference to Coumas' children. That information was and is readily available in other public records if you know where to look.

The vast majority of copied documents that I subsequently reviewed were largely duplicates of documents I had previous received from other sources, and appeared to have been received in Washington, DC from the San Francisco INS District office and other places and for purposes I have already mentioned here. There were however a number of documents that I had not seen before. As I reviewed this new material it became clear to me that there seemed to be a story surfacing within this story. Some refer to something along these lines as the "smoking gun". Well, maybe so. This story has had an odd odor to it from the outset, and it was not necessarily coming from Tom Coumas.

CHAPTER TWENTY-FIVE
REVENGE

It will come as no surprise that our federal government happily makes all manner of laws and rules and then just as happily ignores them unless one of us breaks them. In theory it's not supposed to work that way, but all too commonly it does and with great regularity. What is really unfortunate is that anybody who does these things under color of authority is hardly ever punished for it, regardless of the damage that they do to the lives of others.

There exists within this story a series of events that allowed certain other events to take place. Each of these events were influenced by representatives of the government, were they considered local, state or federal, but each playing a small but critical part in the ultimate evolution of acts that would result in the unlawful denial of the lawful rights of Tom Coumas by representatives of the United States government.

In order to lead you through it, we need to agree that on April 2, 1914 the federal government considered Tom Coumas to be a lawful citizen of the United States of America. When Tom Coumas became involved in events that would lead to the death of Olive Taylor and the wounding of William Duval in 1932, Tom Coumas was still a lawful citizen of the United States of America. Under a treaty ratified and duly executed between the United States and Greece, Tom Coumas was also a citizen of Greece. No U.S. law, oath or any other legal finding held the power to change that. Not even Tom Coumas could change that. As I understand the conditions under which the Greek

Government would have given permission for Coumas to renounce his Greek citizenship, he would have had to first fulfill his military service obligation to Greece. Since we know from the record he had not fulfilled that obligation when he was naturalized in Oregon in 1914, such permission would not have been granted to him had he asked for it.

And so, when Tom Coumas fled to Greece in 1932 and the Greek Government decided to hold trial in Greece for crimes alleged by San Joaquin County to have been committed there against Olive Taylor and William Duval, that trial was based on violations of Greek law, not U.S. law or California State law. Following the extradition hearing by the Greek government in Greece, and following the ruling that Coumas was a citizen of Greece, and subsequently deciding to hold him for trial in Greece, nobody in the United States government protested Greece's right to do so. There is not one single U.S. diplomatic document on the public record in my possession that indicates that Greece was wrong, in error or just flat out had no legal right to declare sovereignty over Tom Coumas and jurisdiction in the matter of Coumas alleged criminal conduct in California in 1932. This was pretty much affirmed by the California Supreme Court.

Please bear in mind, that the United States took no action on the matter of the validity of Tom Coumas U.S. citizenship from 1934, when he was first discovered to be in Greece, and in 1946 when he was aggressively seeking the appropriate paperwork for his intended return to the United States. Coumas claimed, and is on the public record in several legal venues as having claimed he sought an American passport from the U.S. Embassy in Athens following the completion of his parole for the crimes for which he had been convicted in Greece in 1935. Here is where this train starts to leave the rails.

The U.S. State Department had in its employ a career foreign service officer by the name of Daniel Gaudin, Jr. In 1934, Mr. Gaudin was the vice-Consul at the U.S. Embassy in Beirut. In 1947 Mr. Gaudin held the title of "Consul" in the U.S. Embassy in Athens. Oddly enough, a person who holds the title of "Consul" in a U.S. Embassy is not necessarily a lawyer. Since it has been my personal and professional experience that there always seems to be a lawyer involved representing an agency of the government at some level, one would think one might have been providing guidance or advice to the Embassy people, but I have no documents that would cause me to believe a lawyer was guiding or blessing anything having to do with Tom Coumas involving either the Embassy or the State Department.

Mr. Gaudin did seem familiar with Tom Coumas self-claimed involuntary induction into the Greek Army, for which Coumas served a term of four months concurrently in 1932-1934. On January 10, 1947, Mr. Gaudin issued a document called a "Report of Expatriation" regarding Tom Coumas. What this document had the effect of doing was to strip Tom Coumas of his U.S. citizenship. I happily reproduce for your edification this document mostly in its entirety as follows:

REPORT OF EXPATRIATION

> I, Daniel Gaudin Jr., Consul of the United States of America at Athens, Greece, hereby certify that Thomas Coumas, who was born at Roino, Mantinia, Greece, on October 28, 1889, and who was naturalized before the Circuit Court of Multnomah County at Portland, Oregon, on February 25, 1914, has expatriated himself pursuant to the provisions of Section 2 of the Act of March 2, 1907, by taking an

oath of allegiance to Greece in connection with his service in the Greek Army. The evidence of such action consists of the following:

1. A certificate of military service issued by the Recruiting Office of Tripolis, Greece, on October 4, 1946, showing that he was inducted into the Greek Army on November 1, 1932 and was discharged on February 28, 1933.

Thomas Coumas returned from the United States to Greece in 1932 and has since resided continuously in this country. He was married to a Greek subject on April 29, 1933 and one child, Mary, was born of this marriage in Greece in 1934.

Thomas Coumas did not protest to an American Consular Mission against his induction into the Greek Army and the taking of an oath of allegiance to Greece.
In testimony whereof, I have hereunto subscribed my name and affixed my office seal this 10th day of January 1947.

/s/
Daniel Gaudin Jr.
Consul of the United States
Of America

The "evidence" to which Mr. Gaudin makes reference is simply a certification of service rendered issued by the referenced Greek office and also indicates the status of any future military obligations, was issued for the purpose of foreign travel, and makes absolutely no reference to any oath of allegiance taken on connection with the military service rendered on the part of Tom Coumas. A very large possibility exists that this particular "certificate" was provided to the Embassy by Tom Coumas for the purpose of showing that his military obligation to Greece had been fulfilled.

There is no record of any hearing having been conducted as to this "expatriation", no copy of any notice of appeal rights as to the decision, nor any copy of any notice given of this action on the part of Mr. Gaudin to Tom Coumas. In other words, there is no evidence on the public record of any due process having been accorded Coumas with regard to the action taken by Mr. Gaudin on January 10, 1947.

In order for the INS to later charge Coumas with violating the Immigration Act of March 26, 1924, which was the sole basis for the INS arrest warrant issued by the San Francisco District office on February 12, 1948, Coumas had to have been an alien when he landed in Norfolk, Virginia aboard the S.S. Ameriki on September 4, 1947 without a valid visa. Had Coumas been a U.S. citizen, he would not have been subject to a visa requirement and even though he entered the United States at that time without a valid U.S. passport, that would not have been a deportable offense. Had Gaudin not taken it upon himself to strip Coumas of his U.S. citizenship, the INS would not have had any jurisdiction over him when he returned to the United States in 1947.

As you have read here, there has been no shortage of allegations about expatriation throughout this entire story due to this oath of allegiance regarding the Greek military. Coumas always maintained that he never took such an oath, and everybody else claimed that he did, solely based on a written statement by the Greek Minister of Foreign Affairs that such an oath was compulsory. There has yet to surface any document that certifies as evidence that Coumas actually took such an oath as administered or witnessed by anybody. Gaudin took the position that because the Greek military certified that Coumas served in the Greek Army that he had taken an oath of allegiance to Greece. This is like the Army saying Private Jones received dental care because it is the policy of the Army that all soldiers receive dental care. When that was questioned, U.S. authorities got the Minister to certify that such an oath was compulsory, but that did not happen until August 1949, some two years and eight months after Gaudin stripped Coumas of his U.S. citizenship.

Want to know what all the fuss was about? Here then is the translated version of the Greek "Oath of a soldier":

> "I swear that I will bear allegiance to the country and the Democratic regime of the Hellens, support the Constitution, laws and regulations of the State, bear obedience to my superiors, execute willingly and without reservation their orders, defend the flags with faith and devotion until the last drop of my blood, that I shall not abandon them, or I shall never part from them, and respect to the letter the military laws and behave in general as a loyal and proud soldier."

Did you read anything in there about "absolutely and entirely renouncing and abjuring allegiance to the United States"? I have found no statement from Tom Coumas that it was his intent to renounce his U.S. citizenship. More importantly, I have found no statement that anybody asked him whether it was his intent to renounce his U.S. citizenship. Coumas claimed that he was administered the U.S. oath of allegiance at the U.S. Embassy in Athens when he applied for a U.S. passport in 1946. Coumas also claimed that he had been told by an unnamed official at that same Embassy in early 1947, that the U.S. State Department in Washington, DC had ruled that he had expatriated himself. There is no such document in the copies of official government records I have been provided by multiple agencies of the government. The only document on record in my possession from any federal agency only refers to the Gaudin report of January 10, 1947.

What was so difficult to come up with a witness to this oath taking business? More importantly, who cares if Coumas did or didn't take an oath, if it was not his intent to renounce his U.S. citizenship? After all, he was a Greek citizen. I think the general rule when it comes to penalizing people for various things, that the burden of proof rests with the government, not the accused.

When Coumas was in the custody of the INS in San Francisco, a district INS Expulsion Section official by the name of Stan Olsen sent a memo to the Commissioner of the INS in Washington, DC requesting a certified copy of Coumas' passport application from the U.S. State Department. Olsen also wanted copies of any decision that might have been reached by State regarding Coumas' right to claim U.S. citizenship. What Olsen got back was a memo from W.F. Kelly, an assistant INS commissioner who quoted a FBI report which summarized the attempt to extradite Coumas, his subsequent trial in Greece and sentence received on conviction. Kelly sent along a copy of the Gaudin "Expatriation" report, previously quoted here. Kelly concludes that since Coumas "lost" his citizenship (based apparently on the Gaudin report) "it does not appear that a certified copy of his application for a United States passport is necessary at this time." Huh? Coumas is claiming that he attempted to repatriate himself by making application for a U.S. passport in Athens, Olsen is trying to corroborate by asking for the passport application, and this guy Kelly does not think it necessary to acquire the requested application and send it to Olsen in San Francisco?

There existed in January 1949 a letter authored by a person known as R. B. Shipley, Chief of the Passport Division of the U.S. Department of State. The letter was addressed to INS Commissioner Watson B. Miller. Miller had apparently written to State inquiring about the status of Tom Coumas' U.S. citizenship. Shipley, in his response references a "certificate of expatriation" which is noted was transmitted to the INS on June 10, 1947, and concludes,

> ".....this Department was of the opinion that in the absence of evidence to the contrary Mr. Coumas must be regarded as having taken the usual oath of allegiance in Greece in connection with his service in the Greek Army from November 1, 1932 to February 28, 1933."

Excuse me? In the <u>absence of evidence to the contrary</u>? Who would be the party responsible for evidence to the contrary? Where is the evidence of beyond a reasonable doubt? What on Earth is the "usual" oath of allegiance? Shipley does not confirm or even reiterate that Coumas is considered by State as no longer a U.S. citizen as of some sort of effective date. I'm troubled about the declaration that in light of the "certificate of expatriation" the passport application, which if existed would tend to validate Coumas' claim of acts of repatriation while still in Greece as not necessary.

I have no idea what the protocol was in the State Department in 1947 for stripping a person of their U.S. Citizenship, but in the present world a document would be issued by the State Department known as a "Certificate of

Loss of Nationality". Such a certificate would be issued by the U.S. State Department on the recommendation of an American Consul in a foreign country meeting the legal tests necessary to be stripped of U.S. citizenship. I have not found any such document regarding Tom Coumas. I do have a copy of the original of Coumas' Certificate of Naturalization stamped "Cancelled". There is no date or office of record with regard to this stamp. In the case of the Gaudin "Report of Expatriation", it would appear that this was accepted as a lawful declarative order under Section 2, of the Immigration Act of March 2, 1907.

You may recall that I have previously expressed great umbrage here at what appeared to be a lack of understanding of the law on the part of the San Joaquin County District Attorney's Office and a whole host of other state and federal officials regarding the matter of double jeopardy. There was a federal INS Inspector by the name of Mark D. Conroy working out of the Stockton, California INS office. Inspector Conroy began his investigation into the matter of Coumas' immigration status around September 26, 1947. This seems a little odd to me. Why would the INS be called in on the same day Coumas was arrested in Manteca? Conroy interviewed several San Joaquin County officials, and even Coumas, who at the time was indeed a resident of the San Joaquin County jail. On February 3, 1948, Inspector Conroy filed a Report of Investigation in which he noted the following:

> "Brad Crittenden, Assistant District Attorney was interviewed in December, 1947prior to arraignment of the subject on the charges stated. Mr. Crittenden stated that his office will proceed on the 1932 indictment and will seek the death penalty, providing the matter can be taken to trial."

What this entry in Inspector Conroy's' report suggests to me that some doubt existed on the part of Mr. Crittenden that the "matter" would actually be taken to trial. Conroy's' report goes on to explain about Coumas' arraignment, the plea to the charges entered, and the filing for a Writ of Prohibition against San Joaquin County's intent to proceed with a trial of Coumas:

> ".....asking for a ruling as to whether or not subject's conviction and sentence in Greece for the commission of crimes in this country may be set up as a valid defense against the present prosecution. Section 793 of the California Code makes it apparent that subject possibly has a point, and if the Supreme Court rules in his favor, he will be discharged."

Conroy goes on to make reference to the points presented in the Supreme Court filing and suggests that certain facts included in the filing might be useful to the INS in seeking a warrant for Coumas' deportation from the United States. This Conroy concludes, is based on Coumas resisting extradition to the U.S. while in Greece, his residence there, and "his stand on his Greek citizenship to avoid extradition." In other words, there appeared to be a scramble going on to find a means to arrest Coumas and deport him should the California Supreme Court rule in Coumas' favor. Conroy noted in another report that Coumas was being uncooperative and refused to give a statement to Conroy during the period in which Coumas' case was pending before the Supreme Court. The INS issued an arrest warrant anyway, and put a hold on Coumas pending a ruling by the Supreme Court.

Conroy must have been reporting his early investigative findings up the chain of command, because also on September 26, 1947 the Officer in Charge of the

Stockton INS office, a man by the name of Walter T. Peyton, sent a memorandum to the San Francisco INS District Director that noted the following:

> "The subject [Tom Coumas aka Spiros Smyrnogeanes] is presently detained in the San Joaquin County Jail awaiting trial for murder. He killed a woman in Manteca, California in 1932, fled to Greece, and remained in Greece until about two months ago when he claims he was smuggled ashore from a Greek vessel in New York. This subject claims he was naturalized in Portland, Oregon Feb. 25, 1914, and that he recently filed application for a duplicate certificate of naturalization with your office. Preliminary investigation indicates that the subject probably lost citizenship following his departure to Greece in 1932, and will be amenable to deportation proceedings based on his last entry. If there is a San Francisco file, please forward it to this office."

Couple of interesting observations regarding this memo: first I have a copy of a recreated application for a replacement copy of Coumas' naturalization certificate, on that document, an INS San Francisco official certifies that Coumas appeared on September 24, 1947 at their office to file the application, this application gives a residence address in San Mateo, California (a community just south of San Francisco); second, the San Francisco office recommended that the application be granted on September 26, 1947 the same day as Coumas was arrested in Manteca. The San Francisco office did not receive Peyton's memo until October 2, 1947 and there is a stamp on the memo that indicates that "no previous record found", I assume, regarding Coumas. Peyton concludes in his memo that Coumas "probably" lost citizenship following his departure to Greece, and therefore subject to deportation. Isn't this a little early in the game? After all, Coumas had just been arrested, and apparently the San Francisco office had no idea he was wanted and that is citizenship status was in question. From all of the records that exist in this case, we clearly know that departing the country for Greece was not just cause for loss of U.S. citizenship because the INS took no action on the matter prior to 1947. Perhaps odder still, that Peyton reaches all of these conclusions before Coumas appears before any judge for arraignment on the charges for which he was arrested, that arraignment not having occurred until 27 days after being jailed in San Joaquin County. The timing of all of this seems off to me. Government agencies just do not move this fast, particularly when it involves multiple levels of government and various officials having to be briefed and decisions on how to proceed needing to be reached. Particularly in light of the record indicating that the INS had really not had a whole lot of time in which to conduct any sort of investigation. Usually when someone is arrested they must be processed into custody. That is to say that often interviews may be conducted for the purpose of gathering information from the accused, personal property is taken and inventoried, the person is fingerprinted and photographed, and issued jail clothing. All of which take a certain measure of time. I have no idea the time of day that Coumas was arrested on September 26, 1947 because if any incident or arrest reports existed at the time, they did not survive in the custody of the San Joaquin County Sheriff's records division or the Manteca Police Department. That noted, it does not appear to me that there would have been a whole lot of opportunity on that day for outside agencies such as the INS to learn a whole lot from Coumas, and by Conroy's own report Coumas was not being cooperative, and what Coumas was quoted as having said by Conroy were obviously fabrications by Coumas. In other words, there was probably insufficient time on September 26, 1947 to conduct much of an investigation into whether Coumas was an American citizen or an alien. So it would appear that somebody was trying to stack the deck against Coumas from the moment he was arrested on September 26, 1947 even though he set off no alarms by appearing before the INS in San Francisco two days previous. Equally as curious I find no response from the District Director to Peyton regarding this memo in the multitude of documents I was provided by several government agencies.

It's interesting to note here that the INS warrant issued February 12, 1948 carried with it a bond (bail) amount of $500.00, about $4,425 in 2008 dollars. Somebody thought that $500.00 was too puny and jacked it up six times to $3,000.00 or around $26,549 in 2008 dollars. The bond was eventually lowered to $1,500.00, still a lot of money in 1948 and all over a charge of being an alien in the U.S. without a valid visa? Just a tad excessive?

And now we come to the absolute best part of this royal goat rope and that would be Robert S. DeMoulin, Presiding Inspector of the INS San Francisco District Office. If you look back to Chapter Twenty-One you will find Mr. DeMoulin charging Coumas with violation of the Immigration Act of February 5, 1917 in that he was convicted of a felony, or other crime or misdemeanor involving moral turpitude prior to entry into the United States, to wit: murder. And here is where Mr. DeMoulin committed an illegal act by exceeding his authority and thus violated Coumas' rights under the 5th Amendment of the United States Constitution, along with the protections afforded Coumas under California law for which the Supreme Court in that State had already ruled.

Tom Coumas was convicted in Greece of certain crimes under the Greek Criminal Code. Coumas was never convicted in Greece or anywhere else for that matter for crimes under any U.S. federal or state law as they related to the death of Olive Taylor or the wounding of William Duval. With regard to the death of Olive Taylor, look back to Chapter Seventeen and you will find the section of the Greek Criminal Code under which Coumas was convicted. That would be involuntary manslaughter. Unfortunately for Mr. Demoulin's purposes, involuntary manslaughter was not a crime that was considered to involve "moral turpitude". Neither was the weapons charge for which Coumas was also convicted by the Corinthe Court. The oath of allegiance business was a little thin, so what was needed was something else to give positive weight to a deportation finding. Mr. DeMoulin decided to convict Tom Coumas of violation of Section 192, sub-section (1) of the California Penal Code, a crime of "voluntary" manslaughter. Bear in mind that Coumas had never been charged in any indictment for violating Section 192 of the California Penal Code and the Corinthe Court did not convict Coumas of violating it either. That goes to the 5th Amendment requirement of due process. I do not believe enforcement of the California Penal Code was within the jurisdiction of the INS at the time Mr. DeMoulin arrived as his conclusions regarding the crimes for which Coumas had been convicted. That is to say that the conviction would have only been valid due to a judgment rendered by a court having lawful jurisdiction over Section 192, and Tom Coumas. Here is Mr. DeMoulin's "opinion" regarding the matter dated February 23, 1950:

> "On the basis of the respondent's conviction in Greece on October 16, 1935 on the charge of "murder" committed at Manteca, California on April 20, 1932, the charge: The Act of February 5, 1917 in that he has been convicted of a felony or other

crime or misdemeanor involving moral turpitude prior to entry into the United States, to wit: murder, was lodged (p.46). It will be noted that the crime of murder, for which the respondent was convicted as set out in the decision of the Greek court (Exhibit 5), is defined as Voluntary Manslaughter under California statutes (Sec. 192 Cal. Penal Code) and was referred to in the decision of the California Supreme Court on the respondent's petition for Writ of Prohibition (Exhibit 7) as "manslaughter". As Voluntary Manslaughter (under the circumstances of the respondent's conviction) is a crime involving moral turpitude, the lodged charge is sustained."

What is fascinating to me in all of this is the insistence on the part of the government to use the term "murder" in connection with the conviction by the Corinthe Court and the term "manslaughter" interchangeably when they are two separate and therefore distinct with their own separate and therefore distinct legal definitions. Lets first straighten out the facts: 1) regardless of the language used by the jury in their verdict statement, there was no conviction of "murder" within the definition of American or Greek law by the Corinthe Court in 1935 in Greece, 2) the California Supreme Court made no reference to the California Penal Code in its decision with the exception of Section 793 as it relates to the issue of double jeopardy, 3) the reference to the Writ of Prohibition and the word "manslaughter" appears on page 4, line 31 of the petition submitted on behalf of Tom Coumas to the Supreme Court on March 2, 1948 by Stan Mamalakis, Coumas legal counsel, with no reference to the word "voluntary" and 4) there are no legal documents in this matter that finds Coumas guilty of "voluntary" manslaughter against Olive Taylor. What Mr. DeMoulin chooses to leave out of the record is that the Corinthe Court found Coumas, "....that the acts for which he was sentenced guilty are foreseen and punished by Articles 287, 293, para 3 of the Criminal Law and Articles 2 and 13b. of Law 286.....". No mention there of Section 192 of the California Penal Code. I am quoting from the same document that presents the findings of the jury in Greece and is dated October 16, 1935.

DeMoulin lists as item #12 in his list of "Proposed Findings of Fact/Upon the basis of all the evidence presented", "That the respondent committed the crime of murder on April 20, 1932 at Manteca, California". This "finding of fact" is in the same report that finds Coumas guilty of "Voluntary Manslaughter". It probably would be helpful to actually look at Section 192 of the California Penal Code at this point:

> "Manslaughter defined. Voluntary and involuntary manslaughter. Manslaughter is the unlawful killing of a human being, without malice. It is of two kinds: 1. Voluntary – upon a sudden quarrel or heat of passion. 2. Involuntary – in the commission of an unlawful act, not amounting to a felony; or in the commission of a lawful act which might produce death, in an unlawful manner, or without due caution and circumspection."

Let's deal with this once and for all here. Without malice you have no crime of murder. You may recall that Section 293, sub-section (3) of the Greek Criminal Code refers to the penalty if the crime involved aggravation by grave slanders and malice and committed in "excitement of passion". Here is what I believe, from all of the evidence I have read on this subject, that DeMoulin took the "excitement of passion" clause from the Greek Criminal Code, and applied it as a test as to whether the finding of the jury was actually Voluntary (heat of passion) rather than involuntary under the California Penal Code. On the basis of that comparison, DeMoulin concluded that Coumas had been convicted by the Greek Court of voluntary manslaughter (while still naming it murder) and thus a crime involving moral turpitude in justification of a finding of violation of the Immigration Act of 1917, a deportable offense. Mr. DeMoulin justified his findings on the basis of a ruling never made by the Greek Court, or any other Court.

Later, in this same "opinion", in Section III Proposed Conclusions of Law, under item (3) on page 8, "That under Sections 19 and 20 of the Act of February 5, 1917, the respondent is subject to deportation on the ground that he has been convicted of a felony or other crime or misdemeanor involving moral turpitude prior to entry into the United States, to wit: murder;" none of which was proven, except within the mysterious depths of Mr. DeMoulin's noodle. And what is even more incredible than this is that DeMoulin's position on this issue was sustained all the way to the Board of Immigration Appeals. Nobody in the INS had a problem with this thing. Certainly Judge Harris didn't have a problem with it, and I think if Mamalakis caught on to what was being pulled here, the mechanics of it did not come out in U.S. District Court trial. The INS district hearing examiner Harold DeMello pretty much ratified DeMoulin in a hearing on May 10, 1950 in which DeMello more or less parroted DeMoulin on the California Penal Code Section 192 rationale. Mamalakis objected but only to the use of the term "murder" in conjunction with the charge of conviction of a crime of moral turpitude. Mamalakis tried to assert that the conviction was for manslaughter, not murder, but neither DeMoulin nor DeMello were having any part of it. When DeMello filed his "Opinion" on the case, he generally reached the same findings and conclusions as DeMoulin and even quoted the Section 192 comparison as the basis for concluding the conviction was for "Voluntary Manslaughter". Mamalakis had the opportunity to respond to this "Opinion", which

Mamalakis did on July 14, 1950. Mamalakis did not challenge the Section 192 stretch, and in his "Counter-Proposed Findings of Facts and Conclusions of Law" he made a critical error, in my opinion, by referring to the conviction as "Voluntary Manslaughter" on line 14 of page 13 of the document. Mamalakis made the same error twice in his opening remarks before Judge Harris, later correcting himself, but by then even the judge was using the term voluntary. Now Mamalakis claims in his transmittal letter to the INS San Francisco District office that his conclusions document was "hastily prepared because of the amount of work involved, and because I have been ill the last week." Since DeMello actually quotes Section 192 in his "Opinion", Mamalakis could hardly miss it if he read it. Apparently Mamalakis did not comprehend that DeMoulin, with the approval and concurrence of DeMello, was using Section 192 as the definition of the crime for which Coumas was convicted in Greece. It think it reasonable to conclude that Mamalakis had other cases that were commanding his attention, but he had an opportunity to challenge a critical factor in this deportation case and for whatever reason it got passed him. Certainly Coumas should not have been penalized by that. Adequate evidence exists in documentary form that DeMoulin's rationale was provided on appeal to the Commissioner of the INS and subsequently the Immigration Board of Appeals.

Somebody up the chain of command must have concluded that DeMoulin's shuffle on the Section 192 comparison was legal, or they missed it, which at face value seems unlikely. That could be construed as the appellate officials as having sustained an illegal act by at least two of their own employees at the district office level.

That Coumas was essentially discredited, as a believable witness on his own behalf was a foregone and probably rightful conclusion given all of the deceptions he was openly and widely practicing. But, that should not have negated the evidence that did exist and in particular the evidence that did not exist. Maybe all of the documents that I have been able to find were not available at the time to Stan Mamalakis. I find that a little hard to believe, but I suppose it might be possible. What I did not find is anybody picking up on the burden of proof issue, and that if the government held that burden that they did not prove the essential facts to warrant conclusions of violations of various versions of the Immigration Act. Again, the finding of Mr. Gaudin and the evidence he cited only proved that the Greek Government had a policy, and there was no proof that the policy had been applied to Tom Coumas. There was no evidence of due process having been provided as required by the 14th Amendment of the U.S. Constitution in depriving Coumas of his citizenship. And the most egregious of all was convicting Coumas of a law for which he never was indicted, for which he never stood trial and for which he was never convicted. What is even more amazing than that is that DeMoulin went on the record with this bizarre finding and conclusion without an apparent legal leg to stand on and took the whole department with him. DeMoulin also embraced the "theory" of expatriation in his "findings" but again without conclusive evidence. DeMoulin also found fault that Coumas did not protest his induction into the Greek military and protest that he was required to take an oath of allegiance to Greece, in connection with his service in the Greek Army. He was a lawful citizen of Greece, being required under Greek law to serve a term in the Greek Army. What's to protest? Protesting to the United States government would not have changed his status as a Greek citizen under all known circumstances of this case. DeMoulin concluded that Coumas didn't protest because he didn't want to come to the attention of either U.S. or Greek authorities. Here is another slice of Mr. DeMoulin's "Opinion" of February 23, 1950, under the heading of "Discussion of the Evidence":

> "....the respondent has not asserted that he entered into unwilling military service in Greece without protest because of any feeling that such a protest would be futile. Indeed, such a protest to the American Consul would have defeated the respondent's desire for anonymous asylum by bringing him prominently to the attention of both the Greek and American authorities."

It always amazes me how so much conjecture and supposition finds its way into findings of fact, and thus "evidence". How one could serve in the Greek Army and not come to the attention of at least the Greek authorities is way beyond my ability to comprehend, with all due respect to Mr. DeMoulin. The simple fact that Coumas was inducted would seem to be prima facie evidence that Coumas came to the attention of the Greek authorities, otherwise how would the Greek Government know to induct him? Perhaps Mr. DeMoulin meant that by not protesting his military service Coumas did not want to come to the attention of either the American or the Greek Government as Tom Coumas. In fairness, Coumas military service was under the name of Spyridon Smyrnogiannis not Tom Coumas. So from the record, it would appear that Coumas was operating in Greece in 1932-1933 under the name given to him at birth. Even if true, I still don't find any of this relevant to an act of expatriation, but rather one of deception for which Coumas was a demonstrated master. Acting to deceive U.S. authorities of his true identity is hardly an act demonstrative of Coumas intent to renounce his U.S. citizenship. All of this was rendered moot by the extradition hearing in 1934 in Greece, so going back over that ground after the fact is hardly meaningful on the part of the INS. Unless one was engaged in a straw grasping exercise, which from all appearances seems to be the case here. Please note there is also nothing on the record that suggests that the INS did not seem at all troubled by Coumas using multiple false names beginning with his entry into the United States in 1907 and continuing through his naturalization petition of 1910 and again in 1913, and specifically at the time Coumas submitted his petition, and petition information clarification responses to the INS in Washington, DC., all of which contained factual errors supplied by Coumas.

That efforts to deport Coumas was sort of tilting toward the "foregone conclusion" department on the part of various INS officials, consider this; while still released on the $1,500 bond Coumas applied for a rectifier's license from the California State Board of Equalization in February of 1951. The Board wrote to the INS in San Francisco to seek clarification as to Coumas citizenship status as being "in dispute as a result of a felony conviction and other related matters." Perhaps Coumas was seeking employment involving distilled spirits and thus needed a State license as a condition of employment. The INS District Director in San Francisco replied by letter to the Board on March 8, 1951 under the signature of the district Chief of the Detention, Deportation and Parole Section. The second paragraph of which I find interesting:

> "Our file, relating to Mr. Coumas reveals that he is an alien citizen of Greece. Deportation Proceedings are now pending against him and Record of Hearing, accorded him under Warrant issued for his arrest, is now before our Central Office in Washington for decision as to his deportability. The evidence contained in the file reveals that Mr. Coumas at one time did have the status of a citizen of the United States. However, it appears that he divested himself of such citizenship by activities in which he engaged during a rather lengthy residence in Greece. The definite adjudication as to his

citizenship will be rendered by our Central Office and when the decision is received we will be glad to communicate with you further on the subject."

Wow, is that letter just crawling with "read between the lines" stuff. The entire matter had been under appeal once San Francisco issued their rulings. It "appears" that he divested himself of such citizenship? Here I thought all along that was a foregone conclusion.

Of perhaps some interest is that the INS in Washington on February 5, 1949 notified the Circuit Court in Multnomah County, Oregon that Coumas had expatriated himself by taking the oath in Greece in 1932. This is interesting because the SF INS office had not yet completed its review of Coumas' immigration status and was in the process of conducting a deportation hearing. It would appear that Washington was acting solely on the basis of the Gaudin report and still no record of any hearing having been conducted with Coumas participation or with his knowledge. Why the rush all of a sudden two years after the Gaudin report? Makes you wonder why Mamalakis didn't subpoena anybody from the federal government in the District Court trial. DeMoulin certainly would have been a likely candidate to be made to appear and show cause, and most certainly whichever federal official had a hand in jerking Coumas citizenship without apparent due process. The Commissioner of the INS sustained the INS District Office findings and deportation order of Coumas on June 11, 1951. Mamalakis appealed that finding to the Board of Immigration Appeals on June 20, 1951. The Board of Immigration Appeals sustained the INS on January 8, 1952. Mamalakis did not appear on Coumas' behalf on either appeal, which I find rather odd. Unless Mamalakis sensed an irrefutable climate of bias against his client and the outcome of the appeals process preordained. Meanwhile, the INS went merrily on its way with activities in preparation of carrying out their sustained deportation order. Except that Mamalakis filed suit in the U.S. District Court on March 20, 1952. That should have stopped everything regarding the deportation of Coumas, yet I have a copy of a letter from the Royal Consulate General of Greece in San Francisco to the INS in San Francisco conveying notice (in response to the INS district notification of Coumas' immigration status) that the Consulate will issue a Greek passport for Coumas to be used by the INS for his return to Greece. The Vice-Consul notes that the passport will be issued in the name of Spyridon Smyrnoyannis because that is the name Coumas is "registered" under in Greece. Never mind that Coumas legal name is Tom Coumas. This letter is dated May 26, 1952, during the period in which the District Court lawsuit had already been filed. Also never mind that the military recruiting office in Greece thinks Coumas is Spyridon Smyrnogiannis.

Another odd thing occurred in February 1952, a month prior to Coumas suing in District Court to stop his deportation. Coumas must have expressed an interest in being deported to Canada because a fellow by the name of Arthur MacGregor, an attaché at the U.S. Embassy in Ottawa, Ontario sent a form letter of inquiry to the Canadian immigration authorities also in Ottawa to determine if the Canadians were receptive to receiving Coumas in their country. The inquiry was a little loaded in that Coumas is indicated as being a "criminal" on the form. Apparently a previous informal oral conversation on the subject between the parties resulted in requesting a subsequent formal decision in the matter. Unfortunately I don't have any notes as to what was said in that conversation, but as one would probably conclude Canada declined. It just appears from all of these various events on the public record that nobody in the federal government was working very hard on accommodating Tom Coumas, with the possible exception of sending him back to Greece with all possible speed. I think it also reasonable to conclude from the record that returning to Greece is certainly not what Coumas had in mind.

As you have already learned here, Coumas sued the federal government, appealed the ruling of the U.S. District Court against him, and lost that appeal. It was apparently decided to take the matter no further following the 9th Circuit Court of Appeals ruling on May 9, 1956. Coumas got sand bagged as the great federal machine just ran right over him. Too bad that this thing did not make it to the U.S. Supreme Court. I think had it been properly presented and argued, this would have made a great Constitutional case on due process.

As for other "loose" ends in this story, Coumas was delivered to the SF INS authorities on June 3, 1948 following the May 27, 1948 ruling of the California Supreme Court. The INS SF District Director was the official who increased the 1947 arrest warrant bond on May 6, 1948 from $500 to $3,000. The justification for this was that the $500 bond was deemed insufficient to guarantee Coumas appearance. Coumas was released from INS custody on July 8, 1948 after posting a reduced bond of $1,500. So Coumas spent an additional 30 days in detention on top of his September 1947 arrest and jailing in San Joaquin County. That would add up to nine months of incarceration on bogus charges. Perhaps a small additional restitution for the multiple charges Guard Darrah didn't bring against Coumas in 1934.

Speaking of Darrah, he made reference to a child named Mary as having been seen with Coumas in the taking of the deposition of William Pappas in 1934 (see Chapter Fourteen). Since the daughter of Gregoria Yaitros Coumas is the only Mary to have surfaced in any document

I have reviewed thus far, it might be reasonable to conclude that Darrah was referring to the child Mary born in Greece. Of course I have seen no evidence that this child was in California in 1932, most probably because she was not as yet born. For the record, I have seen at least one other document with a different last name for Gregoria, but there are so many sources of names in this story that contradict one another even the authorities cannot seem to manage to keep them all straight. I'm certain that you spotted the reference to a daughter named Mary in the Gaudin report. I think it reasonable to conclude that Gaudin learned all of this information based on the "papers" Coumas claimed the U.S. Embassy at Athens requested he provide to them in 1946. I think that raises certain suspicions that Coumas must have applied for something at that Embassy.

Further evidence that Coumas' claimed visitations to the Embassy was coming to somebody's external attention is a letter authored by the Commissioner of the INS in Washington, DC to the U.S. Secretary of State on November 7, 1945, and quoting a letter from the director of the Federal Bureau of Investigation regarding Coumas. What was in the FBI letter is not referenced and I don't have a copy of it, but the Commissioner is advising State of Coumas naturalization in Oregon in 1914, and of the fact that the INS has no record of Coumas having lost his U.S. citizenship. You more or less can conclude from this letter that the INS is asking State to verify whether Coumas has lost his American citizenship. The last sentence of the INS letter reads, "The record of this office contains no information indicating loss of Unites States citizenship by the subject." So, if any action was taken to strip Coumas of his U.S. citizenship prior to November 1945, the INS was not aware of it. During the period in which all of these events take place, the INS and the State Department had dual responsibilities over immigration matters but apparently did not communicate all that well with each other. People who are not familiar with how government entities operate should understand that while there is a lot of information gathering going on, seldom is that information freely shared with others. The reason for that is fear that by communicating something to another government entity somebody might discover an act or omission that might cause one or several people embarrassment. I have seen divisions, branches and sections within departments who only speak to each other when absolutely necessary and then generally on the subject of the next office potluck. Local government's operate on the same basis, with each department an island unto itself and fiercely defended from all "outsiders". It is not unusual to have parallel resources tied up in pursuit of some activity completely independent and without the knowledge of the other. Certainly not the most effective way to run the government but essentially that is pretty much how it works. At any rate, because I did not get a copy of the FBI report referenced in the Commissioners letter I really have no idea what it said. Suffice it to say, I do not believe inquiries would have been made regarding Coumas if he wasn't making contact with anybody and not trying to get permission to return to the United States. This letter is a red flag and possibly corroborating evidence that Coumas was attempting to repatriate himself through the U.S. Embassy at Athens. I have no doubt that it is highly likely that San Joaquin County had alerted the FBI that it had an outstanding arrest warrant for Coumas and wanted to be notified if he ever attempted to return to the Unites States.

Here is yet another example of just how goofy this whole business was, and that comes in the form of an INS certification form dated December 10, 1947 of Coumas naturalization record. There is no notation on this form that his naturalization had been cancelled or in any manner invalidated. It would therefore appear that the INS believed that Coumas was a naturalized citizen of the United States as of December 10, 1947. How then, could he be charged with being an alien for entering the U.S. at Norfolk, Virginia on August 16, 1947, three months before his status as a naturalized citizen was verified? As far as the INS was concerned, it would appear that their own official records contradict the justification for having issued a warrant for his arrest on February 28, 1948 in that those records considered him a naturalized citizen at the time the INS claimed he entered the country illegally as an alien. In other words, should Coumas have been considered a U.S. citizen until such time as the State Department properly notified the INS to the contrary, and the INS record could be corrected? Keep in mind that the INS did not even notify Multonomah County to correct their records regarding Coumas citizenship status until February 1949, fourteen months after the same INS previously considered the record valid. This might very well be a minor point, but it certainly appears to confirm the apparent confusion that was going on within the INS over Coumas nationality circumstances. Mamalakis apparently did not pick up on this since he didn't voice a challenge on it, or take issue with it, at least not in any record I have read. Perhaps Mamalakis did not have all of these documents at his disposal, but the fact that he did not pursue the obvious denial of due process to Coumas over being stripped of his U.S. citizenship by the State Department seems a major disservice to Coumas.

Included in the materials I did receive from the Citizenship and Immigration Services office was the transcript of the arraignment of Coumas before the Superior Court in San Joaquin County on October 22nd and 29th of 1947. That would have been before Judge Woodward. This apparently was not a hearing by the Judge on the sufficiency of the evidence against Coumas.

The charges were read, the matter was continued for one week, a week later the Judge heard the plea on the charges, and bound Coumas over for trial. Oddly, the charge of attempted murder of Duval was included, so the statute of limitations apparently did not apply to that charge. I have been happily motoring through life under the obvious misguided understanding that the only crime for which there is no statute of limitations is murder. Murder being a circumstance where somebody is actually dead at the hand of another, with malice aforethought. Mamalakis certainly did not raise that issue at either hearing. No testimony was given and no presentations were made before the Court.

Another situation that has given me great trouble throughout this story is the lack of information regarding the murder weapon. Generally speaking, this is considered by most people in law enforcement as a critical piece of evidence, particularly when the weapon can be tied to the accused. I have a copy of the wanted circular issued by San Joaquin County Sheriff Harvey Odell on May 6, 1932. In that circular, Sheriff Odell notes, "May be armed with a .32 caliber Colt's automatic revolver...." I think it is reasonable to conclude that at least there was some theory over the make and caliber of Coumas gun on the part of the San Joaquin County authorities. Now I suppose, as much as I have made light of it here, that one could have a revolver that was considered "automatic" if it were of the double action variety that advanced the cartridge cylinder one position with each pull of the trigger. The only other type of pistol with which I am familiar is one that uses an inserted magazine which holds the bullets used in the firearm. In my opinion, such a firearm would not likely be a revolver since nothing in its mechanism revolves. That the firearm was an automatic revolver unfortunately would not square with the testimony of either William or Rosiann Duval, and would require assumption that the weapon was fully loaded prior to Coumas' entry into Olive Taylor's classroom. Also unfortunately the matter will remain a mystery as to why it was not addressed in deposition testimony by the Bureau of Identification of the San Joaquin County Sheriff's Office.

Under the heading of activities that don't appear to be coordinated, San Joaquin County Sheriff's deputy Rudy Weber wrote to the Multnomah County Circuit Court in Portland, Oregon in March 1934 asking for immigration information on Tom Coumas. The Circuit Court forwarded Weber's letter to the INS in Washington, DC. During May 1934, Ellis Parker wrote a letter to the INS in Washington, DC from his office in Mt. Holly, New Jersey essentially asking for the same information as Weber's letter to the Circuit Court. The point being, the Parker letter made no reference to the Circuit Court in Oregon as being where Coumas was naturalized. Weber obviously had this information in March, but apparently Parker did not know that in May. Sort of makes one wonder who was coordinating all of this. Guard Darrah sent a letter to the INS in Washington, DC during May 1934 asking if the Greek Government had ever been notified to strike Tom Coumas from its list of names of Greek citizens due to his naturalization as an American citizen. In June 1934, the INS responds to Darrah that the file on Coumas does not reflect that the Greek Government was so notified by the INS. Makes one wonder where Darrah came up with that, and was he trying to find a workaround against the treaty between the U.S. and Greece. Why wasn't Darrah coordinating his information requests through the INS San Francisco District office?

From a letter dated October 10, 1938 I have learned that the San Joaquin County Welfare Department was providing state aid for Coumas' son, John. The nature of this aid or for what purpose is not stated in the letter, only that the aid was being provided because Tom Coumas was incarcerated in Greece. The letter, addressed to the INS in Washington, DC wanted to know if Coumas was still incarcerated in Greece and if so, when he might be released from prison there. There was also an INS field office in Stockton, California also home city of the County Welfare Department. The usual protocol in these matters is to start with the local representative and have them work the organization chart upward as necessary. That keeps everybody advised and you avoid a lot of delays and turf issues that way. Public officials tend to jump the chain of command with great regularity, much to the frustration of those within it, all of which generally creates otherwise avoidable delays in getting information where it needs to be in a timely manner.

When I have made mention here of the Coumas deportation hearing conducted by the INS San Francisco District Office I am referring to a series of hearings convened, then adjourned, then subsequently reconvened over a period of months by that office. There were several hearings over which Mr. DeMoulin presided and one hearing in which Mr. DeMello presided. The purpose of these many adjournments seemed to have been driven by the clock on the wall and the need to pause to gather more evidence. Any quotations that I have included here are from the transcripts of these various hearings, and have included on the basis of their importance and relevance to the story. There was a lot of repetition of ground plowed many times over in those transcripts. Coumas was asked the same questions repeatedly, while Mr. DeMoulin justified this as intended to give Coumas an opportunity to correct his previous testimony. What I think is that DeMoulin was on a fishing expedition trying to find a legal justification for deporting Coumas from the United States. He didn't find it, so he made one up.

On June 28, 1955, Tom Coumas traveling under a variety of aliases was placed aboard United Airlines flight 514 at San Francisco to New York via Chicago. It was requested that Coumas flight be met in Chicago and New York and that he be escorted to the S.S. Gregorios C III, which sailed from New York on July 12, 1955. I have no documentation that certifies that Tom Coumas actually arrived in Greece or if he remained there. At least one thing is certain: it took two months shy of eight years to toss him out of the United States.

I can tell you that somebody claiming to be Tom Coumas, and indicating a residence in Santa Paraskeue, Attikes, Greece sent during June 1956 a request to the San Francisco District Office of the INS for permission to apply for readmission into the United States. The purpose of the request noted that the requester did not intend to violate any laws, that is was very difficult to make a living in Greece, that the requester could not withstand the climate, that it is detrimental to the requester's health, and that the requester would like to be near his three children. A memo dated June 22, 1956 from the Regional Examinations Chief for the INS Southwest Region to the District Director of the San Francisco INS office has this line in it, "A careful review of subject's file indicates that he is not one to be favorably considered under recent instructions." What recent instructions? On June 20, 1956, the District Director (SF) sent a memo to the INS Regional Commissioner for the Southwest Region indicating that the "record establishes that the applicant is excludable from the United States under Section [unreadable on my copy] (a) (9) of the Immigration and Nationality Act as an alien who committed a crime involving moral turpitude to wit: murder." Note the change from the term "convicted of" to "committed". That memo goes on to state, "Denial in this case will result in separating him from his three U.S. citizen children, however all his children are all over 29 years of age who live in various parts of the country." I'll leave it to you to absorb the ramifications of that particular statement. So it would appear that not only was this unfounded moral turpitude business handy for tossing Coumas out of the country, it served equally as well to deny him entry back into the county. On June 27, 1956, Bruce G. Barber, District Director of the SF INS office responded that Coumas request was denied because he was an alien convicted of a crime involving moral turpitude, to wit: murder. Although this notice gave Coumas the option to appeal the decision to the INS Regional Commissioner, I have nothing in the records that shows that he ever appealed this decision.

It wasn't until August 2, 1955 that George Laurentzos was able to recover the $1,500 bond he posted on behalf of Tom Coumas in 1948.

This story came about because of an 8-year old child with a foul mouth in a school classroom in Manteca, California in 1932 ended up taking the life of his teacher at the hands of his father and seriously wounding the school janitor. After reading close to a couple of thousand pages of documents in this case, I have not reviewed one single item of evidence placing Tom Coumas finger on the trigger of his own gun. I have read evidence of a struggle between Tom Coumas and William Duval following a physical assault by William Duval upon Tom Coumas. During that struggle was when the gun Coumas had in his pocket when he entered that classroom discharged multiple times resulting in the death of Olive Taylor, a post-mortem wound to the calve of her left leg, and a gunshot wound to the face of William Duval. At least five shots were fired according to witnesses. There is evidence that the gun remained in Coumas pocket until Mr. Duval physically assaulted him. So, who fired the gun? That Tom Coumas was involved in an act of negligent homicide is pretty much a proven fact, based on the evidence that exists in this case. Yes, Tom Coumas was brought to justice based on the known evidence in the case, and paid for his crimes under Greek Law. In a unanimous decision, the California Supreme Court found that the Greek Court was competent and that under the laws of double jeopardy, Coumas could not be tried again under the 1934 San Joaquin County Grand Jury Indictment. Then the United States Government turned Tom Coumas into a victim by depriving him of his rights as a U.S. citizen and wrongfully convicted him of a crime for which he had never been previously convicted. Many of the theories advanced by the U.S. Government fell to the California Supreme Court courtroom floor with a dull thud. Well, perhaps with the exception of Judge Harris' Court. Coumas was accused of conduct that were not crimes for which he had ever been charged, such as flight to avoid prosecution, and bigamy. The U.S. Government took the position that the burden of proof fell to the accused, not the government. Theories were floated as fact without corroborative evidence. I find such conduct particularly troubling in a nation that prides itself on being a nation of laws. Well of course we are a nation of laws, it's just that way too many of our public officials all too often tend to selectively ignore them. Much has been made here over the oath of a soldier allegedly taken by Tom Coumas in Greece in 1932, and the oath of allegiance taken by an alien who becomes naturalized as a citizen of the United States. What has not been emphasized in all of this is that the U.S. Constitution in Article VI Section 3 mandates that all executive and judicial officers be bound by oath to support the Constitution. This requirement has been extended by federal law to include just about everybody who is employed by the federal government. Support means to uphold all of its provisions, not just the parts you like and ignore those that you don't like. Different offices require different oaths, but they are all generally consistent when it comes to the Constitutional support mandate.

The California State Constitution in Article 20 Section 3 requires an oath that encompasses support for both the California and the U.S. Constitution, and applies to just about every employee of every political subdivision of the State with exceptions only for those that are exempted. That stated nothing in either Constitution represents actual evidence that an oath of office was actually taken by those required to do so. That is why many government agencies also require the oath taker to sign a statement to certify that they have taken the required oath freely and without reservation or with purpose of evasion. How does all of this apply to Tom Coumas? Well, all of the laws for which a legion of public officials are attempting to hold Tom Coumas accountable are accountable themselves for upholding all of the laws, even the ones that protect Tom Coumas.

I have no doubt that the San Joaquin County authorities were greatly disappointed that they were not permitted to hold trial of Tom Coumas on the acts he was alleged to have committed in their county in 1932. I would also imagine that it gave them great disgust to have to let Tom Coumas walk out of their jail in May of 1948 a free man. But it was the law. The very law that they had taken an oath of their own to uphold. Tom Coumas had every legal right to return to Manteca in 1947. The fact that he did was just downright stupid on his part. Certainly Coumas could not realistically expect a lot of sympathy from most that his conviction in Greece constituted justice in the minds of the people of San Joaquin County, and most assuredly the surviving family members of Olive Taylor. Human beings are just not built that way, no matter what our laws provide. I wonder if Tom Coumas ever came to realize that. Still, it does not justify taking the law into one's own hands. Robert S. DeMoulin declared to Tom Coumas in a deportation hearing that Coumas had not paid for the crimes he committed in California in 1932. It would seem that Mr. DeMoulin and the Department of Justice of that era found a way to correct that.

It also seems fairly clear from the record that Mr. DeMoulin was well acquainted with the California Penal Code, and his superiors supported him in his findings in that regard. I wonder if Mr. DeMoulin or anybody else in the Department of Justice who had their fingerprints on this deal was familiar with Section 134 of the California Penal Code. It reads,

> "Every person guilty of preparing any false or antedated book, paper, record, instrument in writing, or other matter or thing with the intent to produce it, or allow it to be produced for any fraudulent or deceitful purpose, as genuine or true, upon any trial, proceeding, or inquiry whatever, authorized by law, is guilty of a felony."

The San Francisco Chronicle – Thursday – April 21, 1932

FATHER KILLS TEACHER IN CLASSROOM

Spanking Row Brings Parent with Pistol: Janitor Shot Battling Slayer

Terrified Children See Woman Murdered in Manteca

Special to The Chronicle

MANTECA, April 20-In a classroom crowded with little boys and girls, Tom R. Coumas, 39, today shot and killed Mrs. Olive B. Taylor of Stockton, the teacher, shot and probably fatally wounded W. J. Duval, janitor at the school, and shot at and missed Mrs. Duval, the Janitor's wife.

The shooting took place at the Castle School, five miles east of Manteca on the Stockton highway. It climaxed two years of quarreling between Coumas and Mrs. Taylor, the father accusing the teacher of "being unfair" to his two children, pupils at the school.

ESCAPES IN AUTO

After the shooting Coumas escaped in his automobile, and was the object of a State-wide search directed by Sheriff Odell of San Joaquin county and every available deputy.

Later tonight Stockton police were informed Coumas had been cornered in a house in Manteca. A police shotgun squad sped here to aid in attempts to capture him.

Coumas wife is an inmate of the Stockton State Hospital for the Insane. A son, Chester, is in the Ione State Reformatory. Mrs. Cora Hickman has been keeping house for Coumas since he moved back to his ranch after several months spent in Stockton.

Mrs. Hickman came to the school early this morning and engaged in a quarrel with Mrs. Taylor.

ACCUSED OF SPANKING

She accused Mrs. Taylor of spanking Helen Coumas, 12, on the hand and demanded that the children be permitted to transfer to another school. Mrs. Taylor granted the request and made out a transfer for Helen and John, 8.

This afternoon the father appeared at the school and began to upbraid Mrs. Taylor for striking the child on the hand. The other pupils told authorities he became obscene and abusive and moved threateningly toward the teacher.

Mrs. Taylor stepped back, and suddenly Coumas whipped out an automatic pistol.

Holding the weapon only a few inches from Mrs. Taylor's breast, he pulled the trigger twice. Both bullets pierced her heart. Then, as she lay on the floor, he leaned over her and crashed another bullet through her brain.

The screams of the children in the classroom attracted Duval, who attempted to grapple with the killer. But Coumas was too quick for the janitor, and shot twice, one bullet going through Duval's mouth and the second, through his shoulder.

FIRST SHOT MISSES

Mrs. Duval then attempted to save her husband, and Coumas turned the gun on her. As the first shot whistled past her face she fell to the floor and the killer evidently believed he had hit her. One of the children attempted to run from the classroom and Coumas fired a shot in his direction, but missed.

Then, his pistol empty, Coumas ran from the classroom where the children huddled screaming under desks and behind the teacher's rostrum, and leaped into his automobile. He drove to his home a quarter of a mile away and bundled Mrs. Hickman and his two children into the machine.

BOY TELLS OF KILLING

One of the older boys of the school ran to the ranch home of Arlo Gustafson nearby and told him what had happened. Gustafson telephone Sheriff Odell immediately and deputies were sent out to investigate.

Coumas had meanwhile driven to the Pappas ranch, near Manteca, where he left Mrs. Hickman and Helen Coumas. He drove into Manteca and left his son, John, at the home of a friend, Peter Kaloutsis.

Then, alone in his automobile with the pistol and a loaded shotgun, he drove away toward the south. Sheriff Odell warned his men to expect a desperate battle if they should encounter and attempt to arrest Coumas.

HUSBAND IN STOCKTON

Mrs. Taylor is the wife of Ethan A. Taylor, 1144 West Walnut street, Stockton, owner of a gasoline service station in Stockton. She has been a teacher at the Castle School for eight years, before that having taught in Sonoma county. A daughter, Mrs. Mildred Cohen, is a teacher in Pleasanton.

Coumas, according to the descriptions given the Sheriff, is 5 feet 7 inches tall, weighs 167 pounds, has dark brown hair and brown eyes, is dark-skinned. He was driving a green Essex sedan with license number 9C-6704.

Mrs. D. O. Castle, secretary of the Board of Trustees of the Castle School, said Mrs. Taylor was highly regarded by all of the parents of the district except Coumas. Two years ago when Coumas put his children in the school there had been words between Coumas and Mrs. Taylor, and the teacher complained the Coumas children were unruly and caused frequent disturbances in the classroom.

Copyright 1932 – The San Francisco Chronicle

Here is a listing of all of the names of the various people associated in some way or other with this story. They appear in no particular order:

THE LAWYERS

Guard C. Darrah – District Attorney San Joaquin County
Chester E. Watson – District Attorney San Joaquin County
Harry C. Stanley – Assistant District Attorney San Joaquin County
Bradford M. Crittenden – Assistant District Attorney San Joaquin County
Frederick L. Felson – San Joaquin County Counsel
Fred N. Howser – California State Attorney General
Clarence A. Linn – California Deputy State Attorney General
Herbert Brownell, Jr. – Attorney General of the United States
James P. McGranery – Attorney General of the United States
J. Howard McGrath – Attorney General of the United States
Watson B. Miller – Commissioner of U.S. Immigration and Naturalization
Lloyd H. Burke – United States Attorney
Chauncey Tramutolo – United States Attorney
Charles E. Collett – Assistant United States Attorney
Edgar R. Bonsall – Assistant United States Attorney
Anthony J. Chargin – San Joaquin County Public Defender for Tom Coumas
Stanley P. Mamalakis – for the Consul General of Greece – San Francisco – Counsel for Tom Coumas
Andrew J. Eyman – Counsel for Tom Coumas
Bernard B. Glickfeld – Counsel for Tom Coumas
I.A. Lougaris – Counsel for Tom Coumas (Nevada)
Kendrick Johnson – Counsel for Margaret Coumas (Nevada)

THE VICTIMS

Mrs. Olive Luella Taylor – Teacher – Castle School – Manteca, California
Mr. William J. Duval – Janitor – Castle School – Manteca, California
Mrs. Rosiann Duval – Wife of William J. Duval – Manteca, California
Mr. Joe Coniglio – Rancher – Manteca, California
Mr. Steve Souza – Dairy Farmer – Manteca, California
Miss Dorothy Helen Coumas – Child of Tom Coumas – Manteca, California
Master John R. Coumas – Child of Tom Coumas – Manteca, California

Master Peter Coumas – Child of Tom Coumas – Manteca, California
Mrs. Margaret M. Coumas – Wife of Tom Coumas – Stockton, California
Mr. Tom Coumas – Husband of Margaret Coumas – Manteca, California

CRIMINAL CONDUCT BY TOM COUMAS

Murder of Olive Taylor
Abuse of a corpse of Olive Taylor
Attempted Murder of William Duval and Assault with a deadly weapon
Assault with a deadly weapon on Rosiann Duval
Assault with a deadly weapon on Helen Coumas
Kidnapping of Joe Coniglio and Steve Souza
Assault with a deadly weapon on Joe Coniglio and Steve Souza
Child abandonment of Helen, John and Peter Coumas and perhaps one other Coumas child, Cornelius Coumas
Adultery with Clara Hickman
Bigamy with Gregoria Yaitros
Abandonment of Margaret Coumas
Possible Kidnapping of unidentified victim

CRIMES COMMITTED BY OTHERS

Battery by William Duval on Tom Coumas

CRIMES PROVEN

Involuntary manslaughter of Olive Taylor (Greece)
Use of a forbidden firearm on Olive Taylor (Greece)

CRIMES ALLEGED BUT NOT PROVEN

Invalid Immigration Visa 1947 against the U.S. Government (United States)
Conviction of a crime involving moral turpitude, murder (United States)

CRIMES FOR WHICH AQUITTED (GREECE)

Murder of Olive Taylor with malice (California)
Attempted Murder of William Duval (California)
Assault With Deadly Weapon on Rosiann Duval (California)

SAN JOAQUIN COUNTY OFFICIALS

Hon. Daniel M. Young – Superior Court Judge
Hon. Marion G. Woodward – Superior Court Judge
Hon. Raymond M. Dunne – Superior Court Judge
Charles C. DeYoung – County Coroner
Dr. William P.J. Lynch, MD – County Medical Examiner
F. A. Dougherty – Foreman of the Grand Jury 1932
Henry F. Ellis – Foreman of the Grand Jury 1934
Eugene D. Graham – Clerk of the Superior Court
Hugo P. Braasch – Deputy Clerk of the Superior Court
Thomas U. Stroup – Deputy Clerk of the Superior Court
R.E. Graham – Chief Deputy Clerk of the Superior Court
Bea Scantlebury – Acting Clerk of the Superior Court
Herman G. Spalinger – Court Reporter 1934
Adaline Galgiani – Court Reporter 1947
Edwin S. Parker – Shorthand Reporter
Crawford Hitchcock – Chief of Police Manteca Police Department 1932
Tom Brockman – Chief of Police Manteca Police Department 1947
Harvey M. O'Dell – County Sheriff 1932
Crawford Hitchcock – County Sheriff 1947
Ernest G. Hill – Deputy Sheriff
Louis Totman – Deputy Sheriff
Martin Ansbro –Deputy Sheriff
Crawford Hitchcock – Deputy Sheriff 1934
Amos Ford – Deputy Sheriff
Jack Cassidy – Deputy Sheriff
Ivan E. Hitt – Deputy Sheriff Investigator
Rudolph Weber – Deputy Sheriff Investigator
John R. Williams – Superintendent of Schools
Mrs. Mary B. Castle – Secretary, Castle School Board of Trustees

THE WITNESSES

Miss Frances Fisher – Student at the Castle School
Miss Mary Kondratenko – Student at the Castle School
Miss Frances Aguilar – Student at the Castle School
Miss Athena Bouzeneris – Student at the Castle School
Mr. Wilbur S. Worcester – Insurance Salesman Stockton, California
Mr. William Pappas – Acquaintance of Tom Coumas – Manteca, California

Mrs. Aristea Kaloutsis – Acquaintance of Tom Coumas – Manteca, California
Mr. John Soukos – Acquaintance of Tom Coumas – Manteca, California
Mr. Christ Morogiannis – Acquaintance of Tom Coumas – Manteca, California
Mr. George J. Lourentzos – Acquaintance of Tom Coumas – Manteca, California
Mr. Arlo D. Gustafson – Rancher – Manteca, California
Mr. Sam Jakson – Acquaintance of Tom Coumas – Portland, Oregon

THE TAYLOR FAMILY

Mr. Ethan Allen Taylor – Husband of Olive Taylor
Mrs. Mildred L. Taylor Cohn – Daughter of Olive Taylor
Mr. Sam Cohn – Son-in-law of Olive Taylor
Mrs. Nancy Maria Hite Bailey – Mother of Olive Taylor
Mr. Floyd P. Bailey – Brother of Olive Taylor
Mr. Terry E. Bailey – Brother of Olive Taylor
Mr. Charles M. Bailey – Brother of Olive Taylor
Mrs. Annie Searson – Sister of Olive Taylor
Mrs. Josephine E. Manhart – Sister of Olive Taylor
Mr. George W. Bailey – Brother of Olive Taylor
Mr. Matthew A. Bailey – Brother of Olive Taylor

OTHER RELATIVES OF TOM COUMAS

Mr. John Smyrnos – A cousin – San Mateo, California
Mr. Sam Stavros – A cousin – Southern California
Mrs. George Paulos – A sister – Southern California

OTHER CALIFORNIA OFFICIALS

Hon. James Rolph, Jr. Governor of California 1932
Hon. Frank F. Merriam Governor of California 1934
Andy Bickerton – Night Policeman - Mill Valley Police Department
Alexander Silveria – Fireman – Mill Valley Fire Department
Alex McCurdy – Chief of Police – Mill Valley, California
Walter B. Sellmer – Sheriff – Marin County, California

CALIFORNIA SUPREME COURT

Hon. Phil S. Gibson – Chief Justice
Hon. Homer R. Spence – Associate Justice
Hon. John W. Shenk – Associate Justice
Hon. Douglas L. Edwards – Associate Justice
Hon. Jesse W. Carter – Associate Justice
Hon. Roger J. Traynor – Associate Justice
Hon. Benjamin R. Schauer – Associate Justice

OTHER FEDERAL OFFICIALS

Hon. Franklin D. Roosevelt – President of the Unites States
Hon. Cordell Hull – U.S. Secretary of State
Hon. Lincoln MacVeagh – U.S. Ambassador to Greece
Mr. Daniel Gaudin – Consul – U.S. Embassy at Athens, Greece
Mr. Arthur H. MacGregor – Attaché – U.S. Embassy at Ottawa, Ontario
W. F. Kelly – Assistant Commissioner INS – Washington, DC
R. B. Shipley – U.S. Department of State – Washington, DC
Hon. William Denman – Chief Judge – U.S. Court of Appeals 9th Circuit
Hon. William E. Orr – Circuit Judge – U.S. Court of Appeals 9th Circuit
Hon. James M. Carter – District Judge – U.S. Court of Appeals 9th Circuit
Hon. George B. Harris – District Judge – U.S. District Court Northern District of California

U.S. DEPARTMENT OF JUSTICE IMMIGRATION AND NATURALIZATION SERVICE – SAN FRANCISCO

Bruce G. Barber – District Director
Stan Olsen – Chief, Expulsion Section
Edward D. Ahrens – Chief, Examinations
Robert S. DeMoulin – Presiding Inspector
Harold D. DeMello – Hearing Examiner
Walter T. Peyton – Officer In Charge (Stockton Office)
Mark D. Conroy - Inspector
Leigh DePellegrinni – Stenographer
Carolyn Jay – Stenographer
Fern T. James – Stenographer

J. Edward Kloske

Kay Artinyan – Stenographer

CONSULTANTS

Mr. Ellis H. Parker – Chief of Detectives – Burlington County Police – Mt. Holly, New Jersey
Ambassador Edward Capps – Professor of the Greek – Princeton University

OTHER FRIENDS OF TOM COUMAS

Sam Jaskon - Oregon

FOR THE GOVERNMENT OF GREECE

Dimitri Sophianos – Consul General – Consulate General of Greece – San Francisco
Mr. George Poulis – Assistant Director of Tripolis Prison
AtH. Georgiou – Corinth Assize Court – Judge
N. Carcadsi – Corinth Assize Court – Judge
P. Profanti – Attorney General – Court of Common Pleas
Crimon Troupi – Secretary of Corinth Assize Court
J. Calliris – Chief of the Jury
P. Toumbas – Assistant Secretary of the Court of Appeals
Const. Petrides – Counsel for Tom Coumas
Const. Papathanasiou – Counsel for Tom Coumas
D. Moravalis – Investigating Magistrate of the Second Department
Arg. Kotoulas – Acting President – Council of the Court of Appeals
Andr. Papatheodoropoulous – Assistant State Attorney – Court of Appeals

TRANSLATIONS OF GREEK DOCUMENTS TO ENGLISH

Greek Ministry of Foreign Affairs
U.S. Embassy – Athens, Greece

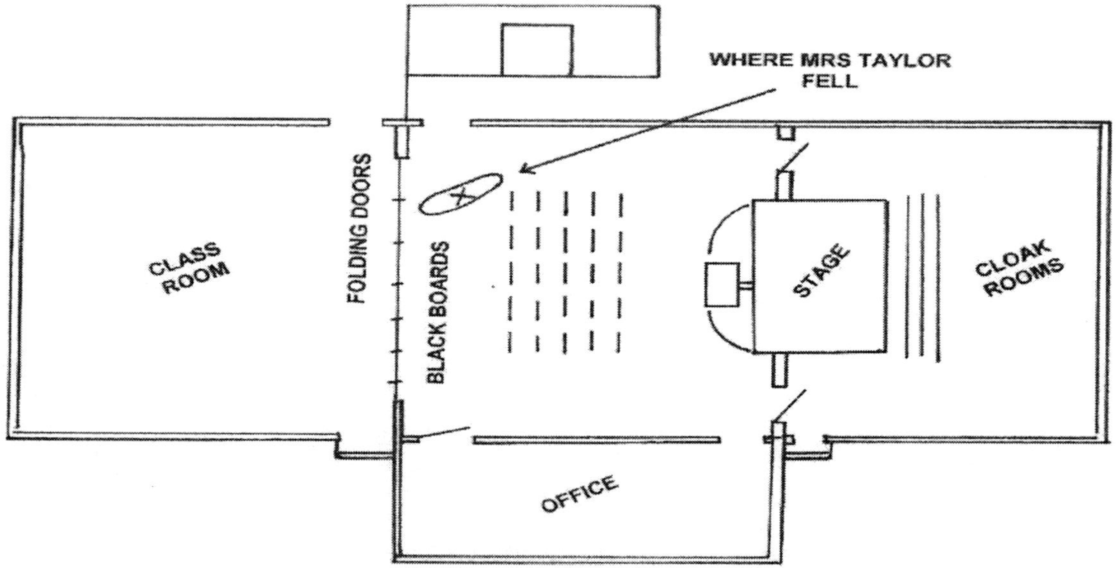

CASTLE SCHOOL – SAN JOAQUIN COUNTY

Recreated by the author from a drawing that originally appeared in the Stockton Record newspaper - April 21, 1932 - Source otherwise unknown

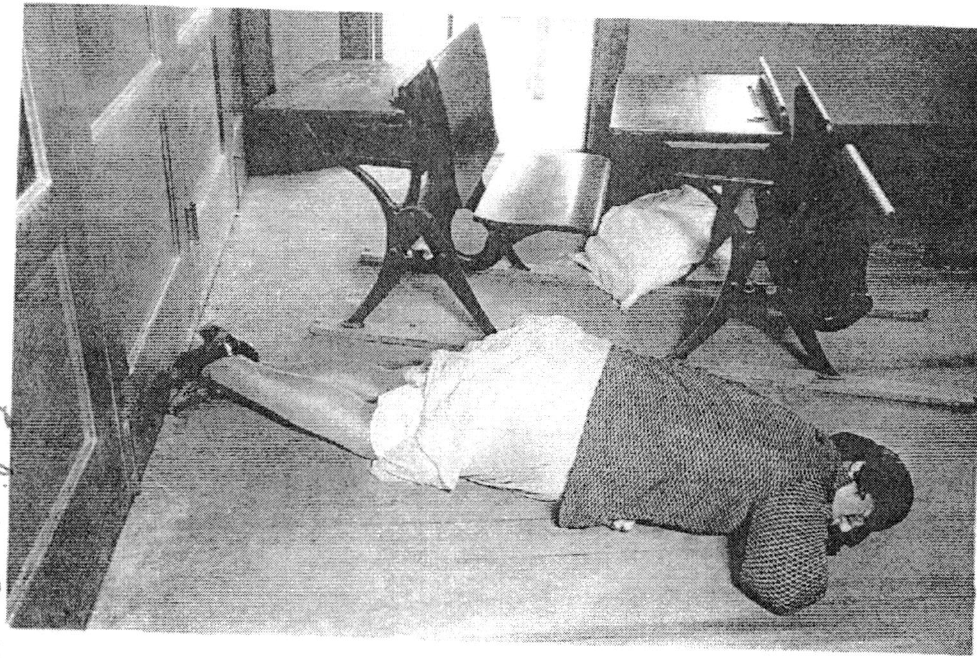

Exhibit No. 10

Olive Taylor on the floor of her classroom where she fell after having been struck by a bullet from the gun of Tom Coumas - Ivan Hitt Photograph 1932

Bloodstained cloth and stains on the floor of the Castle School in the vicinity of struggle between Tom Coumas and William Duval - Ivan Hitt Photograph 1932

CORONER'S RECORD

7696

No. for month 30 No. for cases of term 474

Name in full OLIVE LUELLA TAYLOR

City near Manteca Sex female Race white

Age 50 Single Married Widow married Place of death Castle School Occupation Teacher

Date of Death April 20th, 1932 Date of ~~Inquest~~ Invest. 4/20/32

Length of residence at place of death Many years In California Life

Birth place California Informant Ethan A. Taylor

Name of Relatives Mr. Ethan A. Taylor, Husband, 1144 W. Wallnut St., Stockton.

Disposition of Remains B. C. Wallace, Park View Cemetery, 4/22/32

Detail of Accident aid description of remains Deceased was shot and instantly killed by a revolver in the hands of Tom R. Coumas, Manteca, who was enraged because Mrs. Taylor had chastized Coumas' Children at school. Coumas came into the room of the Castle School where deceased was teaching, and after arguing a few moments he whipped a pistol out of his pocket and shot at Mrs. Taylor. The Janitor, W. J. Duval, tried to protect Mrs. Taylor, but Coumas shot at him and Duval fell down wounded. Coumas fired three shots at Mrs. ~~Taxx~~ Taylor. The shooting occurred at 4:00 PM just as Mrs. Taylor was about to leave for home, with some children.

Witness to accident Mr. and Mrs. W. J. Duval, Manteca, Calif.

Cause of death Exsanguination due to bleeding from ~~xxxxmix~~ ascending aorta as result of gunshot wound.

Post Mortem or inspection by Drs. W. P. J. Lynch

Property found on body none

Disposition of property as below

(RECEIPT)

Stockton, California, April 21st, 1932, Received of C. C. De Young, Coroner

One white metal x ring with white stone ~~xxx~~ one Cameo Brooch and one knife, Miscellaneous papers and letters, one Mercantile Building and Loan Book, five nickels, six penni four five dollarx bills, and one two dollar bill, One Check to W.J. Patmon signed by F. J. Williams, One Check made to E. A. Taylor, for $2.00 signed by Ira L. Flanders, both endorsed. ~~xxxx~~ One checkbook Stockton Savings and Loan, containing miscellaneous papers, One yellow Metal Wrist watch, One fountain pen. Sign E. A. Taylor

Witness E. J. Silva Resd. 1144 W Walnut

Coroner—Form 5—1-M—11/31.

Source - San Joaquin County Sheriffs Office - 2003

Tom Coumas photograph taken from trunk in
Coumas residence by Crawford Hitchcock - 1932

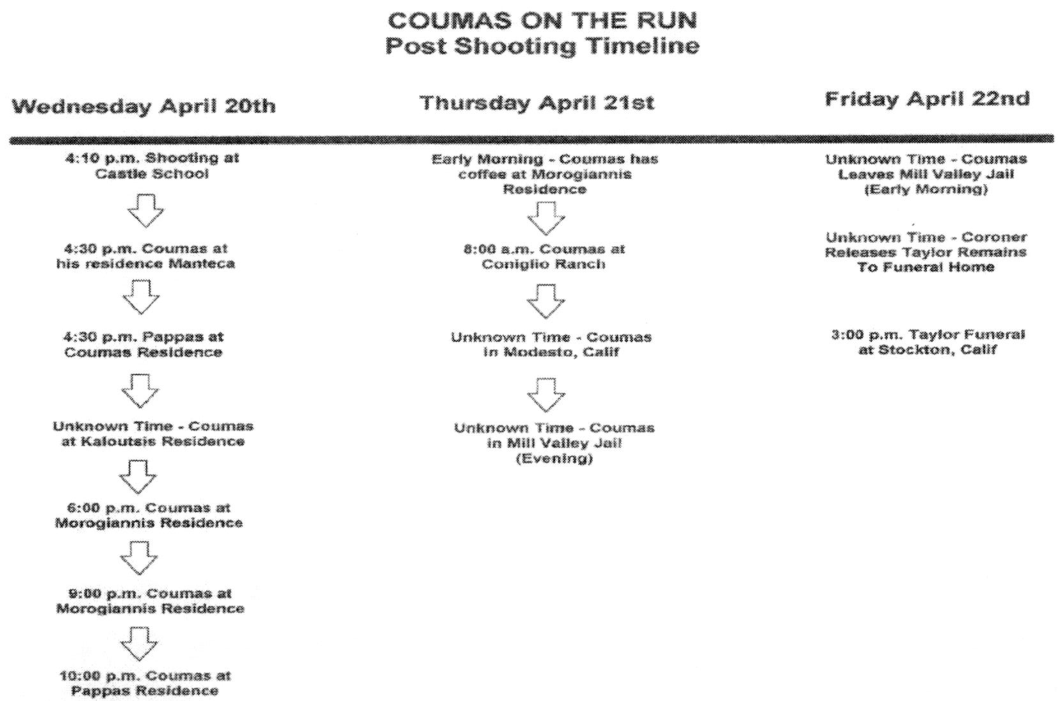

Timeline reconstruction and chart created by the author from public records - 2008

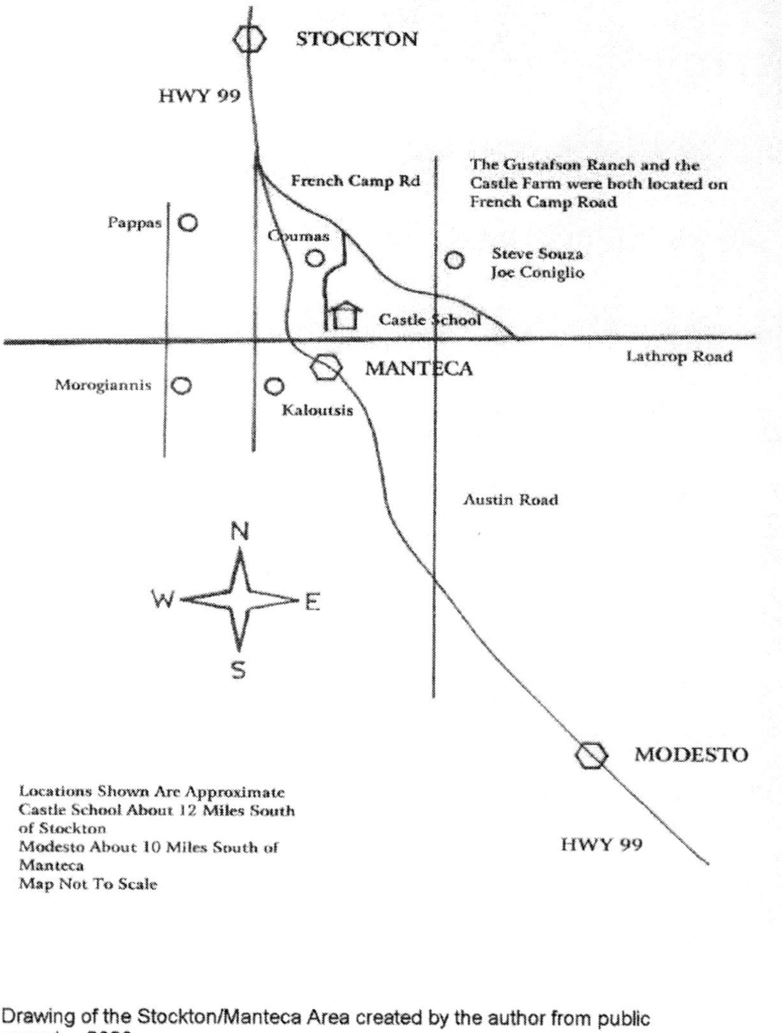

Drawing of the Stockton/Manteca Area created by the author from public records - 2008

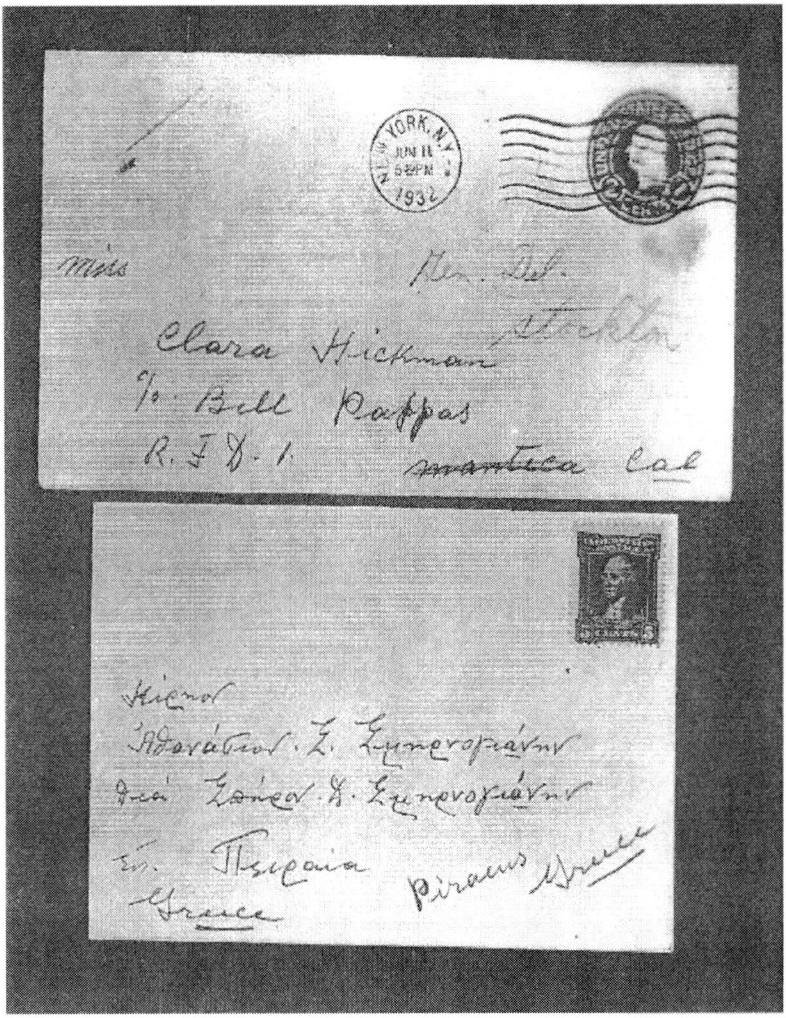

Letter from Tom Coumas, mailed from New York, to Clara Hickman
in Manteca, California - June 1932 - Origin of photograph unknown

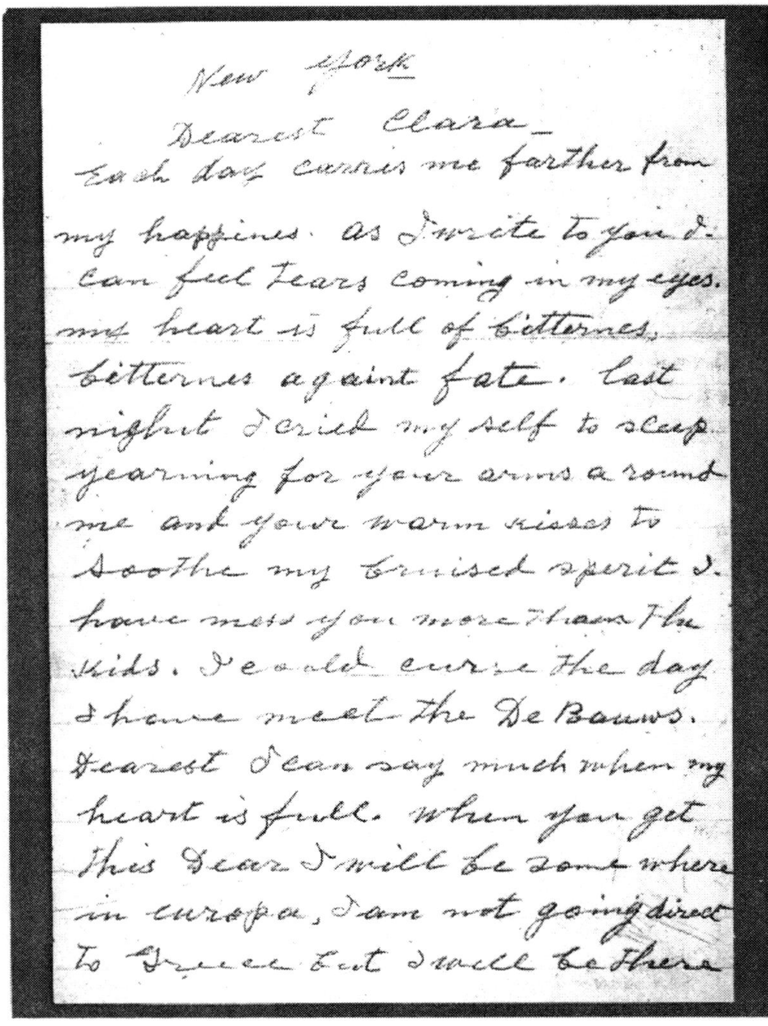

New York

Dearest Clara_

Each day carries me farther from my happiness. as I write to you I can feel tears coming in my eyes. my heart is full of bitterness, bitterness againt fate. last night I cried my self to sleep yearning for your arms a round me and your warm kisses to soothe my bruised spirit I have mess you more than the kids. I could curse the day I have meet the De Bauws. Dearest I can say much when my heart is full. when you get this Dear I will be some where in europa, I am not going direct to Greece but I will be there

Page One of Coumas letter to Clara Hickman - June 1932 - Origin of photograph unknown

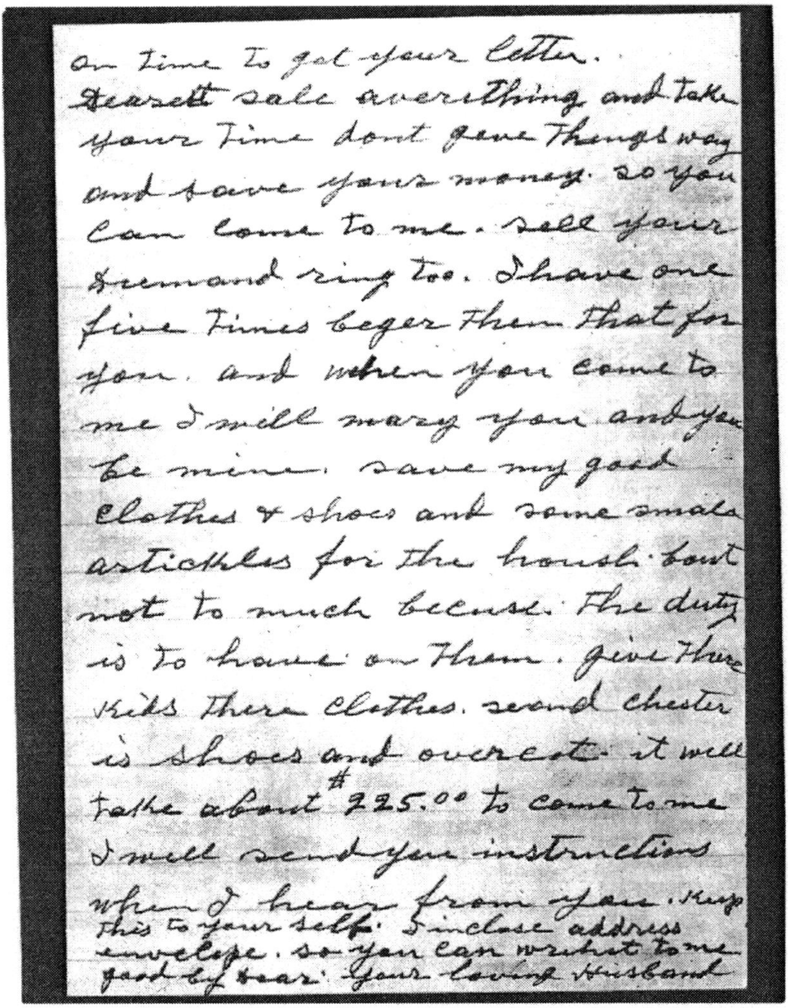

on time to get your letter.
Dearest sale everithing and take
your time dont give things way
and save your money. so you
can come to me. sell your
diemand ring too. I have one
five times beger them that for
you. and when you come to
me I will mary you and you
be mine. save my good
clothes & shoes and some small
astickles for the house. but
not to much because. the duty
is to have on them. give there
kids there clothes. send chester
is shoes and overcot. it will
take about #225.00 to come to me
I will send you instructions
when I hear from you. keep
this to your self. I inclose address
envelope. so you can wright to me
good by dear. your loving Husband

Page Two of Coumas letter to Clara Hickman - June 1932 - Origin of photograph unknown

Tom Coumas with mustache - Photograph provided by the Greek Government to San Joaquin County 1934

Taylor Family Plot - Stockton, California - Photograph courtesy of Kathryn Oehlman Latham

ADDITIONAL CREDITS

Cover and book design by the Author – Author Photograph: Author's Collection – Cover Graphics Services by White House Printing, LLC

Cover photograph – San Joaquin County Courthouse – Stockton, CA circa 1900 – San Joaquin County Historical Society – Lodi, CA - Photographs Collection - Used by permission

Olive Luella Taylor photograph circa 1910 – Courtesy of the Terry Bailey Family

San Francisco Chronicle Newspaper Article – April 21,1932 – Copyright 1932 The San Francisco Chronicle – Reproduced with permission

Stockton Record Newspaper Crime Scene Drawing - April 21,1932 – The Stockton Record – Stockton, California - Reproduced with permission

Sir Francis Bacon quotation from "Bartlett's Familiar Quotations" by John Bartlett - Courtesy of the publisher - Little, Brown and Company